WARSPEAK

WARSPEAK

Nietzsche's Victory over Nihilism

Lise van Boxel

political animal
PRESS
TORONTO · CHICAGO

Political Animal Press
www.politicalanimalpress.com

Distributed by the University of Toronto Press
www.utpdistribution.com

Cataloguing data available from Library and Archives Canada
ISBN 978-1895131-49-9 (paperback)
ISBN 978-1895131-50-5 (ebook)

Typeset in Adobe Caslon, designed by Carol Twombly,
and UWR DIN, designed by Volker Schnebel.

Printed and bound in Canada.

Contents

Publisher's Note

LISE VAN BOXEL approached us with the manuscript of this book in September 2019. She presented it to us as a finished work, indicating that she planned to add an Introduction and to ask Michael Grenke to write a Foreword.

During van Boxel's illness, which began shortly after we undertook this project, she reaffirmed that the work was complete, she chose the title, and she expressed her desire for it to be published as it is here, with an Introduction written by Michael Grenke. Only a small number of superficial changes have been made to the text to prepare it for publication, all of them approved in consultation with Michael Grenke.

This is the authoritative version of *Warspeak: Nietzsche's Victory Over Nihilism*, as Lise van Boxel directed it. It is an extraordinary book by an extraordinary thinker, and it is our honor to publish it.

Lewis Slawsky and Alexander Wall,
Publishers – Political Animal Press,
October 2020

Introduction*

Nothing. Too often that is the answer we give ourselves these days to our most important and defining questions. What can I know? Nothing. What ought I to do? Nothing. What can I hope? Nothing. When we think of the future, either our own future or the future of humanity more generally, what do we find? Nothingness. Perhaps not a pure absence but a set of possibilities for which we do not long or in which we are not interested. Everything that the future seems to offer looks already pre-tested and prejudged, empty of promise, worn out. This is nihilism as Friedrich Nietzsche came to understand it. Such nihilism means a settled, weary despair regarding all future possibilities of human growth or improvement (See GM 1,12).

Some who are deeply concerned by nihilism seek to escape it by a return to the conditions of earlier times, times when people were not so worn out and believed in truth. But such projects of return do not offer viable means. Aside from the fact that projects that seek to recreate the conditions of the past are by their very own actions of recreation never

---

* Before her passing, Lise van Boxel intended to add an introduction to her book. That task has fallen to me. I am not working blind here, as I discussed the introduction with Lise a couple of times. I have tried to produce here an introduction in accord with the author's intentions. Lise wanted an introduction that would make some of the major ideas and methods of the work immediately clear and easily accessible. To do that, I have presented some of the ideas as simpler than they are. I have neither offered proper genealogical accounts of things that are moving and changing nor have I written in the lively literary style that is meant to engage the fullness of the reader's humanity. Thus, while I have attempted to present the ideas of the book in accessible clarity, both this accessibility and this clarity are distortions. This introduction is no substitute for the book that follows. I have attempted to present here the ideas of the book or ideas compatible with the book. But this book is an inspiring and challenging work. I am not done learning from it and I do not yet claim to understand it fully. I hope in this introduction that I have not needlessly misrepresented anything – but about those things I do not understand, I really cannot be sure.

the same as the past was, the return to the truth as it has been known for millennia is no way out. Nihilism is not primarily a disbelief in truth, rather nihilism is the result of a belief in truth of a certain kind. The belief in a truth that is based upon a realm of absolute and unchanging beings is a belief that ultimately leads to the weary despair of nihilism. The ascetic ideal, which for a long time has been the only ideal, has told us that the source of what is good and true is not the world we experience with its continually changing and perishing beings, rather it is the other world of unchanging and absolute being. The ascetic ideal offers otherworldly goals and goods that lead us away from all this-worldly goals and goods. The goods of this world are made to look dissatisfying in comparison to goods of another world that we have never experienced. By this comparison, this world has been denigrated for a long time, and our attachment to this world has been worn down and tired out. The nihilism that we encounter today, the nihilism that Nietzsche already saw in his today, is the product of the long rule of the ascetic ideal.

The confrontation that is required to win a victory over nihilism does not just involve encountering and solving a thought problem. It involves recognizing that a psychological war has been waged with all manner of secrecy, subterfuge, and dishonesty against all healthy and growing human life. The ascetic ideal has to be recognized as a product of and an instrument of this secret war against all that is high. And with this recognition, what needs to be done is to engage this war on its own grounds. The means to victory here is a superior psychology, a physio-psychology. These means are employed here by a new kind of writing, one that attempts to capture the dynamic liveliness of beings that are ever changing and growing, one infused with courage and other warlike virtues, warspeak.

The subtitle of *On the Genealogy of Morals* is "Streitschrift," "A Polemic." This is often taken to mean that the rhetoric of the work is skewed or corrupted by its warlike purpose. Some interpreters have taken Nietzsche to exaggerate certain things here, again in the service of waging a war. This present book reveals that the language appropriate to war, warspeak, is not to be understood as being in need of a correction by the reader. Warspeak is the correction. To combat the psychology employed as a weapon by the ascetic ideal, a psychology that treats words as unchanging, dead beings; <u>words must come alive as the actions of, and</u>

thus the very becomings of, living beings. Streitschrift, polemic, fighting writing, is the proper way to address the psychological war that has been waged for millennia against all that is high. And warspeak is the proper language of a life affirming ideal that can replace the nihilistic ascetic ideal.

In order to see this life affirming ideal emerge in its fullness and vitality this book focuses its attention on Nietzsche's ownmost problem as it develops and transforms into his confrontation with nihilism in *On the Genealogy of Morals*. This book offers a close and focused reading of Nietzsche's book, making much of seemingly small details. Although one might expect or even fear a certain narrowness from a close reading, this fear should be alleviated by the focus here on the central issue of Friedrich Nietzsche's thought, the problem of nihilism. The fact that a victory over nihilism emerges from a careful reading of *On the Genealogy of Morals* decisively marks the *Genealogy* as a central work within Nietzsche's corpus. Around the center swirls everything else. Nietzsche's philosophy is his attempt to say what is, what can be, and what cannot. His whole philosophy is necessary both to diagnose the problem of nihilism in its full extent and to marshal the resources to overcome nihilism. Thus, the investigation of the central issue is necessarily a comprehensive investigation of his thought as a whole.

One gets to the whole through the details. A truly close reading respects the text and pays attention to all the details, no matter how small. For example, this present book makes much of one small detail presented in the Preface to the *Genealogy*. The moral-theological prejudice, mentioned in a story about Nietzsche's thirteen-year-old theological efforts turns out to be a key that unlocks many doors. It helps to understand the related prejudice involved in the faith in opposite values. It shows itself to be equivalent to the ascetic ideal. Again and again, it appears as the underlying belief propping up some obstacle to any way of human life that offers genuine hope for the future.

In this biographical attention to early Nietzsche is an example of the genealogical presentation of the evolution of the philosophic type that winds like a guiding path throughout this entire book. In what could be brushed off as an indulgent or meaningless anecdote, Nietzsche calls our attention to two prejudices early on in the Preface to *On the Genealogy of Morals*. The two prejudices are entangled as one, the moral-theological prejudice. Their combined effect prevents a very young Nietzsche from making progress with the problem that he thinks is his problem, the problem of evil. Learning to disentangle the two prejudices let Nietzsche see them as the prejudices they are and freed him substantially from their sway. In thinking through the separated moral and theological prejudices, Nietzsche's approach transforms. He sees a world of things that come into being out of modified forms of what was there before. "Only that which has no history is capable of definition" (*On the Genealogy of Morals* 2, 13.). By definition here, Nietzsche means a unified, unchanging statement. What is needed in the place of such a definition is a genealogical account. To say what a moving, changing thing is, philosophy must be genealogy.

From the same thinking about the moral and theological prejudices, Nietzsche's attention is directed to the human inventors of the systems of moral value. The realm to be investigated is no longer some other world behind the world we experience, it is now the world that we do in fact experience, understood as the world comprised by the human experience and significantly shaped by our mind and its creations. Nietzsche turns to the psyche, the mind, the soul, of the human being as the place where the genealogical history of the world is to be investigated. Philosophy must become psychology (again).

This turn to psychology is not a turn to a subjective interior realm separate from some outer realm of matter. To think of it this way is to continue under the sway of the moral-theological prejudice. Instead mind and matter have to be understood as one and the same. This is not to reduce mind to matter, rather it is to rethink both. Psychology, which is the science of souls, must become physio-psychology, the science of souls that are understood to be something about the body. What thinks and what does not must be reconsidered. Even what is alive and what is not. Thoughts become events, actions.

Through unentangling the moral and theological prejudices, Nietzsche's ownmost question transforms from the problem of evil to the problem of the value of any system of good and evil. Here Nietzsche begins to confront nihilism

Now, not all of this book is occupied with a painstaking interpretation of each and every detail. This close reading is mingled with selected deployments of lively literary interludes. Here the reader is shown a special kind of respect and courtesy. Not every detail is worked out thus leaving plenty of opportunity for the readers to employ their own powers of observation and interpretation. In these interludes we return to the spirit of warspeak. These interludes broaden out the picture and remind the reader of the overarching themes. Within this broadening out, many aspects of Nietzsche's thought are addressed and developed.

It is worth highlighting two examples here. These ideas are not the central concern of this book, but they are developed as the presentation of the life-affirming ideal unfolds and they both help to flesh out that ideal. First there is a very big claim Nietzsche makes in *Beyond Good and Evil* 257. It has attracted a good detail of attention and has puzzled many. *Beyond Good and Evil* 257 begins, "Every enhancement of the type "human being" has been up till now the work of an aristocratic society..." Nietzsche roots this claim in the growing pathos in the soul that aims ever to widen the gap between its low and high parts. The analysis of pro-active human beings and their creations, in this book, offers another, perhaps better foundation for Nietzsche's big claim. What is shown in this book is that only pro-active, superabundantly vital human beings, who create spontaneously out of their own fullness, can create new things. The pro-active are super-full. Their needs are fulfilled. They do not depend upon external stimuli to prompt their actions. The only antecedent for their actions is their own inner self. In this way they are spontaneous. Enhancement of the human type depends upon the creation of new things. The reactive type of human being does not produce new things, only responses to existing things. If there is to be a better future, it depends upon the creation of new things, and the only sources of humanly new things are pro-active human beings.

Second is the revelation that true love also is the province of pro-active human life. In fact, in Chapter Three love is presented as *the* teaching of *Thus Spoke Zarathustra* and as the genuine experience of the super abundant vitality that is the supreme good for human beings. This presentation should help us to understand why Nietzsche says at the end of *Beyond Good and Evil* 260, "love *as a passion* ... must be of noble origin." It should also help us to understand differently the well known statement of *Beyond Good and Evil* 153, "Whatever is done out of love, always occurs beyond good and evil." If we take Nietzsche's hint from the end of *On the Genealogy of Morals*, 1.17, that beyond good and evil does not mean beyond good and bad, then we see section 153 is not saying that the actions of love are simply outside the moral realm. But he is saying love is incompatible with the morality, good and evil, that is professed by the reactive type.

The two examples above are not the biggest concerns in the *Genealogy*, nor are they the narrowest. The task of reading well requires that one read on multiple levels. It is not just the details, but their sum that offers challenges. In the *Genealogy*, Nietzsche has woven a text of dizzying complexity. The incoherence that sometimes seems to inhabit Nietzsche's texts is artful. Nietzsche himself left many clues to teach us how to read his works. It takes a subtle and multifarious art of reading to see how it all fits together. To match Nietzsche's many ways of conveying his message the reader must pay attention not only to the twists and turns of the argument but also to the gestures and music of the writing. Passions must be engaged as well as reason. The human being, who is not merely a calculating machine, must allow as many parts of his being as possible to be enlivened by the kind of writing that is meant to engage and enliven their whole being.

This is why the section of *Thus Spoke Zarathustra* entitled "On Reading and Writing" is so important for understanding *On the Genealogy of Morals*. Not only is a part of that section pinned to the beginning of the third essay of the *Genealogy*, but reading and writing, interpreting and acting, are a large part of the solution to the problem of nihilism. The third essay is presented by Nietzsche as an example of exegesis. Nietzsche is offering a school for reading. Learning to read such lively writing, and maybe learning how to write along the way, is itself also a school for living. The affirmative ideal requires a reinterpretation and a rewriting of the narrative of the world.

The ascetic ideal has controlled how we see the world and what the words we use mean. The vast cultural edifice that has grown out of and around the ascetic ideal has to be torn down or repurposed. The world needs to be un-poisoned. Reinterpretation and re-writing invade the psychic realm of the ascetic interpretation of the world. It takes the ascetic interpretation's own terms and subverts and transforms them. The universal good that is the same for all and is based upon a world of absolute being is gone. But there is a supreme good that is between being and becoming and is recognized by all human beings. Creation ex nihilo in the strict sense is gone, but there is a real genesis of new things in the "spontaneous" creations of pro-active human beings. There is a kind of resurrection in the continuous self-regeneration of living beings. There is transcendence, not of the kind that escapes this world, but of the kind, in comedy, that escapes the seriousness of this world. Giving these old words new meanings is part of the practice of warspeak. This reinterpretation and re-writing make the inherited traditions of the ascetic interpretation speak a new language and convey new affirmative messages. This clears away or repurposes the old traditions to create a context suited to the new, affirmative ideal.

The big problem with the war against the nihilism that stems from the ascetic ideal is that a viable counter-ideal has been lacking. But the *Genealogy* gives us a viable counter-ideal in the concept of super abundant vitality. Super abundant vitality turns out to be the consensus supreme good from the stand point of both types of morality, pro-active and reactive. Within the pro-active moralities this is rather straightfor-wardly evident. Within the reactive moralities the fact that they secretly honor and admire superabundant vitality is shown by their envy and by the way they portray the goods they expect to receive as rewards in the other world.

Superabundant vitality is the consensus supreme good, but it cannot serve its purpose if it remains merely a formal concept. At any given time, the most highly evolved human being must manifest superabun-dant vitality in order to give it content. This embodied manifestation makes superabundant vitality an affirmation of this world. It also makes superabundant vitality a changing thing. With each subsequent growth of the highest human type new content is added. In considering the highest human type, the fullest expression of superabundant vitality, the philosophic type emerges as the highest type so far. A genealogical account of the evolution of the philosophic type is thus woven through-out the narrative of this book.

At the end of this book the challenge is posed that we human beings take charge of our own future, our own evolution. The term evolution, as used in this book, means not just change but progress, improvement. Its alternative is degeneration, decline, devolution. Taking charge of our own evolution is a daunting task, but we are given guidance both by the supreme good of super abundant vitality in general and by the genealogy of the philosopher. What is possible for the immediate future is determined by the state in which we find ourselves, what we have inherited. At each stage of development, the highest human being offers new possibilities to explore, and the concept of the supreme good helps us to determine which experiments are likely to yield the best results.

There is no easy choice available to us by which we could play it safe. We could try to choose not to experiment. But if we leave things alone, they still will not stay the same. They will change. And they will change in a direction that has no intrinsic relation to our hopes for the future. An experiment will have been carried out without intention and without making use of the guidance we have. Only if we take our future into our own hands can we be sure that it will be a genuine future that offers genuine hope. There is only one direction that offers us hope – forward.

Michael Grenke,
Tutor, St. John's College
October 2020

Chapter One

Philosophy Is Genealogy Is Psychology

Friedrich Nietzsche thinks the human being, and in fact every being, is a kind of moving, or developing, or becoming. To see a being as Nietzsche sees it is to see its history, its genealogy. It follows from this that philosophy is genealogy. In coming to understand what Nietzsche means by genealogy, we also come to realize he thinks genealogy is psychology. The human psyche, or physio-psychology to be more precise, proves to be the realm in which the historical development of beings takes place. Thus, we can infer that philosophy is the study of souls in their genealogical aspects: philosophy is genealogy is psychology. As an inroad to this genealogical thinking, we will use Nietzsche's own presentation of his biographical development as a philosopher. This philosophical biography is found in the "Preface" to his book, *On the Genealogy of Morals*. Since Nietzsche explicitly links this book with another of his books—*Beyond Good and Evil*—we will move between the two works to elucidate the announced equivalence: philosophy is genealogy is psychology.

Of the three terms in this equivalence, genealogy is least familiar to students of philosophy and political philosophy. We will therefore spend most of our time developing our understanding of it. Following in Nietzsche's footsteps, our advance toward comprehending genealogy will be indirect. He begins by introducing himself. He tells us he may almost be defined by what he calls "a scruple" peculiar to him concerning morality. By his own account, it entered his life "so early, so uninvited, so irresistibly, so much in conflict with ... [his] environment, age, precedents, and descent that ... [he] might almost have the right to call it ... [his] '*a priori*'" (GM, "Preface," 2). This scruple soon took the form of a question: "What is the origin of good and evil?" (GM, "Preface," 2).[1]

He goes on to report that, at the ripe age of thirteen, he dedicated his "first philosophical effort" to this question. In the essay that was the fruit of this effort, he gave the "honor" of having generated evil to God, a conclusion he judges "was only fair" (GM, "Preface," 3). The older Nietzsche may be delighted by his younger self's answer. Nevertheless, he is proud to report that his development as a philosopher advanced because he *rejected* this response. He explains, cryptically, that this rejection followed from the fact that he "learned early to separate theological prejudice from moral prejudice" (GM, "Preface," 3). Precisely what are these prejudices?

Nietzsche speaks frequently in his writings of the moral prejudice. It is the conviction that good and evil are universal values. The good is allegedly good for all human beings, and evil is held to be wicked for everyone. What Nietzsche means by the theological prejudice, is less clear. Two possible interpretations present themselves. First, it might refer to the conviction God exists in a transcendent realm. Second, it might denote God is the supreme good. The second option amounts to the belief in a universal good. Thus, it resolves into the moral prejudice. Since Nietzsche tells us the moral and theological prejudices are distinct, this second interpretation cannot be what he means by the theological prejudice. It must instead refer to the belief in an eternal, unchanging, and absolute or pure—in other words, unmixed—God. This concept of God is essentially the same as the traditional philosophic notion of eternal, unchanging being, which is absolute or pure because it is wholly unmixed with becoming (see BGE "Preface"). Such being does not exist in the world in which we live, for our world is characterized by transfiguration and becoming. To maintain the truth of this concept of God or being, therefore, one must posit the existence of an otherworldly realm that exists behind our world and that transcends becoming.

As opposites, absolute being and becoming do not exist on a continuum with each other. They are not different by degree. Rather, they are wholly different in kind. Thus, the theological prejudice is an expression of the larger category of prejudice—namely, the *"faith in opposite values,"* which Nietzsche identifies as the "fundamental faith of the metaphysicians" (BGE 2). Almost all philosophers to date have believed in this compound prejudice:

[It] looms in the background of all their logical procedures; it is on account

of this "faith" that they trouble themselves about "knowledge," about something that is finally baptized solemnly as "the truth." … It has not even
occurred to the most cautious among them that one might have a doubt
right here at the threshold where it was surely most necessary—even if they
vowed to themselves ["all is to be doubted"]. (BGE 2)

Nietzsche describes this moral-theological prejudice in the voice of
a philosopher who believes it:

"How *could* anything originate out of its opposite? For example, truth
out of error? Or the will to truth out of the will to deception? Or selfless
deeds out of selfishness? Or the pure and sun-like gaze of the sage out
of lust? Such origins are impossible; whoever dreams of them is a fool,
indeed worse; the things of this highest value must have another, *peculiar*
origin—they cannot be derived from this transitory, seductive, deceptive,
paltry world, from this turmoil of delusion and lust. Rather, from the lap
of Being, the intransitory, the hidden god, the 'thing-in-itself—there must
be their basis and nowhere else." (BGE 2; see also BGE 191; GS 76; GS
110 – 112; GS 357)

Reassuming his own voice, Nietzsche de-composes this compound
prejudice into its two elements, thereby enabling us to identify them as
the theological and moral prejudices respectively. "[F]irst," he says, "one
may doubt whether there are any opposites at all" (BGE 2; see also BGE
24). As we noted, opposites are absolutes. Do we see this absolute opposition in any of the examples to which Nietzsche refers? Is there such a
thing as the "pure and sun-like gaze of the sage"? Or is even the wise
human being's gaze not wholly devoid of the kind of interest that constitutes lust? Nietzsche continues: "Secondly, … [one may doubt] whether
these popular valuations and opposite values on which the metaphysicians put their seal are not perhaps merely foreground estimates" (BGE
2; see also Z, "Upon the Blessed Isles"). In other words, one may wonder
whether the moral prejudice is a superficial value overlying a different,
more profound, and previously unidentified value.

Nietzsche then invites us to reflect on each of these prejudices.
Regarding the moral prejudice, he asks whether attributes characterized
as evil are as valuable to the vitality of the human species as the so-called
good attributes. He then recombines the moral and the theological prejudices and asks us to wonder whether the value of the alleged absolute,
universal good consists precisely in the fact that it is not the *opposite* of
evil but is instead *one* with it:

For all the value that the true, the truthful, the selfless may deserve, it would be still possible that a higher and more fundamental value for life might have to be ascribed to deception, selfishness, and lust. It might even be possible that what constitutes the value of these good and revered things is precisely that they are insidiously related, tied to, and involved with these wicked, seemingly opposite things—maybe even one with them in essence. Maybe! (BGE 2; see also GS 4)

Having clarified the meanings of the theological and moral prejudices, let us return to Nietzsche's claim that their separation was crucial to his development as a philosopher. Remember, Nietzsche tells us that before he learned to separate these prejudices, he attributed the origin of evil to God. What we did not note previously, but what is significant, is that he says nothing of his early conclusion about the origin of the good. Initially, one might think he does not speak of it because the young Nietzsche casually attributes its origin to God, the supreme good. Hence, its source is not a question for him. However, this inference does not adequately explain why the mature Nietzsche, who does not attribute the good to God, nevertheless chooses to speak only of his encounter with the question of the origin of evil. Given that his immediate subject matter is his philosophic growth, it is reasonable to infer that he thinks the question of the origin of evil in particular highlights the hindrance to philosophic development that results from conflating the moral and theological prejudices. More specifically, reflection on the origin of evil illuminates the path to a new understanding of morality, one that is encapsulated in the equivalence philosophy is genealogy is psychology. Let us flesh out how this is the case.

The young Nietzsche initially presumes God created all things. Thus, when confronted with the question of the origin of evil, he concludes it, like everything else, was generated by God. If this is the case, however, then good and evil have a common source. According to the theological prejudice, this is impossible. Opposites cannot have a common source, since their opposition is absolute. Thus, what appeared to be an answer to the question of the origin of evil actually raises more vexing questions, questions that demand some difficult decisions.

If one wants to retain the theological prejudice, one must conclude evil did not originate in anything purely good. For example, evil cannot result from a confusion or dissipation of goodness. Since God is presumed to be not merely good, but the epitome of pure goodness, evil must be generated by a power that is wholly independent of, and absolutely other to, God. Thus, there must in effect be two creators: one purely good and one purely evil. On what grounds are these creators characterized as good and evil? To make comparisons and contrasts, one must slide back and forth along a continuum of similarity and difference that precludes absolute otherness or opposites, and one must have a satisfactory sense of how far into otherness one has moved. In all such movements, one is necessarily adulterated.

Since purely good and purely evil deities cannot intermingle, their moral characterizations must depend on a standard separate from either of them. This standard raises two problems for the hypothesis. First, the necessary recourse to an independent standard means neither the good god nor the evil god is the true authority in moral matters: the authority is the standard itself. Second, by positing the existence of a standard that incorporates both moral values, one effectively returns good and evil to the same source. One has thereby reconstituted the god to whom the young Nietzsche attributed the origin of both good and evil. *This* god is no longer pure. Hence, it cannot be the god of the theological prejudice.

One might try again to salvage the theological prejudice by claiming God is both absolutely good and omniscient, so that he has complete knowledge of evil, despite being wholly and purely good. One would have to admit human beings cannot understand how both of these things can be true, but one might assert they are both true nonetheless. Someone might add that it is precisely *because* we cannot understand such essential truths that we must accept God's authority. The crux of this hypothesis is that the human perspective is insurmountably limited and false, insofar as it is mixed up with becoming. This claim attracts Nietzsche's attention. By thinking through its implications, he realizes moral valuations must ultimately articulate human, not divine, judgments. Follow him.

The premise of this hypothesis implicitly recognizes that our experiences must be filtered through what we are as human beings. Speaking more precisely, they must be filtered through what we are as individuals. These observations do not entail the additional conclusion that either the human perspective or the individual perspective is absolutely or universally true. On the contrary, from within our perspective we can discern that other beings do not have the same perspective as us. Like our own, their perspectives are integrated into, and generally support, their physio-psychologies, which are more or less like ours (see GM 3.12; GS 374).

Dogs clearly experience smells more acutely and vividly than we do. The hummingbird, which moves very rapidly compared to the human being, must have a different sense of speed than humans. What appears to be extremely rapid motion to us must be normal to this bird. If the hummingbird's sense of speed were *not* calibrated to its physio-psychology, but were instead the same as ours, it would be inviable. Similarly, the mayfly, which in its mature form lives only twenty-hours or so, must experience time in a manner calibrated to its physio-psychology in order to complete the activities that constitute a typical lifecycle for its species. If a mayfly could consider an average human lifetime, it might believe this time is unfathomably long—an eternity. If it could reflect on what it might be like to live so long, it might say, "Life is made meaningful by our consciousness of death! If life were significantly longer or—God forbid! —eternal, I would be bored to death! Surely, eternal life is value-less!" Buzz, buzz.

We can try to bridge the gap between non-human and human perspectives. For example, we can use technology to increase our sense of smell in order to gain some sense of a dog's capacity. Even in this case, however, our heightened smell must be experienced by our non-dog selves. The human being will never have the same experience as the dog so long as the two types of beings are distinct.[2]

Our inability to transcend our human perspective in our relations with the other beings in the earthly realm is equally applicable to a world that might exist behind our own and to the other-worldly beings that might populate it. Even if one were to receive commandments directly from a supposedly transcendent realm, the human perspective remains unavoidable and insurmountable for us, since we must still understand the revealed commandment. Understanding requires interpretation, which necessarily entails making judgments about meaning. Having made these preliminary judgments, one must then deliberate about whether to obey the command, as one has understood it. All of these judgments are human. Nietzsche follows this line of reasoning to its conclusion. Since we cannot know anything supra-human, the supra-human simply does not exist for us. With this conclusion, he frees himself from the theological prejudice, according to which there is a true world of eternal, unchanging and absolute being behind our world (See D 130; TI, "How The 'Real World' At Last Became A Myth"; GS 346).[3]

Overcoming the theological prejudice has a decisive consequence for the moral prejudice. People's belief in the authority of the dominant moral values depends on their belief in eternal, unchanging, and absolute being or God. In other words, the moral prejudice depends on the authority of the theological prejudice. With the destruction of the theological prejudice, therefore, the foundation for the authority of the moral prejudice is also overturned (see GM 3.24).[4]

This realization might prompt you to try immediately to discover a new foundation for the authority of an absolute, universal good. Why? What is your motive? Whatever the answers to these questions may be, and they may be different for different people, the effort is premature. At this point, we ought to realize we do not even know adequately what morality is, let alone whether it is worth preserving or whether it can be preserved. We have spiraled back to the young Nietzsche's questions regarding morality, only now the inquiry is on a higher plane than the one on which he, and we, began, for the moral-theological prejudice has now been cast aside. We must survey this new territory and determine what the guiding question of morality has become.

Since everything that exists for us must be interpreted and judged by what we are, valuations are necessarily always human: consciously or unconsciously, we create them. Thus, an investigation of morality and valuation is necessarily an investigation of the human being. Having realized this, we become more interested in knowing the creator—the human being—than the creations. The creations are valuable first and foremost as a means to understanding the creator. Broadly speaking, valuations articulate something about the physio-psychology of the human being or of certain human beings, but what precisely is articulated? —Notions of good and evil or good and bad. Yes, of course, but what do these values *signify?* Of what are they *manifestations?* In sum, the question concerning morality now becomes: What is the value of morality *for human life?*

Brief as his account is, Nietzsche gives us enough insight into the path he took at this juncture of his investigation for us to see we are on the same track as him. He tells us that, after he ceased looking for the origin of evil behind the world, his question regarding morality was transformed. He, too, began to ask what the value of morality is in terms of human life. He fleshes out the meaning of this question by articulating related questions that illuminate it:

> A certain amount of historical and philological schooling, together with an inborn fastidiousness of taste in respect to psychological questions in general, soon transformed my problem into another one: under what conditions did man devise these value judgments good and evil? *and what value do they themselves possess?* Have they hitherto hindered or furthered human prosperity? Are they signs of distress, of impoverishment, of the degeneration of life? Or is there revealed in them, on the contrary, the plentitude, force, and will of life, its courage, certainty, future? (GM, "Preface," 3; see also GM, "Preface," 5)

Having identified the new form of the question concerning morality, Nietzsche reports he "discovered and ventured divers answers" to it, answers that vary according to historical epochs, peoples, and "degrees of rank among individuals" (GM, "Preface," 3). Surprisingly, after speaking of the range and scope of his discoveries, he does not proceed to reveal what these discoveries are. Or at least he does not seem to do so. Rather, he recounts the effects his investigations had on his psyche:

> [O]ut of my answers there grew new questions, inquiries, conjectures, probabilities—until at length I had a country of my own, a soil of my own, an entire discrete, thriving, flourishing world like a secret garden the existence of which no one suspected. (GM, "Preface," 3; see also BGE 292)

Why does Nietzsche choose to prioritize a beautiful description of how his investigations cause his soul to grow into a garden-world over his answers to the question of the value of morality? His choice suggests he regards the growth of his soul as a manifestation of the answer. His use of metaphor and imagery to respond to the question of the value of morality for life further suggests he thinks this mode of speaking is somehow superior to a more scholarly or pedestrian report. How so?

Recollect, he opens his depiction of his development by confessing his awareness of a scruple concerning morality that is so central to who he is that he "almost" has the right to call it his *a priori* (GM, "Preface," 3). His description of his development indicates he thinks this scruple acts like a kind of seed from which his psyche grows into a world. It is as if, propelled by his essential scruple to delve into inter-related questions, he pushes the boundaries of his soul outward, thereby enlarging its comprehensiveness while also maintaining it as a kind of whole. As a result of his greater comprehensiveness, his experience of his own vitality also increases. Stated differently, and in more general terms, the being of living beings consists of a certain form of activity. Therefore, if a being extends its capacities while also increasing the overall activity that is its life-form, its being necessarily also increases: it becomes more alive, more of what it is. Thus, the imagery Nietzsche uses to describe his growth as a philosopher also depicts how the human being's physio-psychology can grow from a simpler, less vital form to one that is manifold and more vital.

The growth Nietzsche describes is commanded by a governing thought, which in his case is his essential scruple. As a commanded motion, this activity is consistent with human willing, as Nietzsche describes it in *Beyond Good and Evil*. In that book, he notes the human will is not a unit, as almost everyone presumes. Rather, it is "above all something *complicated*, something that is a unit only as a word" (BGE 19). He discerns several features of its complexity. First, "in all willing there is ... a plurality of sensations" (BGE 19). For example, there is the sensation of direction, such as *"toward which," "away from which,"* and the sensations of *"toward"* and *"away"* themselves. There is "also an accompanying muscular sensation, which, even without our putting into motion 'arms and legs,' begins its action by force of habit as soon as we 'will' anything" (BGE 19). Second, human willing involves thinking and a commanding thought. Thinking is not external to, or separate from, the sensations and affects—in other words, the drives—that operate together in human willing. Rather, it is a relation of these drives to each other (see BGE 36; see also GM 2.8). The final feature in human willing, and the one that is most characteristic of it, is the "affect"—that is, the experience—of commanding (BGE 19; see also BGE 3). To say the same thing differently, when human beings will, they typically identify themselves only as the commanding thought that organizes their multiple drives into a kind of whole; hence, they glory in this drive's efficacy or power. Because willing entails multiple drives, however, every willing is "at the same time both the commanding *and* the obeying parties" (BGE 19). Whatever glory one feels in willing is therefore at least partly due to a crude inattentiveness to the true complexity of one's self-experience.

Since human willing involves a commanding thought ruling multiple drives that exist in a social structure, Nietzsche argues it is right for a philosopher to characterize willing itself as moral (BGE 19). The governing class in this society of drives has the sense it is entitled to rule the other drives—it *ought* to rule. This "ought" indicates the governing class implicitly or explicitly designates itself as good. In its sense of moral entitlement to rank and rule the other drives in the community, the commanding thought is comparable to the ruling class in a healthy aristocracy, just as the subordinate drives are akin to this regime's lower ranks (see BGE 257).

The morality that characterizes this commanding and obeying is reflected in some moral doctrines, but it is more fundamental than any of them. Hence, it is not reducible to any particular moral doctrine. Nietzsche characterizes this fundamental morality as "the doctrine of relations of supremacy under which the phenomenon of 'life' comes to be" (BGE 19; see also BGE 257; GS 335).[5] He notes, in addition, that "every animal—therefore *la bête philosophe [the philosophic animal]*, too—instinctively strives for an optimum of favorable conditions under which it can expend all its strength and achieve its maximal feeling of power" or vitality (GM 3.7). This goal, which animals desire and seek above all else, is not the animal's "path to happiness, but its path to power, to action, to the most powerful activity, and in most cases actually its path to unhappiness" (GM 3.7). Nietzsche's observation regarding the aim of all animal life, together with his account of what we have called the fundamental morality, suggest he thinks human beings, and perhaps all thinking beings, are characterized by the fact that they bring together multiple drives under a commanding thought that unconsciously or consciously aims to experience the overall growth or enhancement of the being by altering the being's physio-psychology and circumstances. Commanded vitality therefore stands in contrast to vitality that discharges without any intention of self-augmentation.

While the motion Nietzsche describes is commanded, it is also affected by circumstances and external stimuli. Speaking of his own case, Nietzsche claims his development was influenced by "a certain amount of historical and philological schooling" (GM, "Preface," 3). These circumstances do not deter his commanded motion; rather, they help to determine the pathways to his maturation as a philosopher. Thus, they are incorporated into the general intentionality or direction of his commanded motion. We can easily imagine a less successful and more typical case, whereby the commanded motion is undermined, redirected, or destroyed by external circumstances (e.g. see BGE 269).

If we now draw back from the details of the image Nietzsche sketches of his own growth and consider the picture as a whole, we can see that it shows us something of what it is to be a living being and of what genealogy is. A living being has a certain degree of organized, self-directed, and continuous motion, which is affected by things extrinsic to it. The history of this motion and its current condition merge fluidly in a continuum that determines various possibilities for its immanent motion, growth, or decay. This fluid motion—the motion of the becoming that is the being's being—is what Nietzsche means by generation or growth. Thus, genealogy is the study of the changing shape—the morphology—of life.

We can now also see why it is fitting that Nietzsche introduces genealogy with a description and a metaphor rather than a definition—such as, genealogy is the logos (λογος)—that is, the rational account or speech—of generation or growth (γενεα). By so doing, he provokes us to *envision* this particular kind of motion, whereas, if he had immediately offered a definition of the word, people would be inclined, at least initially, to overlook the kind of becoming that is a living being and instead to mistake this being for something static. In other words, a definition would reinforce the error that has plagued almost every thinker to date. While this error is due to the conflation of the two prejudices, it is also bound up with words, which of course are themselves static. We can see continuous motion, but we cannot speak of it directly. While imagery employs words and therefore cannot entirely overcome the stasis they involve, it also provokes us to use our mind's eye to see the motion described. Thus, the image communicates more effectively the becoming that genealogy addresses.[6]

These clarifications of the fundamental good, moral doctrines, and genealogy help us better understand Nietzsche's question of what the value of morality is for human life (GM, "Preface," 3). With this question, he is asking what particular moral doctrines reveal about the vital condition of the human beings who create them and who believe them: "Are they signs of distress, of impoverishment, of the degeneration of life? Or is there revealed in them, on the contrary, the plentitude, force, and will of life, its courage, certainty, future?" (GM "Preface," 3). In addition, he is asking whether and how specific moral doctrines help the human being, or particular human beings, secure the fundamental good—that is, the experience of their maximum vitality: "Have they hitherto hindered or furthered human flourishing?" (GM "Preface," 3). In sum, moral doctrines are valuable to the extent that they promote our growth. From the standpoint of human evolution, moral doctrines—which human beings create—have so far been the most momentous means to our experience of maximum vitality, for they have been one of, if not *the*, most significant factor in determining what we have become (see WP 144; WP 146; WP 610).

Now, see how Nietzsche's description of his own growth illustrates this answer to the question of the value of morality for human life. His moral scruple is the commanding thought that compels him to pursue the question of morality to previously unknown depths of the human physio-psychology. As a result of his explorations, he discovers a new way of understanding the world, which prompts him to reject key aspects of the moral-philosophic tradition as threats to his otherwise ascending vitality. In lieu of them, Nietzsche aims to live according to his understanding of the *fundamental* good. In keeping with his understanding, Nietzsche realizes his philosophic inquiries are good because they develop his soul into a more comprehensive, vital world.

That Nietzsche intends his depiction of his own growth to illuminate the value of morality for human life in general is indicated most clearly by his placement of it at the beginning of a book on the genealogy of morality, which proves to be inextricably intertwined with the evolution of the human being. Additionally, before speaking of his own development, Nietzsche describes the development of all philosophers in terms that accord with his depiction of his own growth. *Every* philosopher's growth is directed by a commanding thought that seeks to develop the philosopher's psyche into a world:

> We [philosophers] have no right to isolated acts of any kind: we may not make isolated errors or hit upon isolated truths. Rather do our ideas, our values, our yeas and nays, our ifs and buts, grow out of us with the necessity with which a tree bears fruit—related and each with an affinity to each, and evidence of *one* will, *one* health, *one* soil, *one* sun. —But what is that to the trees! What is that to *us*, to us philosophers! (GM, "Preface," 2)[7]

Nietzsche depicts the interconnection of morality and growth again in *Beyond Good and Evil,* where he describes the philosopher's growth as a motion ruled by a kind of psychic, moral seed:

> Gradually it has become clear to me what every great philosophy so far has been: namely, the personal confession of its author and a kind of involuntary and unconscious memoir; also that the moral (or immoral) intentions in every philosophy constituted the real germ of life from which the whole plant had grown. (BGE 6)

Later in this book, he presents the development of philosophic inquiry over the course of history not only as an ongoing conversation between philosophers, but also as contributions to the evolution of *the* philosopher, understood as a type of human being. Each individual philosopher, who is himself a world, is therefore also a part of the world that is becoming manifest in the ongoing evolution of the philosopher:

> That individual philosophical concepts are not anything capricious or autonomously evolving, but grow up in connection and relationship with each other; that, however suddenly and arbitrarily they seem to appear in the history of thought, they nevertheless belong just as much to a system as all the members of the fauna of a continent—is betrayed in the end also by the fact that the most diverse philosophers keep filling in a definite fundamental scheme of possible philosophies. Under an invisible spell, they always revolve once more in the same orbit; however independent of each other they may feel themselves with their critical or systematic wills, something within them leads them, something impels them in definite order, one after the other—to wit, the innate systematic structure and relationship of their concepts. Their thinking is, in fact, far less a discovery than a recognition, a remembering, a return and a homecoming to a remote, primordial, and inclusive household of the soul, out of which those concepts grew originally: philosophizing is to this extent a kind of atavism of the highest order. (BGE 20; see also: BGE, "Preface"; BGE 6; BGE 213)

The philosopher is a complex unity that evolves in part by incorporating into himself physio-psychological characteristics that previously existed in separate individuals. This same process occurs in inheritance. Individual human beings are formed not only by their particular history, but also by the histories and physio-psychologies of their ancestors:

> One cannot erase from the soul of a human being what his ancestors liked most to do and did most constantly: whether they were, for example, assiduous savers and appurtenances of a desk and cash box, modest and bourgeois in their desires, modest also in their virtues; or whether they lived accustomed to commanding from dawn to dusk, fond of rough amusements

and also perhaps of even rougher duties and responsibilities; or whether, finally, at some point they sacrificed ancient prerogatives of birth and possessions in order to live entirely for their faith—their "god"—as men of an inexorable and delicate conscience that blushes at every compromise. It is simply not possible that a human being should *not* have the qualities and preferences of his parents and ancestors in his body, whatever appearances may suggest to the contrary. (BGE 264)

Given that genealogies are continuous and interconnected, if we trace the genealogies of human beings back in time, we eventually discover that species distinctions blur. The ancestries of human beings incorporate ancestries of pre-humans, and non-humans. There are no definite boundaries between kinds of beings. Look farther back. More deeply! Everything is connected in a continuum of vitality that runs through all living things. Does it also run through pre-life, the un-generated, the un-alive? The falsity of absolute opposites suggests it does. The concept of individuation—on which all of these distinctions depend, including types, kinds, and even individual beings in the world—begins to reveal itself to be a regulative hypothesis—a hypothesis that is potentially valuable for human vitality—rather than something true (see BGE 15; BT 1 - 15).

While this entire genealogy determines to some extent what we are, the boundaries it imposes on us are not absolute. Given sufficient time, any aspect of what we are could recede or disappear from our physio-psychology, if not from our history:

> That the character is unalterable is not in the strict sense true; this favorite proposition means rather no more than that, during the brief lifetime of a human being, the effective motives are unable to scratch deeply enough to erase the imprinted script of many millennia. If one imagines a human being of eighty-thousand years, however, one would have in him a character totally alterable: so that an abundance of different individuals would evolve out him one after the other. The brevity of human life misleads us to many erroneous assertions regarding the qualities of man. (HH 1.41)

Thus, we come to realize the living being is neither absolutely fluid, nor is it fixed in its present state. It has a past that informs, and to some extent determines, what it is in the present and what it can become in the immediate future. Pathways of development that were available to it at one stage of its development are not available to it in the same way later, after its physio-psychology has been altered. Regarding its future, there is no limit on what a being might become. For example, the current physio-psychology of the human being strongly inclines us to suspect we cannot acquire the capacity to regenerate all parts of ourselves in the next instant or tomorrow. Nor do we expect suddenly to acquire the capacity to see electro-magnetic fields. We regard these conclusions as reasonable because we have not discerned a path to such immediate and dramatic alterations in our physio-psychology. However, the fact that such capacities seem unavailable as the immediate next step in our evolution does not rule out the possibility that the species will acquire them at some future stage of its genealogy. Similarly, while it may be true that every human being that has existed to date has died, this does not mean mortality is necessary to what we are. That a being lives does not necessitate that it also dies.

Such thoughts have not been seriously explored by philosophers prior to Nietzsche, or following him, for that matter. In spite of the fact that most people, including most thinkers and scientists, now accept evolution as a true account of living beings, they continue to hang on to the notion of a final cause or natural limit that determines what a living being is, all that it could ever be, and what it ought to be. However, the notion that a living being is subject to an insurmountable limit that defines both what it is and what is good for it is an expression of the moral-theological prejudice (see BGE 22; BGE 9; GS 37; GS 109; GS 143; WP 12; WP 13; WP 552). There are no such limits, nor is there any reason to think they would be good, if they did exist. The absence of such limits is what it means to be a being that is a becoming, an undetermined being. In other words, traditional definitions of the human being try to define what we are ahistorically, but they fail to offer an adequate definition because a living being is a type of motion that is inseparable from its genealogy. Nothing with a history can be defined according to a single, ahistorical moment in its genealogy, as though this moment encapsulated all that it ever was or could become (see GM 2.13).

In lieu of this traditional approach to understanding a being, Nietzsche's account of his own development indicates that, if one wants to know what a being with a history is, one must know its genealogy— one must know the narrative of its changing shape as a living-form. If one wanted to know something about a living being with a view to determining whether it is evolving or declining, or with a view to guiding its motion, one might reasonably look to the activity that is most vitalizing for it or that has the potential to be most vitalizing. One might seek to augment this activity or to make it more of what it is. Nietzsche does this in his own case when he speaks of his moral scruple. He does it again in the case of the human being. As a result of his genealogical investigations of the species, he concludes the human being's most vitalizing activity to date consists in our ongoing effort to take charge of our own evolution, which we have so far done unconsciously, instinctually, and largely by means of moral doctrines (e.g. see GM 2.1 – 2).

The moral-theological prejudice manifests again in the concept of free will, understood as the freedom to choose one's actions. This concept presupposes that the essence of a human being consists in an unchanging, unitary soul or self that persists throughout an individual's life, and perhaps beyond. Nietzsche attributes the notion that there is such an entity to grammar and the belief that the cosmos is ruled by a mind, a first cause, or a God. This belief is then reflected in the concept of the human being. Pushing this compound prejudice aside, Nietzsche maintains there is no such thing as an unmoved self—an "I"—that stands apart from, and freely determines, the human being's actions. In Nietzsche's language, there is no *doer* behind the *deed*. The doer *is* the deed; the deed is everything (GM 1.13). Hence, we are neither free nor unfree in the way most people believe. We are so far from being free to choose to act or not to act that there is not even a necessary connection between willing an act and that action. We can will an act without that action coming to be. Alternatively, our physio-psychology can move without our having anything of the feeling of command that is most characteristic of human willing. Conditions like Tourette's syndrome and muscular dystrophy illustrate this point. Action and inaction are simply the results of the interplay of multiple drives that exist together in the social structure we identify as the body (see BGE 12 - 19; BGE 21; GM 1.13; GM 2.21; GS 333).

Again, Nietzsche captures the falsity of the concept of free will in his depiction of his own growth and that of philosophers in general. According to Nietzsche, no philosopher experiences his philosophic activity as something he is free or unfree to do or not do. Rather, he experiences it as the expression of what he most profoundly and most powerfully is. This is to say he also experiences himself as more than this most dominant drive: he is *aware* of his own complexity. Thus, he is often in awe of his own thinking, as though it were something external to him. He lives within himself like an adventurer in a land at once familiar and strange:

> A philosopher—is a human being who constantly experiences, sees, hears, suspects, hopes, and dreams extraordinary things; who is struck by his own thoughts as from outside, as from above and below, as by *his* type of experiences and lightning bolts; who is perhaps himself a storm pregnant with new lightnings; a fatal human being around whom there are constant rumblings and growlings, crevices, and uncanny doings. A philosopher—alas, a being that often runs away from itself, often is afraid of itself—but is too inquisitive not to "come to" again—always back to himself. (BGE 292; see also EH, "Why I Am So Clever," 9)

The philosopher philosophizes because the drives that motivate this activity are typically stronger than those that seek to express themselves in other acts. What is true of the philosopher's psychic activity is true of every human being's so-called psychic events. Stronger drives always prevail over weaker drives, just as any stronger force prevails over a weaker one (see BGE 21). Yet, having just spoken of the psyche, we must note that Nietzsche thinks there is no distinction, strictly speaking, between the so-called mind and body. Although he uses these terms, he does so as a kind of shorthand or short cut. When he is speaking strictly, he avoids them and instead speaks of physiology or physio-psychology. His rejection of the mind-body dualism follows from the fact that it presupposes there are pure kinds or types of beings. In this particular case, it presumes the mind and body are wholly unmixed. In its presupposition of purity, this presumption proves to be yet another expression of the theological prejudice. As we have noted, life, as revealed by genealogy, exists on a continuum. It therefore precludes pure kinds. Thus, what is true of the activity and growth of the so-called psyche must be true in some way of the so-called body. If we extend Nietzsche's depiction of psychic growth to the body, we can infer bodily growth occurs when the vitality or strength of the aggregate of drives that constitute it is sufficiently great not only to sustain the being's form, but also to augment and increase it. The form degenerates when the aggregate is overpowered.

Apply this same line of thinking to the genealogy of the species. Nietzsche observes that breeding preserves and augments certain drives while weakening and destroying others. Over generations, the physio-psychology of the species acquires greater stability and predictability (e.g. see BGE 257; BGE 262; GM 2). Yet, this relative fixity still does not imply or require us to revert to the idea that absolute being is in any way involved with the species. As in the case of the individual's form, the species-form is also the effect of an aggregate or society of drives that have become sufficiently strong in their interactions to withstand and overcome opposing forces with some regularity and for some time.

Extend this thinking about vital drives to all things. By so doing, we make this thinking into a physical or cosmic hypothesis that might explain everything in the world. According to this hypothesis, the distinction between what is intrinsic and extrinsic to a being is only a manifestation of the interactions between strong and weak fields of a single kind of drive. This hypothesis does not require us to forego the notion that there are beings. What it does mean is that these designations are more like dynamic force fields, than static, absolute boundaries that are separate from the interacting drives (see BGE 12 - 14; BGE 17; GM 1.13).

This cosmic hypothesis belongs to Nietzsche. He presents it in *Beyond Good and Evil*, the book he writes to redeem the feminine principle of becoming so that it can resume a fecund, dualistic union with the masculine principle of being. By re-establishing this dualism, Nietzsche aims to overthrow the moral-theological prejudice and thus to make way for his teaching on the goodness of generation.[8] It is in the context of this project that he presents this cosmic hypothesis. The name he gives to the hypothetical force that could explain everything in the world is the will to power:

> Suppose nothing else were "given" as real except our own world of desires and passions, and we could not get down, or up, to any other "reality" besides the reality of our drives—for thinking is merely a relation of these drives to each other: is it not permitted to make the experiment and to ask the question whether this "given" would not be *sufficient* for also understanding on the basis of this kind of thing the so-called mechanistic (or "material") world? I mean, not as deception, as "mere appearance," an "idea" … but as holding the same rank of reality as our affect—as a more primitive form of the world of the affects in which everything still lies contained in a powerful unity before it undergoes ramifications and developments in the organic process (and, as is only fair, also becomes tenderer and weaker)—as a kind of instinctive life in which all organic functions are still synthetically intertwined along with self-regulation, assimilation, nourishment, excretion, and metabolism—as a *pre-form* of life.

In the end not only is it permitted to make this experiment; the conscience of method *demands* it. Not to assume several kinds of causality until the experiment of making do with a single one has been pushed to its utmost limit (to the point of nonsense, if I may say so)—that is a moral of method that one may not shirk today—it follows "from its definition," as a mathematician would say. ... In short, one has to risk the hypothesis whether will does not affect will wherever "effects" are recognized—and whether all mechanical occurrences are not, insofar as a force is active in them, will force, effects of will.

Suppose, finally, we succeeded in explaining our entire instinctive life as the development and ramification of *one* basic form of the will—namely, of the will to power, as *my* proposition has it; suppose all organic functions could be traced back to this will to power and one could also find in it the solution of the problem of procreation and nourishment—it is *one* problem—then one would have gained the right to determine *all* efficient force univocally as—*will to power*. (BGE 36; see also BGE 259)

Understood as a cosmic force, the will to power is a thought experiment. Nietzsche comes to it in the same way we did—by thinking through the implications of generation as fully as possible, until one finally arrives at conclusions Nietzsche himself identifies as nonsense. In addition to completing the investigation of generation, this cosmic hypothesis serves the purpose of undermining metaphysics on its own terms. By means of it, Nietzsche cuts all metaphysical doctrines that arise from the moral-theological prejudice to ribbons with Occam's razor, the scientific principle according to which greater simplicity is proof of greater plausibility. The authority of Occam's razor is inherent to the moral-theological prejudice. Yet, Nietzsche's hypothesis reflects it more fully than any other metaphysical doctrine, for his cosmic hypothesis does what these metaphysical doctrines fail to do: it explains everything with only *one* term.

While the will to power, understood as a cosmic hypothesis, is a brilliant play, it is not Nietzsche's primary interest. By far the lion's share of his attention is focused on living beings and on human beings in particular. With respect to living beings, he also speaks of the will to power, but here it denotes what we have so far called vitality. It is the activity or motion that is life. Nietzsche makes this point explicitly by equating the will to power with the will of life (BGE 259).

In light of this clarification of the often misunderstood term—the will to power—we can restate the definition of genealogy we offered earlier using Nietzsche's language. Previously, we described genealogy as the study of changing shape—the morphology—of life. Since life is will to power, we can now say genealogy is "morphology and *the doctrine of the development of the will to power*" (BGE 23). This definition of genealogy is precisely the same as Nietzsche's definition of psychology:

> To understand ... [psychology] as morphology and *the doctrine of the development of the will to power*, as I do—nobody has yet come close to doing this even in thought—insofar as it is permissible to recognize in what has been written so far a symptom of what has so far been kept silent. (BGE 23)

Thus, after spending much time fleshing out what genealogy is, we suddenly discover that this investigative work reveals with surprising ease both the definition of psychology *and* its equivalence to genealogy.

Nietzsche introduces the definition of psychology with an observation: "All psychology so far has got stuck in moral prejudices and fears; it has not dared to descend into the depths" of "the most spiritual world"—the world of the mind, the intellectual world—where one must go if one is first to face and then to answer the question of the value of morality for the life of the human being (BGE 23; see also TI, "What I Owe to the Ancients," 2; GS 340; BT, "Attempt at a Self-Criticism," 1). He implicitly indicates neither moral prejudices nor fear has kept him from these depths. Since he alone has descended into that profundity, he is the first to see psychology—and hence genealogy—for what it is. Reflecting on his travels and their implications, he makes a proclamation of victory. He announces that, as a result of his discovery of what psychology truly is, "psychology shall be recognized again as the queen of the sciences, for whose service and preparation the other sciences exist. For psychology is now again the path to the fundamental problems" (BGE 23).

Although Nietzsche identifies himself as the first to know adequately what psychology is, he indicates here that this science at least held its proper rank and was used as a means to fundamental questions at some point in the past. When?[9] Most philosophers think metaphysics holds the highest position amongst the sciences. However, one philosopher makes a point of saying he rejects metaphysics. Paradoxically, that philosopher is Socrates, the very individual whom Nietzsche charges with having originated the moral-theological prejudice that entangled every major thinker who lived after him.[10]

Socrates, as depicted by Plato, says he was interested in metaphysics at one time in his life, because he thought it would be a means to the rational accounts of all beings. He believed these accounts would be grounded in a divine mind or first cause. However, he found this approach to the beings to be unavailable and therefore unfruitful for himself and everyone else. Thus, he turned away from metaphysics and toward human accounts or speeches as a way of learning about the beings. He calls this turn to human things a "second sailing," which is a term the ancient Greeks use to describe their recourse to oars—to human power—when the invisible power of the winds proves inadequate for our needs (Plato, *Phaedo*, 99d – 101a; see also BGE 191).

Speech makes the psyche manifest. Thus, Socrates' analysis of the things people say belongs to psychology—the logos (λογος) of the psyche (ψυχη). Since Socrates is the most renowned and influential practitioner of the science of souls prior to Nietzsche, we can reasonably infer psychology was the queen of the sciences and the path to fundamental problems when Socrates and his students employed it.

Perhaps in order to indicate the earlier epoch to which he refers when he claims to have returned psychology to its proper place and employment, Nietzsche makes what seems to be an allusion to Socrates' sailing metaphor: he completes the section in which he presents the first *true* definition of psychology with a sailing metaphor of his own. He warns the bold traveler who investigates the value of morality adequately that he will suffer like someone with seasickness from what he discovers. He will "have to contend with unconscious resistance in the heart" when he begins to see that all good impulses are derived from wicked ones. His rebellion against himself will become even stronger in the face of his discovery that evil and bad affects, such as "hatred, envy, covetousness, and the lust to rule … must be present in the general economy of life (and must, therefore, be further enhanced if life is to be further enhanced)" (BGE 23; see also BGE 295; Z, "On the Higher Man," 5). In light of this foreseeable war within oneself and the suffering it will necessarily involve, Nietzsche advises everyone who can keep away from such explorations to do so.

Then, he adds:

> On the other hand, if one has once drifted there with one's little ship, well! All right! Let us clench our teeth! Let us open our eyes and keep our hand firm on the helm! We sail right over morality, we crush, we destroy perhaps the remains of our own morality by daring to make our voyage

there—but what matter are *we!* Never yet did a *profounder* world of insight reveal itself to daring travelers and adventurers. (BGE 23)

Nietzsche knows Socrates is the archetypal philosopher, or at least he was before Nietzsche conceives of an enhancement of the philosophic type. Socrates, like Nietzsche, makes no distinction between psychology and philosophy. He is the embodiment of the equivalence between the philosopher and psychologist. However, we do not need to look to Socrates to see this equivalence. Nietzsche characterizes himself inter-changeably as a psychologist and philosopher. In one of his most explicit moments of self-identification, Nietzsche audaciously and elegantly announces: "That a psychologist without equal speaks from my writings, is perhaps the first insight reached by a good reader—a reader as I deserve him, who reads me the way good old philologists read their Horace" (EH, "Why I Write Such Great Books," 5; see also EH, "Why I Write Such Great Books," 6; EH, "Why I Am A Destiny," 6 - 7). In addition to identifying himself as a superlative psychologist, he observes one can only know from experience what a philosopher is. He then describes this experience—firsthand:

> A philosopher who has traversed many kinds of health, and keeps traversing them, has passed through an equal number of philosophies; he simply *cannot* keep from transposing his states every time into the most spiritual form and distance: this art of transfiguration *is* philosophy. We philosophers are not free to divide body from soul as the people do; we are even less free to divide soul from spirit. We are not thinking frogs, nor objectifying and registering mechanisms with their innards removed: constantly, we have to give birth to our thoughts out of our pain and, like mothers, endow them with all we have of blood, heart, fire, pleasure, passion, agony, conscience, fate, and catastrophe. Life—that means for us constantly transforming all that we are into light and flame—also everything that wounds us; we simply can do no other. (GS "Preface," 3. See also EH, "How One Becomes What One Is," 3; BGE 211; BGE 292).

Since genealogy is psychology and psychology is philosophy, we can conclude all three are "morphology and *the doctrine of the development of the will to power*" (BGE 23). To say the same thing more rousingly, philosophy is the art of the transfiguring of all that one is into light and flame (GS "Preface," 3; see also GS 26).

Chapter Two

The Genealogy of Morals Begins

Nietzsche identifies the "typology of morals," including the preparatory work for it, as the sole study of morality that is "justified so far" and the only task that is "still necessary here for a long time to come" (BGE 186; see also GM 1.17). He takes up this task by means of the genealogy of morals, which is inextricably intertwined with the genealogy of the human being. By examining genealogies, he unearths and brings to light the proper foundation for a moral typology.

Before turning to Nietzsche's moral typology, we will sketch the philosophic backdrop against which it emerges. The first philosopher who seems to engage in moral typology is Socrates. His work involves examining people's opinions about the moral good. These investigations suggest these opinions can be broadly divided into two categories. People in the first category are pious. They believe the moral good is ultimately grounded in the gods of their city-state and that the gods' wills are reflected in the city's laws and mores. The second group is comprised of people who do not understand themselves as pious. Within this group, natural philosophers are especially noteworthy, for their works seem to lead them to authorities other than the regime's gods. Specifically, they regard the ultimate causes of phenomena as supremely authoritative. These causes are orderly always or for the most part and are therefore predictable, unlike the willful gods. To the extent that these natural philosophers regard the orderliness they see in the cosmos as good, and to the extent they attribute this orderliness to the ultimate causes of things, they believe these causes are good. However, they do not think these causes are invested in the moral concerns of human beings. The causes determine what is necessary, what things are, and what is possible, but they reveal nothing about what a human being ought to be or how we should act, for they are mindless rather than conscious entities. Hence, these philosophers do not look to the causes as moral authorities: that is, as guides for actions that pertain to relations with other creatures.

In lieu of obedience to the causes and the city's gods, the philosophers' apparent obedience to the regime's laws is the effect, not of obedience or duty strictly speaking, but of their orderly characters, habits, and prudence or something akin to prudence, which advises them not to defy or to seem to defy the city's laws and mores so long as the regime affords them the conditions they need to philosophize. Because these natural philosophers regard nature rather than convention or artifact as authoritative, and because they do not think there is any natural or non-conventional standard of the good, they may be characterized as pre-political philosophers.[11]

Having identified these two broad categories of human opinions about the good, we note that Socrates does not seem to belong to either category. He does not regard the city's gods as morally authoritative, but he also does not share the pre-political philosophers' conclusion that the study of nature yields no answers to the question of the good human life. Rather, Socrates is the first philosopher who thinks the human mind or psyche has a nature that, when adequately understood, reveals what excellence or the good life are for the human being. By elucidating this standard of excellence or the good, Socrates necessarily also articulates the authoritative standard against which all political regimes are properly measured. As he is the first to discover a universally authoritative standard for political regimes, he stands as the founder of political philosophy. Thanks to his political philosophy, we can make the reasonable argument that regimes that promote the full actualization of human nature are good and just according to a supra-historical and supra-political standard—namely, nature and human nature more specifically. By contrast, those regimes that do not promote the full actualization of the human being or, worse, that inhibit this actualization, are bad and unjust.

The nature of the psyche, Socrates argues, is available to be seen by means of the dialectical art—that is, short exchanges of questions and answers. This kind of conversation can occur between two or several people. Since our minds are not simple wholes, we can also engage dialectically with ourselves, as Socrates demonstrates on occasion. In any of these cases, dialectics makes the psyche available for examination in a manner comparable to the way one can examine entities that are more available to our sense perception. Such examination enables one to expose false opinions, ground true opinions with reasoned accounts, and expose the lies people tell others and themselves. By correcting false opinions and removing lies, it is possible to determine the completed end or nature of the human being, which is regarded as excellent or good. Such a nature is embodied in the philosopher, who is most fully what he is when he is actively philosophizing. As the completed form of human nature, the philosopher is the standard of excellence for the human being per se.[12]

Socrates maintains that every human being manifests an inclination to complete his nature by becoming philosophic. While most people do not reach this completed state or natural end, each is nevertheless recognizable as a human being by the fact that each yearns for and participates in this end to some degree. To repeat, this standard of human nature is universally available to be seen everywhere at all times; it is trans-political and trans-historical. As such, it is both more rational than the gods of city-states, whose authority pertains only to the city to which they belong, and it is a more appropriate standard for human excellence than the mindless ultimate causes. It is at least partly for these reasons that excellent or fully actualized human nature becomes the measure of the excellence or goodness and justness not only of every human being, but also of every regime, for every regime explicitly or implicitly claims to be good and just.[13]

This overview enables us to recast the moral typology Socrates seems to initiate in the language of becoming and being. Since the pious and conventional conceptions of the good in Ancient Greece are associated with specific city-states, each of which is transient, these concepts are also transient. They are kinds of becoming. By contrast, the concept of the good that is based upon a belief in a defined, static, and universal nature belongs to the concept of absolute and unchanging being (*The Republic*, 506d – 511d). In this light, it becomes apparent that the conclusion according to which the complete human nature is more authoritative than the city's gods, laws, and mores depends on the prior, deeper conviction that being is superior to becoming. Thus, what initially appeared to be a genuine moral typology proves at a more profound level to be a manifestation of the moral-theological prejudice.

Stride now across the several centuries that separate classical Greece from the modern era. Here, we encounter the English psychologists, whom Nietzsche credits for taking the first step in the direction of a genuine moral typology. They do this by realizing that, if one wants to understand the good, one must attend to history rather than to the concept of an unchanging nature (GM 1.1). However, while they see something of the connection between history and morality, they fail to understand adequately the depth of this connection. They apprehend that the concept of the good has its origin in the past, but they do not realize it develops over time (GM 1.4; BGE 186).

Nietzsche attributes their failure in this regard partly to the fact that they share the "hallowed custom" of all philosophers, which is to think only ahistorically (GM 1.2). Such ahistoricism is yet another manifestation of the moral-theological prejudice, according to which truth is at odds with alteration. Insofar as the English psychologists are guided by this prejudice, their ahistoricism is consciously willed. Yet, their failure is not solely attributable to this prejudice. It is also due to a particular physio-psychological incapacity: they lack "the historical spirit," which one needs to engage adequately in genealogical studies.[14]

Nietzsche describes the historical spirit as "the capacity for quickly guessing the order of rank of the valuations by which a people, a society, a human being has lived" (BGE 224; see also GS 83; GS 337). It is like a sixth sense that has been incorporated into the human being relatively recently, as a result of the kind of breeding that typifies the modern era. Or rather, we have incorporated this new capacity by virtue of the *lack* of breeding that attends all democracies. The mindless democratic mixing of human beings, which transforms the human being in ways that may or may not be salutary, has produced this particular characteristic.

Democracies are always disordered mishmashes. As such, they can never be cultured, for the very purpose and meaning of culture consists in cultivating or determining artfully the development of the human beings who live in a particular political order. Given that culture artfully delimits human beings in this way, it properly belongs only to aristocracies, since only this type of regime arranges people into class structures that form a kind of complex whole. This whole is united by a shared vision of human excellence and a shared project of educating or cultivating the human being so that it incorporates and actualizes this concept of excellence more fully.

To cultivate the human being, the aristocrats strictly circumscribe the perspectives of everyone within the regime, including themselves. These limits help to prevent the development of disparate characteristics while also concentrating the society's focus on the task of integrating, defining, and refining more fully attributes that fall within the cultural horizon the aristocracy demarcates for itself. Thus, the human being becomes more composed, and this composed form becomes more fixed or hardened. Such hardening brings with it pronounced likes and dislikes. In other words, it breeds taste. Since taste is developed within a specific, limited cultural horizon, good taste is inseparable from an intolerance of everything foreign to that horizon. Thus, the most cultured human beings are unable to appreciate and to benefit even from potentially invigorating aspects of other peoples and cultures. Democracies, by contrast, are hostile to shared breeding projects. They are therefore uncultured, strictly speaking. It was and remains the characteristic lack of culture in the democracies of the nineteenth century and thereafter that enables a "mixing of classes and races" that were previously held apart by the strict class hierarchies that characterize aristocracies (BGE 224).

Such mixing has both costs and potential benefits for modern human beings. On the one hand, our physio-psychologies come to reflect the democratic regime's incoherence. "[E]very form and way of life, of cultures that formerly lay right next to each other or on top of each other" coincide in modern individuals (BGE 224). This incoherence costs us a cultural home in the world. No single culture can encompass the diverseness of the modern physio-psychology. Nietzsche expounds upon this homelessness by likening the modern human being to someone who tries constantly to find an outfit that suits him and in which he feels comfortable, but whose efforts in this regard are futile. We moderns may metaphorically don costumes from any and every culture. However, since we are more multifarious than the human beings for whom these costumes were sewn, none simply suffices. We cannot fit fully into any of them:

> The hybrid European—all in all, a tolerably ugly plebian—simply needs a costume: he requires history as a storage room for costumes. To be

sure, he soon notices that not one fits him very well; so he keeps changing. Let anyone look at the nineteenth century with an eye for these quick preferences and changes of the style masquerade; also for the moments of despair over the fact that "nothing is becoming." It is no use to parade as romantic or classical, Christian or Florentine, baroque or "national," *in moribus et artibus [in morals and culture]*: it "does not look good." (BGE 223; see also GS 337)

On the other hand, while our mishmash physio-psychologies come at the cost of a cultural home, they also provide what might be our greatest advantage. We can penetrate and appreciate a great variety of different and even opposing cultures to a degree that is unavailable to truly cultured human beings. In other words, while no costume fits us fully, we can fit tolerably well into a great variety and perhaps even most costumes, at least for a time. It is especially noteworthy for genealogical studies that we can comprehend semi-barbarians and incomplete cultures. The relative formlessness of these conditions renders them opaque to people whose physio-psychologies are more coherent and refined. For them, where there is chaos or semi-chaos, history does not occur. That is, they regard such periods as though they were dark periods or voids in the history of the human being. This is not the case for we moderns with the historical sense.

> Through our semi-barbarism in body and desires we have secret access in all directions, as no noble age ever did; above all, access to the labyrinths of unfinished cultures and to every semi-barbarism that ever existed on earth. And insofar as the most considerable part of human culture so far was semi-barbarism, "historical sense" almost means the sense and instinct for everything, the taste and tongue for everything—which immediately proves it to be an ignoble sense. (BGE 224)

Such boundlessness and lack of measure manifests in the artistic genius who embodies the historical sense. In lesser modern artists or so-called artists, the effect of unbridled mixing of disparate forms is an ugly—that is, enervating—confusion. However, truly great modern artists can amalgamate these disparate elements in a way that invigorates us and that we therefore rightly deem beautiful (see TI, "Expeditions of an Untimely Man," 19, 20, 24). In their hands, art becomes profoundly artificial. Paradoxically, this might mean it becomes most artful, if not most cultured and tasteful.

Nietzsche cites Shakespeare as an example of such an artist, describing him as an "amazing Spanish-Moorish-Saxon synthesis of tastes that would have all but killed an ancient Athenian of Aeschylus' circle with laughter or irritation" (BGE 224). In contrast to the cultured response to Shakespeare, Nietzsche, as a modern human being, expresses profound appreciation for him: "[W]e—accept precisely this wild abundance of colors, this medley of what is most delicate, coarsest, and most artificial, with a secret familiarity and cordiality; we enjoy him as a superb subtlety of art saved up especially for us" (BGE 224).

After weighing the costs and benefits of cultural homelessness, Nietzsche affirms and embraces the physio-psychological advantages that mishmash modernity affords with an exuberant "Yes!" *"Measure* is alien to us; let us own it; our thrill is the thrill of the infinite, the unmeasured. Like a rider on a steed that flies forward, we drop the reins before the infinite, we modern human beings, like semi-barbarians—and reach our bliss only where we are most—*in danger"* (BGE 224). His embrace is apt, for Nietzsche himself is a modern artist. His philosophy is a work of art in the highest, most life-promoting sense of the word.

Like the great modern playwright, the great modern genealogist experiences foreign and past moralities within himself. As a result of his diverse composition, moral concepts and the epochs they epitomize are open to him to a great extent, if not fully. Various moral eras resonate with different components or aspects of what he is. He can employ these resonances like spiritual handholds that guide him into foreign or past realms in which he can dwell either literally, in the case of foreign realms, or imaginatively and spiritually, in the case of past realms, for a significant time before becoming vagabond again. His capacity to live in these foreign or past cultures enables him to discern what other and past peoples believe is most difficult, what they hold to be most important, and what they venerate. He can understand the way their political and social arrangements express their greatest fears, needs, and aspirations. From such things, he can detect how such people, together with the eras defined by their moralities, can be destroyed, overcome, and superseded.

Since the English psychologists lack the historical sense, they cannot do any of the things that depend upon it. Obtuse to genealogy, they do not know that they must peel back the layers of a concept's current shape so that its simpler, earlier forms are exposed. Instead, they believe the concept of the good that dominates in their day, whereby the good is equivalent to the useful, is all that the good has ever truly meant. Thus, while they may think they are seeking the origin of the concept of the good, they are in fact seeking the origin of only one of the concept's meanings. They act like human beings who hold a pattern in their hands and page through a sketchbook that records the pattern's development. Rather than observing the changes to the pattern over time, they seek the page upon which the pattern first appears. Ironically, if they flipped the pages quickly, and thus seemed to search less carefully, they would see something closer to the truth of the matter, for they would see an altering rather than a static pattern.

While the English psychologists insist the good is utilitarian, some and perhaps all human beings lack complete faith in this definition. We retain the sense that there is such a thing as a non-utilitarian good, a good that is always choice worthy for its own sake rather than as a means to something beyond itself. Utilitarians are aggravated and threatened by this persistent sense of a non-utilitarian good. They seek to destroy it by asserting it is a fiction derived from a misunderstanding of the utilitarian good. They "decree" that, initially, "one approved of un-egoistic actions and called them good from the point of view of those to whom they were done, that is to say, those to whom they were useful" (GM 1.2). In this pronouncement, they implicitly indicate the passive human being—one upon whom or for whom an action is done—originates the concept, rather than the actor. They argue that people eventually forgot that the concept originated in the passive beneficiary of the act. Nevertheless, the praise for such acts continued, in spite of people's ignorance of the cause of such praise. Finally, because such acts were stupidly praised continually and daily, people acquired the *habit* of praising such acts. Out of this non-rational habit, the notion of the good per se is born. That is, people no longer knew such acts were originally deemed good from the perspective of the beneficiary, and they inferred they must be judged from the perspective of the actor. Since these acts did not seem useful to the actor, or at least not primarily so, they imputed a different motive to him. They concluded he must act un-egoistically, for a non-utilitarian reason. He must act for the sake of the good-in-itself, the good per se!

Nietzsche concludes his summary of the English psychologists' account by reflecting on its essential components and intended effects. He observes that higher human beings have so far been proud of nothing so much as the human being's ability to comprehend and act in accord with the notion of the good-in-itself. We have regarded it "as a kind of prerogative of the human being as such" (GM 1.2). At the hands of these psychologists, these higher acts are reduced to utility, forgetting, habit, and error. This reduction is intentional. As utilitarians see it, "This pride *has* to be humbled, this evaluation disvalued" (GM 1.2). Who in particular must be humbled? The pro-actor—yes—but above all they intend to humble those who are remarkable for their courage. They focus on courageous human beings because such humans are best equipped for higher actions, for all truly high acts require courage. The highest acts, which are always original, require astounding independence from the status quo. One with such independence necessarily acts without the safety net of common opinion, public estimation, and common sympathy.

Consider the paradigmatic example of a courageous act—the warrior's heroic actions in the face of extreme danger, especially war. Since utilitarians regard the non-utilitarian good as a fiction, the courageous human being—most pointedly, the heroic warrior—is a dupe (GM 1.2). Given the character of his action, this warrior, more than anyone else, acts from forgetfulness, habit, and error. In other words, the heroic warrior is above all else an idiot of the first order (see BGE 190). We are right to be suspicious of an argument that undermines the most lauded and noble actions. What motivates these denigrators of all things high, especially the heroic warrior? (GM 1.1).

Our sense that their motives are suspicious is augmented by the fact that the utilitarian argument is illogical (GM 1.3). Utilitarian concepts are logically secondary to a non-utilitarian good, for they presuppose an answer to the question: "Useful for what?" Utilitarianism claims to be rational, and rational action aims at a final end. This end renders intelligible every action that is subordinate to this end. By contrast, an infinite regression of responses to the question "Why?" implicitly presents every end as merely proximate rather than final. Every proximate end is a means to another, similarly proximate end. All ends thereby dissolve into means, which is to say that the entire chain of dissolving ends is ultimately untethered by a final, rational account. To end the infinite regress and thus to preserve the intelligibility of human action, one must eventually bring the regress of answers to the question "Why?" to a halt. This is done by means of a non-utilitarian good-in-itself. By arguing that the non-utilitarian concept of the good, the good-in-itself, is a product of error rather than a real thing, these English psychologists deny themselves the rational foundation that is necessary to make utilitarianism intelligible and therefore logically sound.

In addition to being untenable logically, the English psychologists' argument is also "psychologically absurd" (GM 1.3). Nietzsche concisely captures the psychological absurdity of this argument with a single rhetorical question: "How is this forgetting *possible?*" (GM 1.3). Those who are familiar with Nietzsche's reflections on forgetfulness will recall that forgetting can result from two causes. One results from a kind of passive dissolution of the associations and details of what is forgotten. We expect passive forgetting to occur over time, as we acquire more vivid memories, which push aside and dissipate those that are less vivid. The other kind of forgetting is actively willed. In this case, one actively endeavors *not* to remember something (GM 2.1 – 2.3). What we now call repression is an example of such forgetting. While passive forgetting is not possible where the association between utility and the good is constantly reinforced, might not active forgetting explain people's forgetfulness of the fact that the non-utilitarian good is an erroneous interpretation of the utilitarian good, as judged from the perspective of the action's beneficiary?

This possibility is not psychologically absurd, but it does not seem to occur to the English psychologists. They say nothing about it. Additionally, they offer no motive for active forgetting. Instead, they seem to have in mind only the more commonplace understanding of forgetfulness— passive forgetfulness. Limiting ourselves, as they do, to only this kind of forgetfulness, it is indeed psychologically absurd to suggest people would forget the connection between the concept of the good and utility, despite the fact that this connection always exists and is highlighted by the continual praise that is lavished upon the utilitarian good.

As an alternative to this absurd argument, Nietzsche considers Herbert Spencer's hypothesis on the origin of the concept of the good. Like the other English psychologists whom Nietzsche addresses prior to Spencer, Spencer also equates the good with the useful. Unlike them, he avoids making a psychologically absurd argument by simply denying that anyone believes or ever has believed there is such a thing as a non-utilitarian good. As Spencer would have it, everyone has always known the good is nothing but the useful. Indeed, he claims it is precisely because everyone knows the good is the useful that the useful can legitimately be called the supreme good. Nietzsche summarizes the essence of Spencer's conclusions:

> [T]he concept "good" is essentially identical with the concept "useful," "practical," so that in the judgments "good" and "bad" mankind has summed up and sanctioned precisely its *unforgotten* and *unforgettable* experiences regarding what is useful-practical and what is harmful-impractical. According to this theory, that which has always proved itself useful is good: therefore it may claim to be "valuable in the highest degree," "valuable in itself." (GM 1.3)

While Nietzsche does not dismiss Spencer's theory as absurd, he does argue that it is false (GM 1.3). As we shall come to see, Nietzsche thinks not only that all human beings are aware of a non-utilitarian good, but also that this concept signifies a very real entity in our earthly world, *the* world. In truth, the good signifies what is most real.

This teaser tempts us to turn aside from erroneous arguments and toward Nietzsche's hypothesis. He tells us he saw a "signpost to the *right* road" toward the origin of the concept of the good in one question: "What was the real etymological significance of the designations for 'good' coined in various languages?" (GM 1.4).[15] By reflecting on the etymology of the word, he realizes the designation "good" has the same first meaning and genealogy in all languages. It denotes political dominance in an aristocratic political order, together with a certain quality of soul that the aristocrats identify as the essence of what they are and of what accounts for and legitimizes their rule:

> [E]verywhere "noble," "aristocratic" in the social sense, is the basic concept from which "good" in the sense of "with aristocratic soul," "noble," "with a soul of a high order," "with a privileged soul" necessarily developed: a development which always runs parallel with that other in which "common," "plebian," "low" are finally transformed into the concept "bad." (GM 1.4)

What could explain the fact that all languages have the same first meaning of the good? It suggests there is a common cause for this first meaning, but what might that be?

Before pursuing the question of who or what might produce the first meaning of the good, we must be sure that we have an adequate sense of what an original concept is. It is neither an imitation or a recollection, nor is it a negation of a pre-existing concept. It is a beginning, a first thing. As such, the creation of any truly original entity, including a concept, is a kind of creation *ex nihilo*.

By characterizing original creation in this way, we do not mean it is the most radical form of creation *ex nihilo*, which entails producing something out of nothing—being out of non-being. Some believers attribute this most radical form of creation *ex nihilo* to Yahweh and the Christian God. Even if this most radical form of origination were possible, it would be wholly unknowable by us. It is unknowable by our perception because, while we might perceive something manifesting where it was not previously apparent, this perception would not enable us to discern whether the suddenly manifest thing was created out of nothing. It is unavailable to reason because it defies the relationship between cause and effect that reason requires. Since this most radical kind of creation *ex nihilo* is unknowable by us, it does not exist for us. This leaves us with only one kind of creation *ex nihilo*. What is it?

Real or true origination involves altering or re-forming existing entities so that they come to have a shape that did not exist for the human being, the individual creator, or both, prior to this creative act. We can envision possible examples of original creations, such as the invention of the wheel, a new mathematical formula, a new kind of engine, the first artificial intelligence that exceeds the current human capacities of the human being. What is unlikely to come to the minds of most people when they think of examples of original creation is evolution. Nevertheless, evolution is arguably the most wondrous version of creation *ex nihilo*. It is also the kind we must understand more clearly if we are to comprehend the origin of the good and the genealogy of morality more generally.

We begin by noting that, as Nietzsche understands them, evolution, generation, and growth are synonyms for same process. All describe the motion by which a being's physio-psychological form or shape is augmented by being extended or by extending itself into ontological territory it did not previously occupy. As a result of this growth, the being's overall vitality is increased. That is, the entity becomes a new shape of itself that is more active in the world than it was prior to this augmentation.[16] Moreover, to say a being is augmented and increases its vitality or its activity in the world is to say it has more being—it is *more* of what it is—as determined by its genealogy, including this augmentation (BGE 36; BGE 259).

Consider the creation of original concepts in terms of evolution, so conceived.

A concept, like perception, is a kind of thinking. Thinking, in turn, is a shape of the motion that is life. As such, thinking can degenerate and grow. Since thinking is a life-form, and concepts are a kind of thinking, concepts are also alive. Hence, they degenerate and grow.

That a concept is alive is strange thought. To clarify this thought, while perhaps not making it less strange, note that nouns are not real things, strictly speaking. That is, a noun is a kind gesture toward the activity that the noun summarizes. There are no unchanging entities that are somehow separate from actions; hence, there are no concepts, understood as self-subsisting, unchanging things. Speaking more mindfully, therefore, when we say a concept is alive, what we truly mean is a concept only insofar as an entity is thinking it. Even more precisely, since the thinking entity is itself a kind of motion, we say that conceptualizing is part of the motion the thinking being is during the time that it is thinking in this way. Finally, we conclude that, since conceptualizing is part of the activity that is thinking in this way, and since we recognize this thinking being as alive, the so-called concept is necessarily also alive. To the extent that a concept may seem to be separate for the conceptualizing entity and as something with fixed or static content, it appears so because we are indoctrinated with the moral-theological prejudice. This misunderstanding of a concept may also arise from and be compounded by the fact that a concept is an abstraction. That is, the fullness of the motion from which the concept is derived and toward which it points has been thinned out and is therefore less apparent to more casual consideration of what a concept is.

Given that a concept is a kind of thinking, and since Nietzsche does not distinguish between mind and body, we can infer that an entity whose physio-psychology is not in a condition to engage in the thinking that the concept represents cannot adequately understand the concept. We can illustrate this by contrasting the different ways in which an adult and a child conceive of what the human being is. A philosopher might describe the human being as a rational animal. While an adult whose physio-psychology is genuinely mature can understand what this means, we do not expect a child to understand fully what this means, because the child's thinking capacity, and his capacity for reason in particular, is not as developed as that of the adult. We implicitly recognize that the child cannot conceive adequately something he cannot adequately experience. If the child's physio-psychology grows sufficiently, he will become able to understand what he previously could not, for his physio-psychology will come to be in a condition to do the thinking signified by the concept. Similarly, the physio-psychology of an adult human being may be augmented, in learning, for example. To the extent that the augmented adult thinks, his thinking will include concepts that are original for him, even if they are not original to human beings. If the thinking individual's physio-psychology evolves beyond what the human being per se has been to date, then his thinking must be original both to him and to the human being. Therefore, whatever concepts emerge out of this thinking must also be original to himself and to every other human being to date. In order to share something of his thinking, this human being may use concepts to try to initiate the growth he underwent in other human beings. Only if other human beings evolve or grow in a manner that is sufficiently similar to this more evolved thinker's growth will they be able to comprehend his thoughts.

In all of these examples, one sees that concepts, including original concepts, emerge out of our physio-psychology and articulate a physio-psychological alteration within us. They can have no other origin other than our physio-psychology. Thus, we have deduced something of the origin of the concept of the good: it must emerge from our physio-psychology.

Origination of an idea out of oneself has an analogue in the Biblical story of divine creation, according to which God generates the idea of an ordered world or cosmos out of himself. Understanding the idea to be good, God then imposes it upon existing material. By forming the cosmos in his image, he implicitly claims the beings who comprise it as his own to some significant degree, if not totally, for they now bear the stamp of his conception; they bear the stamp of him. Since both the human and divine creators' conceptions of the good are without precedent, and since both arise pro-actively out of the creators, we characterize both creative acts as spontaneous.

This consideration of what is entailed in spontaneous origination accords with Nietzsche's account of the origin of the concept of the good, in which he employs precisely this language. He announces it was "plain" to him that an original concept of the good "grows spontaneously," out of its creators (GM 1.10).[17] He goes on to deny explicitly that the concept could have originated in the beneficiary of a good act. In other words, it could not have originated in a reaction. Rather, for reasons we shall illuminate, he concludes it must have been created pro-actively. It cannot and "did not originate with those to whom 'goodness' was shown! Rather, it was 'the good' themselves—that is, the powerful, high-stationed and high-minded who felt and established themselves as good" who created it (GM 1.2). By this self-naming, the pro-active creator does not intend to indicate he is useful to others. Rather, he signifies it is good or choice worthy to be what he is. This pro-actively generated self-glorification— this "Yes!" to himself—is the true origin of the concept of the good-in-itself. In contrast to the utilitarian account of the concept's origin, Nietzsche's conclusion is both psychologically and logically sound.

What prompts these spontaneous creators to generate this concept? Nietzsche hypothesizes that, upon confronting human beings whom they recognize as vitally impotent in relation to themselves, these creators suddenly experience an acute sense of the difference between their vital potency and the vital impotence of these others. This is not to say they conceive of this difference and articulate it as a difference in vitality; rather, they perceive and experience it as a difference of the strength or the power to satisfy one's desire relatively immediately and directly. Moved by this sense of their vital superiority in contrast with these others—a sense Nietzsche calls the pathos of distance—they celebrate themselves in a terrific act of egoism, self-love, and self-glorification: they define themselves as good, in contradistinction to the vitally impotent or weak, whom they designate as bad.[18]

The fact that original morality was generated in the context of an interaction between its creators and those human beings from whom they distinguish themselves will tempt some people to conclude that the creation of the original good was reactive rather than pro-active. This conclusion cannot withstand scrutiny. Action only occurs in relation to one or more other beings or actions. Both pro-actions and reactions are therefore kinds of interaction. Pro-actions are nevertheless distinct from reactions, not because they are non-relational, but because they are manifestations of a super-abundant form of the will to power. To say the same thing more fully, they are manifestations of a form of vitality that is sufficient not only to sustain its form or its activity against opposing powers, but also to overcome these powers. In this overcoming, the pro-action both initiates and determines the shape of its action.

Unlike a pro-action, the impulse for a reaction originates in an external power. If it were not for the external stimulus, the reaction would not occur. Additionally, whereas the form of a pro-action is self-determined, the shape of a reaction is at best only the negation of the previously existing, pro-actively determined form. In other words, the shape of the reaction is limited by the boundary of the power against which the reaction occurs. A reaction can therefore never generate new content. It can only remove, negate, or reorient the pro-actively determined, content-rich original. Since only pro-actions can generate an entity that is content-rich and whose form did not exist previously, and since the original concept of the good is such an entity, the concept must have emerged from the physio-psychology of a pro-active creator.

The rationale for Nietzsche's conclusion that the concept of the good must have originated in a pro-action can be further illuminated by contrasting his thinking with the argument we discussed earlier, according to which all effects must ultimately be grounded in a first cause that is both the cause of itself and that serves as the foundational cause of all other apparent causes and effects. We noted that, since every cause other than the first dissolves into an effect, and since reason finds the infinite regression of effects unintelligible, the first cause serves as a kind of anchor for logic. It terminates what would otherwise be the infinite regression of effects. By so doing, it gives rational legitimacy to the entire chain of reasoning from effects to causes. Hence, the notion of a first cause is necessary to a morality that looks to reason as the authoritative standard. Is Nietzsche's argument for the priority of pro-action over reaction in the creation of original entities a version of the argument from effects to a final cause? Has he merely replaced the words "first cause" and "effects" with the words "pro-action" and "reaction" respectively? In a word, no. Nietzsche's argument does not depend on an abhorrence of an infinite regression of reactions. Rather, he considers what power is necessary for origination. It is this consideration that makes it "plain" to him that origination cannot be derivative. To repeat, a reaction cannot carve out new territory for itself, and this carving out is the essence of what we have characterized as creation *ex nihilo*. Having clarified the differences between pro-actions and reactions and the necessary dependence of creation *ex nihilo* upon pro-action, we return to our investigation of original morality.

As a form of self-glorification, the primary value in original morality is always the good. Its content invariably consists of attributes the pro-active creators associate with themselves and, more importantly, that they recognize as most characteristic of what they are. By contrast, the notion of the bad in original morality is always secondary and vague. It amounts to little more than the "not-good," which means something like vital impotence, weakness, or sickness.

The vagueness of the original concept of the bad is due largely to the fact that its creators do not have a prolonged experience of the weakness that characterizes the human beings with whom they contrast themselves. Their lack of significant experiences of weakness renders them unable to supply the concept of the bad with vivid content. Furthermore, they instinctively guard themselves against developing a more intimate knowledge of weakness or the bad (GM 1.10). Their instinct is right to be wary of such knowledge. Given that the so-called body is truly indistinct from the so-called mind, there is a danger that one will become weak by thinking for a prolonged period about what weakness is. By so doing, one enters more fully into the thought. One keeps company with it, and company—good and bad—can transform us. In colloquial terms, you are what you eat—but you are what you think, too (see BGE 231; EH, "Why I Am So Clever").

By designating weakness or sickness as bad, the creators of original morality articulate their sense that weakness per se is not choice worthy; it is a misfortune. Misfortune in no way indicates those who are weak are culpable for their condition. Nor does it suggest weakness is somehow illegitimate. Rather, as a relative measure of vitality, the concept of weakness belongs, along with strength or health and super-abundant vitality, on the continuum of life. It does not even occur to the creators of original morality to question the ontological legitimacy of weakness or sickness.

To flesh out the sense of misfortune that attends the original concept of the bad, Nietzsche directs us to the Ancient Greek nobility. Their understanding of the bad is typical of the pro-active type:

> One should not overlook the almost benevolent nuances that the Greek nobility, for example, bestows on all the words it employs to distinguish the lower orders from itself; how they are continuously mingled and sweetened with a kind of pity, consideration, and forbearance, so that finally almost all the words referring to the common man have remained as expressions signifying "unhappy," "pitiable" ... and how ... "bad," "low," "unhappy" have never ceased to sound to the Greek ear as one note with a tone-color in which "unhappy" preponderates: this as an inheritance from the ancient nobler aristocratic mode of evaluation, which does not belie itself even in its contempt. ... The "well-born" *felt* themselves to be "happy"; they did not have to establish their happiness artificially by examining their enemies, or to persuade themselves, *deceive* themselves, that they were happy. ... [T]hey likewise knew, as rounded men replete with energy and therefore *necessarily* active, that happiness should not be sundered from action—being active was with them necessarily a part of happiness (whence *eu pratein* takes its origin). (GM 1.10)[19]

It is not accidental that Nietzsche can look to the ruling class in Ancient Greece to elucidate the original concept of the bad. Spontaneous valuators necessarily rule as kings or aristocrats in any political regime that emerges out of a pre-political condition. This is because such political orders, like the original concept of the good, are unprecedented and must therefore be pro-actively generated. The first regime seems to be generated simultaneously with the first meaning of the original concept of the good. In naming themselves as the good, pro-active valuators implicitly give voice to their sense of their right to rule over weaker human beings. They impose their sense of rank upon these weaker human beings, thereby forming an aristocracy in which they rule and the weak are ruled (see GM 2.17).

The genealogy of the original concept of the good supports Nietzsche's hypothesis that the pro-active creators ruled in the earliest regimes, for its first meaning is associated with signifiers of political power such as "the possessors," and "the masters" (GM 1.5). However, while this meaning of the good is intertwined with trappings of political power, Nietzsche observes that such trappings are not essential to the concept (GM 1.5). Rather, the concept essentially signifies "one who *is*, who possesses reality, who is actual, who is true" (GM 1.5). These first valuators are aware that what they are is the maximum degree of life in its human form, and they equate this maximum form of vitality with the real and the true (GM 1.5). Their recognition of the goodness, reality, and truth of their maximality can be expressed in a proclamation attributed to Yahweh: "I AM THAT I AM" (Ex. 3:14 AV).

Since super-abundant vitality is necessary for pro-action, it necessarily remains the essential attribute of all pro-active valuators. However, all degrees of vitality, including super-abundant vitality are accompanied by a shape or form. The shape of the super-abundantly vital human life-form alters over time. This means every concept of the good that super-abundantly vital human beings generate out of their physio-psychology articulates something of the growth of the most vital form of the human being at a given epoch of our human evolution (see GM 2.12). We can therefore move from definition to definition, so to speak, to see something of how we have evolved over time.

Nietzsche identifies three distinct definitions of the original concept of the good over the course of the concept's genealogy. We infer from this that there are also three definitive eras in the genealogy of the human being, as represented by the super-abundantly vital human life-forms. The first meaning, which we have examined, indicates its creators do not recognize a standard of the good that is separate from what they are. In other words, they do not seem to regard themselves as subjects to which the predicate "good" pertains. They make no distinction between subject and predicate. Rather, they equate themselves with the good without any mediation, without much or any thought or consciousness about whether there could or should be a distinction between themselves and the good. They feel or know instinctively that they are good. If we could remove the grammatical distinction in English between the subject, the verb, and the predicate, so that they were all one and the same, we would have a more accurate conception what these first valuators mean when they assert: "I am the good; the real; the true" (GM 1.5).

In the second era, the concept takes what Nietzsche calls a "subjective turn" (GM 1.5). By this, he means the pro-active valuators no longer equate the real and the good directly or in an unmediated way with themselves. Instead, they now understand themselves as subjects about whom predications, such as "good," can be made. The distinction the value-creators now make between themselves and the concept of the good is reflected in the concept's second meaning, according to which the good signifies "the truthful," "the honest," human being, in contra-distinction to the "lying common man" who populates the lower classes and who, as a liar, is unqualified to be a law-giver and ruler (GM 1.5). By distinguishing between themselves and the good, they make the concept of the good into an objective standard against which they can measure not only themselves, but also all other human beings. In theory, there-fore, human beings other than these pro-active valuators might be good.

The third stage in the concept's genealogy brings us to the modern era. It arises in conjunction with the degeneration of aristocratic regimes. This degeneration is marked and at least partly caused by the fact that the super-abundant human type no longer holds political power. If any such human beings remain in the ruling class, they hold their political power alongside vitally impotent human beings. These weak rulers dilute to the point of virtual ineffectiveness whatever political consequences these remaining super-abundantly vital human beings might otherwise have.

In keeping with this change in political circumstance, the third meaning of the good includes no new trappings of political power. Rather, these creators glorify something new in their physio-psychology; namely, a significant development of the soul, spirit, or mind. More spe-cifically, the good is indicative of a certain "nobility of soul," in contradis-tinction to ignobility of soul (GM 1.5). Spiritual or intellectual courage is singled out in this era as especially noble; hence, spiritual cowardice is regarded as particularly bad or base (GM 1.5; see also Z, "On the Vision and the Riddle").[20]

To say spiritualized courage is especially celebrated in the third meaning of the concept is not to say courage does not belong to the concept's earlier meanings. In truth, it belongs to every meaning of the original notion of the good. Together with self-rule, courage seems to be the most persistent character trait super-abundant vitality has in its human form. That said, the courage that characterizes the super-abun-dant creators who live prior to the third epoch is simpler than it is at this later stage. Earlier, it is not especially involved with mind. As such, it is akin to animal ferocity and steadfastness. The later meanings of courage encompass something of the earlier meanings while also augmenting them with new content. This development of the concept indicates that the super-abundant creators who generate the later meanings similarly incorporate into their physio-psychologies something of the earlier forms of courage while also developing beyond them. Thus, in this third stage of the genealogy of the original concept of the good and of the human being, courage is recognized not only in overt acts of bravery, but also and most especially in the self-imposed command to seek out and confront terrible truths in the arena of the intellect. In *The Gay Science*, Nietzsche speaks of such heroes of the mind as "preparatory" human beings. These rare ones can lead the way into a new era of human evolution:

> I welcome all signs that a more virile, warlike age is about to begin, which will restore honor to courage above all. For this age shall prepare the way for one yet higher, and it shall gather the strength that this higher age will require some day—the age that will carry heroism into the search for knowledge and that will *wage wars* for the sake of ideas and their consequences. To this end we now need many preparatory courageous human beings who cannot very well leap out of nothing, any more than out of the sand and slime of present-day civilization and metropolitanism—human beings who know how to be silent, lonely, resolute, and content and constant in invisible activities; human beings who are bent on seeking in all things for what in them must be *overcome*; human beings distinguished as much by cheerfulness, patience, unpretentiousness, and contempt for all great vanities as by magnanimity in victory and forbearance regarding the small vanities of the vanquished; human beings whose judgment concerning all victors and the share of chance in every victory and fame is sharp and free; human beings with their own festivals, their own working days, and their own periods of mourning, accustomed to command with assurance but instantly ready to obey when that is called for—equally proud, equally serving their own cause in both cases; more endangered human beings, more fruitful human beings, happier beings! For believe me: the secret for harvesting from existence the greatest fruitfulness and the greatest enjoyments is—*to live dangerously!* Build your cities on the slopes of Vesuvius! Send your ships into uncharted seas! Live at war with your peers and yourselves! Be robbers and conquerors as long as you cannot be rulers and possessors, you seekers of knowledge! Soon the age will be past when you could be content to live hidden in forests like shy deer. At long last the search for knowledge will reach out for its due; it will want to *rule* and *possess*, and you with it! (GS 283; see also GS 2; WP 64)

Not only is the complexity of courage increased in proportion to its involvement with mind, but the power of the mind or intellect is also increased in proportion with its involvement with courage. Hence, Nietzsche indicates that, today, the most spiritual human beings—that is, those with the most highly developed minds—are also the most courageous. He then adds that this combination of highly developed courage and intellect necessarily involves the one who embodies them in "by far the most painful tragedies" (TI, "Skirmishes of an Untimely Man," 17). These tragedies are not an argument against life, according to these heroes. On the contrary, they honor life in such tragedy. In these very tragedies, they see life pitting "its greatest opposition against" them. They want to face such opposition, for in it they feel their strength most acutely (TI, "Skirmishes of an Untimely Man," 17; see also BGE 227; BGE 230; EH "How One Becomes What One Is," 3; EH, "Why I Write Such Great Books," 3; Nietzsche, "On the Pathos of Truth").

Now, we must pause for something of a confession. The way we have presented the path to the modern era by means of the changing meanings of the original concept of the good has made the journey seem straight-forward. It is not. We attained the appearance of straight-for-ward development by ignoring up to this point Nietzsche's discovery of a second morality that branches off relatively recently from the evolution of the original, pro-actively generated concept. This second morality comes into being when reactive creators say "No!" to the primary con-cept of the good. This "No" thereby becomes the primary concept of a derivative or reactive morality. Let us further investigate this reaction, together with the concepts it yields.

The reactive "No!" inverts the orientation of the original concepts good and bad. Initially, we might think this reaction simply inverts the relative positions of the original concepts of good and bad so that the original good becomes the reactive bad, and the original bad becomes the reactive concept of the good. This conclusion is not entirely wrong, but it is insufficient for our investigation of the good. The most salient point of the reaction is that it seems to entail a rejection of vitality as the standard that had always been implicitly recognized as authorita-tive. Only by rejecting this original standard can the reaction plausibly reorient the two original values, good and bad. To replace the standard of vitality, reactive morality posits the existence of a transcendent realm that allegedly exists behind our world. In this transcendent other-world, it goes on to say, there exists a universally authoritative, perfectly rational God that does not alter in any way. By positing the existence of this God, slave morality finds a way to usurp the standard of vitality, at least explicitly, and replace it with reason as the ultimate authority.

In keeping with this deification of reason, concepts are held to be more authoritative than perceptions. They wield this authority, not because they are believed to be more vital than perceptions, but because they are more intelligible—more available to reason. This proclaimed basis for the authority of concepts is strange indeed, since concepts are derived from, and secondary to, the very beings in the world that reactive morality devalues by its deification of reason.

This inversion of reality, according to which vitality is held to be inferior to reason, prepares the way for reactive morality's claim that absolute opposites are more real than beings that are available to our sense perception, since the beings we perceive are never absolute opposites. The fact that we can encounter them means they necessarily exist on a continuum of similarity with, and difference from, ourselves. They are reflections of us. To say the same thing differently, they must be filtered through our physio-psychology, which is to say they bear the stamp of what we are. However, once the authority of absolute reason and hence of opposites is accepted and we apply this standard to the perceptible world, it no longer seems necessary to regard these beings as existing on a continuum with each other. Absolute opposites replace or seem to replace similarities and differences. This replacement enables reactive morality to claim the right to push the original good entirely out of the realm of valid existence. Thus, the original good is characterized, not merely as the bad, but as evil.

Unlike the original concept of the bad, which denotes something unchoiceworthy but nevertheless ontologically valid, evil signifies ontological invalidity: evil ought not to exist; the world would be better if evil were wholly absent from it. What does this mean? Since the parameters of the original concept of the good are defined by, and consist of, the essence and attributes of super-abundantly vital human beings, and since reactive morality cannot transcend these boundaries, the reactive notion of evil essentially amounts to the assertion that super-abundantly vital beings are ontologically invalid. All embodiments of super-abundant vitality are gathered together under the general concept of "The Evil One."

The concept of evil is the primary value in reactive morality. Its primacy is due to the fact that the derivative morality is created by a reaction against the primary value in the original, pro-actively created morality,

which is the good. The reaction against the original good does not oblit-
erate the concept's robust or vivid content, or at least it is not obliterated
immediately. Rather, in its inverted form, the concept retains its vividness. Hence, it says very clearly what evil is—it is what was deemed good
in the original, in rich detail. By contrast, the reactive notion of the good
is vague. In its nebulousness, it is akin to the original concept of the bad.
The vagueness of both values is due to the same cause: both are secondary. As such, they are derived by negating the primary concept of the
morality to which they belong. Thus, as we noted, the original concept of
the bad amounts to the "not-good." Similarly, the reactive concept of the
good amounts to nothing other than the "not evil." To speak less cryptically, the good in reactive morality is that which is not super-abundantly
vital. Hence, we can infer that the more vitally *impotent* something is,
the *better* it is. This inference is consistent with the deification of reason,
which abstracts or strips attributes from individual, perceptible beings so
as to make a general concept from them.

While the secondary concepts of both pro-actively and reactively
created morality lack content, this absence is much more serious when
it pertains to the good than when it pertains to the bad. Only a content-rich concept of the good can give us a clear notion of what constitutes an enhancement or an augmentation of our being; only a positively
determined goal can direct our growth. When the good is negatively
defined, as it is in reactive morality, it tells us something about what to
avoid, but it says nothing about what constitutes growth. Hence, it offers
us nothing to direct our lives, and especially our growth, consciously or
mindfully.

This failure is perhaps most apparent in the most fully developed
reactive concept of God, which Nietzsche identifies as the holy God.
This God's holiness consists in the fact that it lacks to a maximum degree
all characteristics not merely of thriving human life, but of all degrees of
life (GM 1.8; GM 2.22). What began as a concept of a perfectly rational
God thereby paradoxically becomes so abstract as to be unavailable to
thought. Thus, while reactive morality might initially seem to offer an
alternative standard to vitality, further examination of the concept of the
holy God, which is the mature form of this alternative, reveals that reactive morality ultimately fails to offer any standard, for what is inconceiv-

able is unhelpful as a guide for human life. Hence, it is also helpless in giving the human being a genuine future, which is to say future growth.

Having worked through some of the details of these two kinds of moralities, consider their significance within the framework of Nietzsche's call for a moral typology (BGE 186). His discovery of two distinct types of morals leads him to a momentous realization. Since the content of every morality reveals the mode of valuation or the kind of action that generated it, and since there are only two modes of action— pro-active and reactive—all morals can be categorized by one or the other of these two modes. These modes therefore prove to be the proper foundation for moral typology.

We have so far called these modes pro-active or spontaneous on the one hand, and reactive on the other. Nietzsche typically refers to them as noble and slavish respectively (BGE 260). We have avoided these terms until now partly because Nietzsche's designations risk being misinterpreted as narrowly political or economic. Such an error leads one to draw the additional false conclusion that Nietzsche thinks anyone who is politically powerful or wealthy is noble, and anyone who is polit- ically disempowered or poor is slavish. To recap, as Nietzsche employs them, the designations noble and slavish are only directly political and economic to the extent that they reflect the fact that the noble type nec- essarily rules in the first and early regimes that emerge from a pre- or post-political condition, while the slave type always constitutes the ruled classes during these same epochs.

Given that the typological designations Nietzsche employs are lia- ble to being misunderstood, we may wonder why he employs them. He likely does so because every regime in which the noble human type does not rule nevertheless depends upon this type's morality. This is true even where reactive morals are dominant since these morals must be derived from the noble concepts. Every regime and all moral language therefore point explicitly or implicitly toward their origin in the physio-psychol- ogy of the noble type, of which the archetype is the warrior. Thus, the true moral typology returns the warrior to the helm of humanity.

Chapter Three

The Slave Revolt in Morality

You might not know it, but you are engaged in a war of the slave type against all that is noble, and against the noble warrior in particular. We have been engaged in this war, consciously or unconsciously, for at least the last twenty-four hundred years. It has now reached a critical point, a point at which we will either consciously take hold of a genuine future—a future in which the human being can grow—or we will degenerate. What is this war, and how did we come to this point?

Nietzsche investigates this question at length in all three essays of his book, *On the Genealogy of Morals*. He tells us this book "contains the first psychology of the priest.'²¹ The priest's psychology is relevant to our questions, because it is the priest who creates slave morality, and it is slave morality that initiates the war in which we are now most perilously immersed. Understanding the priest psychology is therefore the first step in understanding the war—and winning it.

The first essay of *The Genealogy* is entitled, "'Good and Evil,' 'Good and Bad.'" In it, Nietzsche considers the circumstances surrounding the slave revolt. Partly by tracking the genealogies of concepts back in time and partly by reasoning from current and historical evidence, he develops the hypothesis that the slave revolt originates in a schism between the two ruling factions within the Jewish people: the priestly-aristocrats on the one hand, and the warrior-aristocrats on the other.

Prior to the slave revolt, these two groups share the activities that constitute their aristocratic rule. Together or in coordination with each other, they wage wars against foreign powers; they determine their people's moral values, including justice; and they execute religious rites. Over time, however, a certain unhealthy physio-psychological inclination in the priests toward inactivity and hesitation before overt action is exacerbated by their priestly activities. More specifically, these duties limit their opportunities for a direct and full expression of their vitality, which in turn causes their unhealthy inclinations to develop. Hence, the priests begin to degenerate. Their devitalization eventually progresses to the point where they are no longer able to hold their own against the superior vitality of their ruling warrior counterparts.

The priests recognize their own impotence, along with the probable implication of it, which is that they will become subordinate in political power to the warriors. They are unwilling to lose this power; yet they know they are no longer able either to overthrow the warriors overtly. They also know they are unable to defend themselves directly against the warriors, for, in addition to being vitally potent and therefore more willful and determined, the warriors are trained and experienced in direct combat.

Faced with these circumstances, the priests devise a weapon that had never previously been conceived. This weapon is psychological warfare, which takes the form of slave morality. This stealth weapon is designed to pass undetected by the warriors, and this is precisely what it does. Let us flesh out details of the world-historical event that is the creation of slave morality.

We begin by recollecting some of Nietzsche's discoveries that are relevant to our current investigation. The original concept of the good is spontaneously generated by the noble human type as a form of self-glorification. With it, the noble human being designates himself as the good, the true, and the real. Because the noble type necessarily rules in original and nascent political orders, the first and early meanings of the good that emerge from a pre-political condition are also associated with the trappings of political power and the habits of these super-abundantly vital rulers. Over time, the concept's meaning transforms in conjunction with transfigurations in the physio-psychology of the noble human type and changes to the type's political circumstances.

In the sixth section of the first essay, Nietzsche remarks that the general rule, according to which the meaning of the concept develops from a signification that includes trappings of political power into one that denotes a quality of soul, is not violated when the governing class is occupied by priests (GM 1.6). The priestly-aristocrats, like all true aristocrats, pro-actively generate a concept of the good that glorifies the attributes and activities that pertain to their specific role in the regime. In particular, they extol the concept of purity. Hence, they speak of the concepts good and bad as pure and impure respectively:

> [W]hen the highest caste is at the same time the *priestly* caste ... [it] emphasizes in its total description of itself a predicate that calls to mind its priestly function. It is then, for example, that "pure" and "impure" confront one another for the first time as designations of station; and here too there evolves a "good" and "bad" in a sense no longer referring to station. (GM 1.6)

When these concepts are first created and for a long time thereafter, they are, from our complex perspective today, almost inconceivably simple. Their simplicity follows from the fact that the physio-psychologies of these priestly-aristocrats are themselves simple compared to ours. More specifically, these early priests do not have a well-developed interior world of the mind. Hence, their sense of pure and impure denote nothing of what we now identify as the soul. For them, the real world, the world of meaning, is in large part if not totally limited to the external world. This emphasis on the external realm as the meaningful world is reflected in their notions of pure and impure. Purity signifies nothing more than bodily cleanliness. "The 'pure one' is from the beginning merely a man who washes himself, who forbids himself certain foods that produce skin ailments, who does not sleep with the dirty women of the lower strata, who has an aversion to blood—no more, hardly more!" (GM 1.6). Conversely, the impure one is merely the human being whose body is typically dirty.

The priests' avoidance of sex with dirty women sheds light on their characteristic inclination to hesitate before exhausting their drives or desires. In this particular circumstance with dirty women, for example, they likely feel simultaneously their attachment to bodily cleanliness and hence revulsion at these women, and sexual desire for these same women. Thus, their drives oppose each other. We suspect this kind of opposition is what causes their characteristic hesitation, for the conflict must be resolved sufficiently, if not totally, before they can act. Since they define themselves as clean, and they equate their cleanliness or purity with the good, we expect their will or drive to cleanliness typically overrules competing drives. Nevertheless, the fact that their drives battle each other, even if only temporarily, testifies to Nietzsche's observation that there is something unhealthy from the start in these priests. That is, internal opposition or incoherence is almost invariably enervating, and enervation is another word for degeneration or sickness. While the degree of opposition between their drives does not yet produce any significant alterations to their physio-psychology, it does lay the foundation for the development for such alteration in the form of interiority, as we shall learn.

Having pointed a finger at hesitation as an attribute that is suspicious, we must pause to explain why it is so. Today, the inclination to hesitate before acting is typically believed—without adequate reflection, ironically—to be good always or for the most part. Is this opinion sound? It presupposes that considered actions, which always involve a delay of some time, are a sign of some kind of human excellence. Yet, as we have suggested, Nietzsche thinks hesitation itself is not typically indicative of vital potency. To the contrary, it is usually a manifestation of vital impotence or sickness. Such sickness is not limited to the so-called body. Rather, given that mind and body are not distinct, insofar as one's so-called body is sick, one's thinking must also be so: thoughts that emerge from sickness must manifest this sickness. Thus, the hesitation that is lauded as a sign of thoughtfulness is, in fact, typically bad when judged according to the standard of vitality. One ought not to want it, or at least one ought not to want it in it insofar as it is the manifestation of degenerating life.

Although the priests' sickness is undesirable, it is not initially sufficient to render them incapable of pro-action. However, the priests' habits and duties not only make them sedentary, but also tend to keep them out of direct combat and the vigorous action combat entails. At a basic physio-psychological level, inactivity or low -level activity causes "that intestinal morbidity and neurasthenia that has afflicted priests at all times" (GM 1.6). Thus, the very practices that are peculiar to the priests and that are associated with their political power exacerbate their degeneration.

Over time, their vitality declines to the point where they no longer belong to the noble type. They become slavish. In a twist of irony, their deterioration advances largely because of their own misguided efforts to treat their sickness. One such "treatment" consists of throwing themselves suddenly into extreme activity or inactivity. The shock to their

physio-psychologies that such behavior produces temporarily invigorates them, but it is followed by increased enervation. In addition to
such sudden and extreme shifts in behavior, they also attempt to treat
themselves by withdrawing even further from direct action. Nietzsche
reflects on both the priests' illness and their reactions to it:

> There is from the first something unhealthy in such priestly aristocracies
> and in the habits ruling in them which turn them away from action and
> alternate between brooding and emotional explosions ... but as to that
> which they themselves devised as a remedy for this morbidity—must one‾
> not assert that it ultimately proved itself a hundred times more dangerous
> in its effects than the sickness it was supposed to cure? Humankind itself is
> still ill with the effects of this priestly naïveté in medicine! (GM 1.6)

The priestly-aristocrats' deterioration manifests in their concept of
the good so that its meaning eventually comes to diverge so greatly from
the noble warriors' concept of the good that the two notions cannot be
reconciled. Nevertheless, each faction still wants to impose its own concept of the good upon the ruled classes so as form them in its own image.
Thus, they find themselves "in jealous opposition to one another and
are unwilling to come to terms" (GM 1.7). "[C]hasms are torn between
human being and human being that a very Achilles of a free spirit would
not venture to leap without a shudder" (GM 1.6).

If it was not previously clear to the priests, it now becomes all too
obvious that they are no longer vital enough to overcome or even to
sustain themselves against the warrior-aristocrats, or at least they cannot
do so by overt acts. Faced with their own impotence, the priests begin
to hate the warriors. Since they are weak, however, they are forced to
hate secretly, discreetly, behind closed doors. Frustrated by its inability
to exhaust itself openly and immediately, this hatred turns inward and
acts against the priests themselves. Its inward action digs out a kind of
metaphorical space or realm of action in the priests' physio-psychology.
It creates the expanded interior realm that we recognize as consciousness. In this inner realm, the priest's hatred deepens and is transfigured
by becoming involved with mind. It "grows to monstrous and uncanny
proportions, to the most spiritual and poisonous kind of hatred" (GM
1.7).

Their spiritualized hatred now becomes creative in a new and very
specific manner. It consciously falsifies its enemy to make it seem like
an abomination and thus infinitely more hateful than it is or could be.

Nietzsche elaborates on the characteristic way hatred falsifies its enemy by contrasting the lies such hatred produces about the noble type with the errors made by the noble type in its estimation of the slave type. Whereas the slave type has enough knowledge of the noble type and noble individuals to be aware that it falsifies them, the noble type's errors are the effect of ignorance. In turn, this ignorance is produced at least in part by the noble type's healthy instincts, which guard against knowledge of what they recognize as base. These instincts realize that knowledge of the base can diminish their vitality. In other words, knowledge of, or familiarity with what is base can make one base. Because they are healthy, the instincts rightly choose vitality over knowledge:

> When the noble mode of valuation blunders and sins against reality, it does so in respect to the sphere with which it is *not* sufficiently familiar, against a real knowledge of which it has indeed inflexibly guarded itself: in some circumstances it misunderstands the sphere it despises, that of the common man, of the lower orders; on the other hand, one should remember that, even supposing the affect of contempt, of looking down from a superior height *falsifies* the image of that which it despises, it will at any rate be a much less serious falsification than that which is perpetrated on its opponent—in *effigie* of course—by the submerged hatred, the vengefulness of the impotent. There is indeed too much carelessness, too much taking lightly, even too much joyfulness, for it to be able to transform its object into a real caricature and monster. (GM 1.10. See also TI, "Skirmishes of an Untimely Man," 20)

In addition to the noble type's instinctive protection of its super-abundant vitality, its characteristic inattention to slavish human beings, whom it is typically inclined to regard as inconsequential, precludes it from exerting the care that is required to concoct an elaborate lie about the slave type or slavish individuals (GM 1.10). Indeed, left to himself, the noble individual does not regard slavish human beings as enemies at all. To be clear, this is because he does not have the same concept of the enemy as the slave type. Far from hating his enemy and regarding him or trying to regard him as monstrous, the noble individual desires an enemy whom he recognizes as his equal. His enemy is a kind of second self whom he holds in the highest esteem as a worthy opponent against whom he can test himself. Thus, while he aims to overcome his enemy, he is also quite willing under certain circumstances to help his enemy improve his chance of victory. To the extent that his competitor becomes better, his victory over his enemy is sweeter, more thrilling, and more deserved both in his eyes and in those of his enemy. We see something of this noble behavior when Homer's Achilles grants Priam—the father of the vanquished hero, Hector, and the king of the enemy Trojans—as much time as Priam says he needs to hold a funeral for his son. A less noble human being might not grant this respite, or he might grant it deceitfully and then take advantage of it. Achilles ensures that Priam's request is honored (Homer, *Iliad*, XXIV).

Given the equality and thus the mutual respect that exists between noble enemies, it would not be surprising if, under different circumstances, they were friends. By contrast, friendship is never possible between the slavish human being and his enemy (GM 1.10). The slavish human being is aware he is vitally inferior to his enemy. This inequality makes his bitter sense about his own vital paucity more vivid and painful. He responds to his feelings of disgruntlement, which arise from what he is, by blaming noble human beings and the noble type in general for his condition. By bolstering his hatred for the vitally potent type with false reasons, this spiritualized passion is reinforced and burrows further into the priest's physio-psychology.

Return to the circumstances in which the ruling priests now find themselves. Whereas most slavish human beings must resign themselves at most to secret or semi-secret, small acts of revenge against their noble enemies, the priestly-aristocrats break this mold for the first time ever by conceiving of the most brilliant and "most spiritual revenge" (GM 1.7). We have identified this revenge already as psychological warfare in the form of slave morality. This new kind of weapon does not merely target the warrior-aristocrats with whom the priests' share the political power to rule their people. It extends beyond these immediate enemies to include everyone and everything noble in the present, the future, and across the globe.

Nietzsche argues the priests even include the past in this war. They do so by re-writing and over-writing the original version of Jewish scripture or Old Testament. Nietzsche sees this book to the extent that it still communicates its unadulterated form, as the manifestation and record of a people that remains unsurpassed in strength of soul and nobility:

> In the Jewish "Old Testament," the book of divine justice, there are human beings, things, and speeches in so grand a style that Greek and Indian lit-

erature have nothing to compare with it. With terror and reverence one stands before these tremendous remnants of what man once was, and will have sad thoughts about ancient Asia and its protruding little peninsula Europe, which wants by all means to signify as against Asia the "progress of man." (BGE 52)

This tremendous nobility persists in the Jewish warrior-aristocrats. However, after the priests initiate their ideological warfare, they edit the original form of the Jewish scripture so as to remove, obscure, and reinterpret the nobility it expresses. Thus, they make the book appear to be in accord or more in accord with slave morality (BGE 52). Indeed, they even present it as "The Old Testament"—and thus a harbinger of Christianity, which Nietzsche argues is a slave morality. As part of this latter project, the priests omit or obscure the fact that morality belongs to, and defines, a specific, limited group of people who have a shared history and heritage and who are relatively identifiable by their mores and customs. That is, they replace the morality of a particular people—the Jews—with the notion of a universal morality (GS 3.22). Unlike Judaism, Christianity is in principle open to all human beings, regardless of their history, heritage, or the regime in which they live. As such, it is antithetical to the very notion of a people.

This universalization of a morality that previously belonged to a specific people is the first step toward the much more radical and ingenious move to obscure the religious character of the values slave morality promulgates. According to Nietzsche, these values appear in a variety of masked forms, including certain strains of democracy, communism, socialism, anarchism, and even atheism (e.g. see BGE 225; GM 3.24). They can even appear to be non-political and uncommitted to any moral judgments, including notions of justice and the good. In other words, they can appear to be objective. This seeming objectivity belongs most notably to modern science. Whatever form the mask assumes, slave morality can nevertheless be recognized for what it is by the fact that those who pride themselves for adhering to these values presume there is a universal good that includes specific dictates that are universal and everlasting.[22] The fact that these values can present themselves as non-religious and non-political enables them to slip into multiple and various forms of regime throughout the globe without being recognized as belonging to a doctrine that in truth has profound ramifications both for politics and for the future of the human being per se. By means of this morality the priests not only overthrow the political power of the original, noble morality, they also bring the noble type to the brink of extinction.

This effectiveness of the psychological weapon that is slave morality is rooted in the fact that it takes advantage of the noble type's characteristic reliance on instinct rather than reason. Because the noble type's instincts are healthy, they are typically excellent guides to the maximum expression of the noble type's will to power. Since this expression is good, and since the noble type's instincts reliably guide him to this end throughout most of history, the type had little or no cause to develop alternative guides to action. Hence, reason or deliberation first develops to a significant degree in the slave type, which is too vitally impotent to express its will to power immediately and openly and is therefore forced to find a means of supplementing its vital paucity. Slavish human beings find this supplement in reason, which, among other things, directs them to act indirectly and to lie, which is a form of indirection, as means of expressing their will to power. Given these differences in the behaviors of the two human types, noble human beings are not well equipped to identify slave morality as a threat. They are the targets of this psychological war, and they do not know it.

The priests employ slave morality in three different ways against the noble type. First, this morality seduces noble human beings to self-destruct. How? Consider the typical noble human being of this era. To recap, he does not have a significant degree of interiority, and he typically does not act indirectly. He is therefore unfamiliar with telling lies and with recognizing them when they are told to him. How does the saint, whom we might reasonably characterize as the most authoritative of priests, portray himself as the archetypical practitioner and advocate of slave values? He says he is strong. Yet, he acts in ways that are characteristic of vital impotence. Since the noble human being is unfamiliar with deception, he does not conclude that the saint may in truth be significantly different from what he claims to be. Rather, he takes the saint's claim to preternatural strength largely at face value. Thus, he falsely concludes the saint might be like himself. Confronted with this conclusion, the noble human being must ask himself: "If this human being is strong, why does he act as he does? Why does he not express and satisfy himself as I do?" Perhaps the saint is engaged in some previously unknown test.

Or perhaps the saint knows something very important about a great danger. Nietzsche describes the encounter between the noble being and the saint, who serves as the paradigm for the ascetic priest and ascetic human beings more generally:

> So far the most powerful human beings have still bowed worshipfully before the saint as the riddle of self-conquest and deliberate final renunciation. Why did they bow? In him—and as it were behind the question mark of his fragile and miserable appearance—they sensed the superior force that sought to test itself in such a conquest, the strength of the will in which they recognized and honored their own strength and delight in dominion: they honored something in themselves when they honored the saint. Moreover, the sight of the saint awakened a suspicion in them: such an enormity of denial, of anti-nature will not have been desired for nothing, they said and asked themselves. There may be a reason for it, some very great danger about which the ascetic, thanks to his secret comforters and visitors, might have inside information. In short, the powerful of the world learned a new fear before him; they sensed a new power, a strange, as yet unconquered enemy—it was the "will to power" that made them stop before the saint. They had to ask him– (BGE 51. See also HH 1.126 – 127; HH 1.136; HH 1.143)

By misinterpreting ascetic behavior, the super-abundantly vital human being is seduced to compete with the ascetic. However, he is oblivious to the fact that the ascetic human being is cheating, since the ascetic pretends that great potency accounts for his actions, whereas in truth they are the result of his vital impotence. To compete with the ascetic human being's deceptive self-presentation, the noble human being's strong drives must be turned against each other, in all their potency. He initiates a ferocious war within himself, one that typically causes his drives to weaken or destroy each other. Thus, he disintegrates, degenerates, finally self-destructs. In short, he is unwittingly seduced into transforming himself into a slave.

The second way the priests use slave morality is as a means of co-opting a vast army of people to their side of the battle against all that is noble. This is not to say most people necessarily share the priests' desire to eradicate the noble type. They may be co-opted without being aware they are becoming embroiled in this war. Nietzsche argues that this unwitting participation is possible because the priests secure the people's support indirectly, by giving a moral interpretation to bad conscience. In truth, bad conscience is nothing other than a painful physio-psychologi-

cal alteration that occurs in vitally impotent human beings. According to
the ascetic priest's moral interpretation of bad conscience, however, this
pain is not an evolutionary development. Rather, it is divine punishment
for our moral transgressions, the existence of which is allegedly proved
precisely by the supposed fact of our punishment.

Nietzsche arrives at these conclusions about bad conscience and its
moralization by tracking the genealogy of the modern concept of guilt to
its origin. He tells us in the second essay of *The Genealogy*—"'Guilt,' 'Bad
Conscience,' and the Like"—that he began this part of his investigation
of the psychology of the ascetic priest very simply, by noticing the shared
etymology of the modern German words for guilt (*Schuld*) on the one
hand, and debt (*Schulden*) on the other (GM 2.4). From their shared etymology, he infers that the two concepts are inter-related and likely have
a shared origin. He reasons further that, since both guilt and debt are
associated with punishment, alterations in the concept of punishment
over time must also be relevant to understanding the genealogy of guilt.
What is punishment? What does it mean?

Today, punishment is typically understood and defended as a means
of arousing the sense of guilty conscience in the criminal. Yet, Nietzsche
observes that it typically has precisely the opposite effect. It tends to
make human beings "hard and cold; it concentrates; it sharpens the feeling of alienation; it strengthens the power of resistance. ... [Its effects
are characterized by] a dry and gloomy seriousness" (GM 2.14). Given
the usual results of punishment in the punished, it is unlikely that the
purported meaning or reason for punishment truly explains it.

This line of thinking leads Nietzsche to suspect punishment is so
embedded in our human genealogy that we continue to perform the various actions associated with it, out of instinct or ritualized habit, and we
then find justifications or reasons for this instinctual or habitual behavior. As Nietzsche states it, "the custom, the act, the 'drama,' a certain
strict sequence of procedures" is "relatively enduring," but the "meaning,
the purpose, the expectation associated with the performance of such
procedures" is fluid (see GM 2.13). This distinction between the content
and its meaning leads Nietzsche to realize, once again, that if one wants
to understand punishment, one must not ask for its meaning. Like any
entity with a history, punishment has had so many meanings that no
single one can encompass it. It defies definition, as do all things with a

genealogy. To understand punishment, one must instead comprehend the transformations it has undergone (GM 2.14). Hence, to understand guilt, which is tied up with punishment, one must understand the interaction and convergence of the genealogies of three distinct things: the debtor-creditor relationship, punishment, and bad conscience.

Having prepared us for the kind of thinking that moves backward in time from a complex thing through its simpler form and finally to its original, simplest form, Nietzsche takes us to a former era. Specifically, he takes us to a time before punishment becomes enmeshed with the doctrine of free will. It is this doctrine that lends at least the appearance of legitimacy to the modern notion of punishment. Dwelling upon these earlier ages, Nietzsche observes that "a *high* degree of humanity had to be attained before the animal 'human being' began even to make the much more primitive distinctions between 'intentional,' 'negligent,' 'accidental,' 'accountable,' and their opposites and to take them into account when determining punishments" (GM 2.4; see also BGE 32). For most of history, punishment was nothing more than the angry lashing out at someone who caused one harm or injury. Such anger is later "modified by the idea that everything has its *equivalent* and can be paid back."[23] This notion of commensurability and repayment is rooted in the debtor-creditor relationship, as is the feeling of guilt.

This economic relationship is "the oldest and most primitive personal relationship" that exists between human beings (GM 2.8). It is in these relations that one human being first "*measured himself* against another. No grade of civilization, however low, has yet been discovered in which something of this relationship has not been noticeable" (GM 2.8). The determination of values in such interactions—the "contrivance of equivalences, exchanging"—was so central to the "earliest thinking" of the human being that "in a certain sense they constitute thinking *as such*" (GM 2.8). The human being took such pride in this thinking and regarded it as so superior to the capacities of other animals that he designated the human as the "'valuating animal as such'" (GM 2.8).

The capacity for exchange, especially exchange that is not completed immediately and therefore involves promises, was chiefly the effect of cultivation. This project of human self-creation or self-breeding was conceived and effected primarily by instinct rather than reason (GM 2.1 – 2.2; GM 2.17). Crucial to such exchange and the capacities it required was the creation of memory, which was not always sufficiently developed in us to make exchange broadly practicable. It was therefore here, in the context of economic valuation and the debtor-creditor relationship, that a significant degree of domestication and memory was implanted in the human being. This was done largely by establishing an association in the human physio-psychology between breaking promises and contracts on the one hand, and terrible pain on the other. It is in this same context that the concept of guilt first appears. Originally, it signified indebtedness. Neither this indebtedness nor the harm that accrued from defaulting on a loan—unredeemed guilt—were laden with the modern, moral meaning of guilt.

Since the painful punishment that followed from defaulting on a loan was not consciously employed with a view to burning into the human being both memory and the related capacity for keeping promises, there must have been some other reason for involving punishment in the debtor-creditor relationship. Nietzsche finds this reason in the notion of commensurability. This notion enabled the creditor to feel compensated for what the debtor owed him by causing the debtor pain. This recompense in the form of the sanctioned pleasure to do harm is the first meaning of punishment:

> To inspire trust in his promise to repay, to provide a guarantee of the seriousness and sanctity of his promise, to impress repayment as a duty, an obligation on his own conscience, the debtor made a contract with the creditor and pledged that if he should fail to repay he would substitute something else that he "possessed," something he had control over; for example, his body, his wife, his freedom, or even his life (or, given certain religious presuppositions, even his bliss after death, the salvation of his soul, ultimately his peace in the grave—and among the Egyptians such peace meant a great deal). Above all, however, the creditor could inflict every kind of indignity and torture on the body of the debtor; for example, cut from it as much as seemed commensurate with the size of the debt. ... Let us be clear as to the logic of this form of compensation: it is strange enough. An equivalence is provided by the creditor's receiving, in place of literal compensation for an injury (thus in place of money, land, possessions of any kind), a recompense in the form of a kind of *pleasure*—the pleasure of being allowed to vent his power freely on one who is powerless, the voluptuous pleasure *"de faire mal pour le plaisir de le faire,"* [*of doing harm for the pleasure of doing it*] the enjoyment of violation. (GM 2.5. See also GM 2.6)

Once the associations between "exchange, contract, guilt, right, obligation, [and] settlement" had been adequately established in the human being, these ideas and their interconnections spread "inexorably" to the simplest, most primitive social complexes. There they became the foundation for the "oldest and naïvest moral canon of justice," according to which justice is "the good will amongst parties of approximately equal power to come to terms with one another... —and to *compel* parties of lesser power to reach a settlement among themselves—" (GM 2.8).

Having come along the tracks of these multiple genealogies and seen how they interpenetrate, we must leave this trail temporarily. We depart from it, as does Nietzsche, to follow the genealogy of bad conscience. As we shall see, its genealogy will intersect with our current location. Remember it.

In making this demand, we admit it is confusing to follow Nietzsche's investigations into each of these genealogies. In defense of our approach, which is modeled on Nietzsche's, we note that it is the course we must follow if we are to understand a complex entity adequately. Additionally, to the extent that the plot of the second essay of *The Genealogy* is much more complex and harder to follow than that of either of the other two essays, it illustrates how evolution has proceeded to date. Thus, what might appear to be artlessness in the plot of the second essay proves, in fact, to be artful. By giving us such a convoluted plot, Nietzsche shows us that evolution has not been carried out lucidly, as though a mind were intentionally weaving together different genealogical threads with a view to growth or to any other goal. Insofar as the intersections and interpenetrations of these various genealogies are intelligible, they are so because Nietzsche's mind illuminates and gives sense to an otherwise mindless imbroglio of genealogies.

We begin a new path. In its original meaning, guilty conscience is equivalent to bad conscience, which Nietzsche describes as a most "serious illness man was bound to contract under the stress of the most fundamental change he ever experienced"—namely, the founding of the first political regime (GM 2.16). Immediately prior to this founding, vitally potent human beings lived in tribes or packs that are akin to wolf packs or lion prides. Appropriately enough, Nietzsche calls the beings who comprise these tribes "beasts-of-prey" (GM 2.17). They are ready, willing, and able to attack. Their tremendous vitality and the capacity for ferocious, aggressive action that is inherent to super-abundant vitality gives them the capacity to impose order first and foremost upon them-selves, and also upon others. Such conquest is driven primarily by an unconscious artistic drive to re-form other beings in their own image (see GM 2.18). By this re-making or re-formation, they expand their influence, which is to say they expand themselves. They appropriate what is foreign and thereby grow. Such expansion by appropriating the other and making it one's own is the way of all growing beings (see BGE 259).

Human beings who lack this vital potency live in much looser or less organized associations, more like herds than hierarchically ordered packs. Their co-habitation is not so much for the purpose of growth as it is for the sake of safety and comfort. They are relatively peaceable or un-warlike. This is not to suggest they do not act in accordance with the will to power or the will to life. Rather, their actions merely manifest the amount of vitality they have, as human beings.

At some point, the tribespeople encounter the herdspeople and attack them. Although the herdspeople were "perhaps tremendously superior in numbers," they lack the vigor, together with its attendant capacity for organization and efficacy in war, that characterizes the tribespeople. They stand no chance of escaping these beasts-of-prey. Nietzsche hypothesizes that the tribespeople's victory and their subse-quent incorporation of the herdspeople into the first political order must have been "too terrible, too sudden, too convincing, too 'different' even to be hated" by the vanquished (GM 2.17). His reasoning here is based partly on his observation that human physio-psychology as we know and experience it has an unusually developed consciousness or inner world, together with a highly developed capacity for reason or deliberation. If we evolved from much simpler beings and likely even the simplest of beings, then these attributes were not always a part of what we were. They must have come into being as we evolved. In other words, it is not as though we always had these capacities but did not always use them. Rather, we did not use them because we did not have them. As Nietzsche understands them, the calculative capacity is produced by drives acting inwardly, against the individual, rather than outwardly. Since the individual is comprised of a community of drives, we can state the same observation more strictly. Inwardly directed drives act against the community to which they belong in some way. Their inward direction is a reversal of the more long-standing direction of the drives, which is outwardly. In their outward action, they typically sustain or augment the vitality of the community, whereas this reversed, inward direction pits them against the community in a manner that has so far almost invariably undermined its integrity and hence its vitality. To the extent that, in a healthy being, the community of drives is integrated so that the entity as a whole thrives, the inward action of a drive that enervates the community's overall vitality is perverse or unhealthy. This kind of unhealthiness characterizes most human beings, and it is available to be seen. Precisely this perversity suggests to Nietzsche that the circumstances of a significant number of human beings must have altered so suddenly, violently, and with such tremendous force that their physio-psychology lacked the time that would be required for it to adapt in a healthier way to the new circumstances that overtook these human beings. The tribespeople's attack and imposition of the strictures of the first and early political regimes upon the herdspeople meets the criteria necessary for effecting this perverse development in the human being. This alteration was then inherited by all or almost all human beings.

Nietzsche likens the circumstances facing these vanquished and enslaved human beings to those confronted by sea creatures when they were precipitously compelled to leave the ocean and take to land. Like these sea creatures, these human beings were well adapted to their previous environment, but not to the new one they were forced to enter. To begin, their actions in their former circumstances were primarily in the external realm rather than in the internal realm of consciousness or mind. One's orientation in the external realm is largely spatial; hence, it is determined by sense perceptions, which were acutely developed in these human beings and indeed all humans. This is not to suggest sense perceptions do not involve mind. To the extent that the sentient being is conscious of its perceptions and interprets them, mind is necessarily involved. However, these activities do not require a significantly developed capacity for calculation or deliberation. In other words, they do not require to a significant degree any of the attributes that depend upon interiority (GM 2.16; see also GM 1.10). Whereas the external world is primarily experienced in terms of space, the interior world of consciousness is primarily experienced temporally or sequentially. At least partly because the inner world is not experienced spatially, the instincts that had commanded human actions so successfully in the outer world had to be augmented or replaced by a commander that was adequate to the primacy of temporality. This commander is reason, understood as the calculative or deliberative aspect of the drives. Reason is therefore thrust by necessity to a place of prominence in the physio-psychology of these human beings, despite the fact that it is the most recently developed, weakest, most fallible aspect of the drives (GM 2.16).

As in the case of the priestly-aristocrats' internalized drives, although the direction of the drives reverses and turns inward, the drives necessarily still express themselves to their full capacity. They must act to the extent that they can, for they are nothing but forms of action, and they have no means of restraining themselves (GM 2.16; BGE 259; GM 3.7). The first "subterranean gratification" these internalized drives find for themselves consists in ferociously carving out a kind of metaphorical hole or arena for operation within the individual who harbors them (GM 2.16). In a way, they do to the community of drives to which they belong what vitally potent human beings do by imposing a new form upon other, weaker human beings. This uncanny, reversed action of the drives develops what we now identify as the soul, mind, or consciousness. The devitalizing, painful excavation that produces it is all that bad conscience originally signifies:

> All instincts that do not discharge themselves outwardly turn inward—this is what I call the *internalization* of man: thus it was that man first developed what was later called his "soul." The entire inner world, originally as thin as if it were stretched between two membranes, expanded and extended itself, acquired depth, breadth, and height, in the same measure as outward discharge was *inhibited*. Those fearful bulwarks with which the political organization protected itself against the old instincts of freedom—punishments belong among these bulwarks—brought about that all those instincts of wild, free, prowling man turned backward *against man himself*. Hostility, cruelty, joy in persecuting, in attacking, in change, in destruction—all this turned against the possessors of such instincts: *that* is the origin of the "bad conscience." (GM 2.16)

We see something of this internal distress and torture in other captured animals that were once wild or that belong to a species that has not been tamed sufficiently for them not to suffer from the restrictions that attend domestic or captive life. Granted, we do not necessarily see such a sophisticated expression of inwardly directed drives. Rather, we see an outward manifestation of something more like the distress of sea creatures forced onto land. For example, the polar bear that is caged in an enclosure that is too small for the creature to get adequate exercise or stimulation paces around and around in circles. It swings its heads neurotically back and forth and may even disintegrate into madness. The caged parrot that pulls out its own feathers seems to be another example of a creature whose drives are unable to express themselves adequately in the circumstances in which it is held. Its drives therefore express themselves against the bird. Something comparable can happen to human beings whose drives do not have sufficient means to express themselves in a manner that promotes the overall vitality of the community of drives that constitute this complex creature. The resulting behavior need not be so obvious as that of the distressed polar bear or the parrot, but the same principle is at work. Drives that cannot express themselves in the external world will act inwardly, often to the detriment of the individual.

With such thoughts and observations in mind, Nietzsche judges the physiological development of bad conscience against the authoritative standard of life and finds it wanting because it brings with it a decline in the human being's overall vitality (GM 2.16). In keeping with this decline, our most sophisticated thinking has almost invariably expressed our physio-psychological distress and disintegration. It, too, has been enervating, or rather, it has been the expression of degenerating life (see GS, "Preface," 2). Because conscience and its effects have typically been bad, Nietzsche characterizes it as

> the gravest and uncanniest illness, from which humanity has not yet recovered, man's suffering *of man, of himself*—the result of a forcible sundering from his animal past, as it were a leap and plunge into new surroundings and conditions of existence, a declaration of war against the old instincts upon which his strength, joy, and terribleness had rested hitherto. (GM 2.16)

Having presented his hypothesis on the origin of bad conscience, Nietzsche goes on to investigate how the illness of bad conscience was moralized and thereby brought to "its ultimate height" (GM 2.19). To do this, he now recollects the interconnected genealogies we explored and set aside earlier. He notes that the ascent to this perverse peak begins when the human conception of the debtor-creditor relationship, together with the notions of guilt, punishment, and the pain associated with punishment, become involved with the genealogy of religious belief.

At the time of this merging, "[t]he conviction reigns that it is only through the sacrifices and great accomplishments of the ancestors that the tribe exists" (GM 2.19). This conviction now becomes involved with the debtor-creditor relationship. Hence, the present generation both feels increasingly indebted over time to its ancestors, and it believes it must recompense them with commensurable sacrifices and deeds. Fear of punishment for defaulting on a debt has also been bred into human beings by this time, and it increases in proportion with one's debt. Thus, so long as the tribe continues to prosper, the present generation's fear of its ancestors and of the consequences it will suffer if it does not redeem itself continues to increase. Eventually, the current generation comes to believe that the ancestors' power and fearsomeness are of "monstrous dimensions" (GM 2.19). The concept of the ancestor is thereby transformed into the concept of god.

Although this sense of guilty indebtedness develops before the first state is founded, it does not disappear when political regimes replace the tribes. Rather, it is inherited along with the household gods that pre-date the regime. Once these gods are incorporated into the political order, their genealogies come to reflect the regime's victories and losses, just as they previously reflected the fortunes and misfortunes of the tribes. The genealogies of the gods thereby become the genealogies of political regimes (GM 2.20).

Following through on the interconnection between a regime and its gods, Nietzsche infers that a despotic form of government is always accompanied sooner or later by a monotheistic god: the one form reflects the other. Hence, because a despot holds maximum political power, despotism must sooner or later introduce a monotheistic god that is all-powerful, at least with respect to these particular people. Furthermore, since a monotheistic god is maximally powerful, the human beings who believe they are subject to this god feel maximally indebted to it—maximally guilty.

Apply this reasoning to the most powerful gods in human history. Although the Jewish God comes to be understood by the Jews as a universal ruler, this God limits his allegiance primarily to the Jews, The Chosen People. By contrast, the Christian God is not understood as a god of a particular people; rather, this God is unqualifiedly universal. With this move to universality, divine power rises to a new, previously unknown level. In other words, the Christian God is the maximum God conceived and attained so far. In keeping with this God's maximality, belief in the Christian God is accompanied by "the maximum feeling of guilty indebtedness" in the genealogy of the human being to date (GM 2.20).

Nietzsche observes that the Christian God has since been murdered by Christians themselves. Modern human beings live in this God's mere shadow, unaware both of this God's death and of the impending, catastrophic consequences of this death (GM 3.27; GS 108; GS 125; GS 343). In non-metaphorical language, the death of God means Christians no longer truly believe in their God (GS 125). Their disbelief is apparent in their sense that they are entitled to interpret moral teachings and laws for themselves, independently of Church authorities who were previously widely regarded as the divinely ordained representatives of God. The structure of the Christian Church is falling down. Its deconstruction signifies the demise of its God, just as increasing disbelief on the part of a citizenry in the legitimate authority of their government signifies the demise of a political regime.

Despite the death of God, the human sense of guilty indebtedness is not waning, as one might reasonably expect it would (GM 2.20). Why not? Nietzsche argues the priests prevent the onset of a second innocence by giving a moral interpretation to bad conscience. He identifies three stages in this moralization (GM 2.21; see also BGE 55). Each signifies an increase in the spiritualization of internalized cruelty, an increase in the scope of influence of the moral interpretation of bad conscience, and an intensification of the pain that accompanies moralized bad conscience.

In the first stage, the concepts of guilt and the duty to repay a debt are applied to the concept of the human being. Thus, human beings torture themselves with the notion they are indebted to God. Since God is believed to be extremely powerful, the human beings' sense of guilt increases to the point where they eventually think their debt is irredeemable. The notion of irredeemable debt then gives rise to the concept of eternal punishments, like those associated with the concept of hell (GM 2.21).

In the second stage, the concepts of guilt and duty are turned against the creditor, understood either as Adam, the alleged progenitor of all human beings; or nature; or existence. Where Adam is the creditor, he is

blamed for having perpetrated the first transgression against God by dis-
obeying God's laws in the Garden of Eden. All of Adam's descendants
are believed to inherit his guilt, inescapably. None can avoid it, for none
can unmake the past. Faced with such an inheritance, human beings
come to resent the past (GM 2.21; see also Z.3, "On the Vision and the
Riddle"). Something comparable occurs when the concepts of guilt and
duty are mixed with the concept of nature. In this case, not Adam but
nature is "diabolized" (GM 2.21). This demonization is apparent in the
condemnation of bodily appetites as wicked temptations to sinfulness.
It manifests also in the idea that nature, as an enemy, must be put on
the rack, tortured, controlled. Finally, where existence is believed to be
the creditor, it comes to be regarded as *"worthless as such* (nihilistic withdrawal from it, a desire for nothingness or a desire for its antithesis, for a
different mode of being, Buddhism and the like)" (GM 2.21).

The illness of bad conscience reaches its ultimate height in its third
stage of its moralization. Here, "we stand before the paradoxical and hor-
rifying expedient that afforded temporary relief for tormented humanity,
that stroke of genius on the part of Christianity.

> God himself sacrifices himself for the guilt of humankind, God himself
> makes a payment to himself, God as the only being who can redeem the
> human being from what has become unredeemable for the human being
> himself—the creditor sacrifices himself for his debtor, out of *love* (can one
> credit that?), out of love for his debtor!— (GM 2.21)

God's act is characterized as an act of love for us, his debtors. By
sacrificing himself, he allegedly assumes our guilt and thereby redeems
us. Implicit in this apparently loving act is God's conclusion that human
beings will *never* be good or potent enough to redeem themselves. In
other words, God takes pity on us in his knowledge that the human
being cannot have a genuine future—that is, a future involving growth
or enhancement—let alone a genuine future that is self-directed (see
AC 47; BGE 225). The kind of pity that manifests disbelief in a genuine
future for its object is nihilistic (see AC 47; BGE 225). Thus, at this peak
of the moralization of bad conscience, nihilism moves from the human
withdrawal from existence to God, the alleged creator of all things, the
absolutely pure source and authority of all goodness: God has become
a nihilist. Believing themselves to be the objects of God's nihilistic pity,
we are led to agree that the human being is indeed future-less, a hopeless

case of a creature. Such pity thereby proves enervating not only for the one who pities, but also for the one deemed pitiable.

In addition to being nihilistic, God's self-sacrifice does not present a coherent picture of love. Nietzsche draws attention to this fact by posing the rhetorical question of whether love can be credited. With this question, he indicates true love does not belong to the debtor-creditor relationship. It is not a matter of exchange. However, if Christianity disagrees and wants to argue that love does belong to economics, it must explain how God's assumption of our debt does not leave us further indebted than we were before he acted. It makes no sense, economically, to suggest a creditor can recompense himself on behalf of the debtor by expending more of himself on the debtor's behalf. Nor can one argue God offers us loan-forgiveness. If this were the case, God's self-sacrifice would be redundant, as would repayment by anyone else for past guilt.

The Christian account of God's love has still more problems. In addition to claiming implicitly that love belongs to economics and can therefore be credited, the concept of the holy God brings with it an implicit claim that God's love is unegoistic or altruistic. Altruism signifies a concern for the well-being of others, absent all concern for oneself. This notion is nonsensical, for in the absence of all self-interest in the relationship between oneself and another being there is no motive for one's drives or passions to act in any way with respect to this other. To say the same thing differently, a drive or passion is responsible for the actions of all living beings, and a passion inherently denotes some degree of interest for itself. Passions are necessarily egoistic. Perhaps you will retort that the holy God is not a living being; hence, His passions cannot be compared to ours? Of what, then, are we speaking? Certainly, we are no longer speaking of love.

By exposing this tangle of thinking in the account of God's self-sacrifice for our sins, Nietzsche leads us to see that God's act is incommensurable, not so much because it is too grand-scale or magnanimous to be matched by us, but because it is nonsensical and impossible, at least as it is characterized by the ascetic priest. God's act is neither super-natural nor supra-natural; it is *anti*-natural; it is absurd. Since human beings continue to feel indebted to God despite being faced with a debt that is impossible to repay, the human being's pride in himself is crushed (GM 2.23; GM 1.2). The destruction of human pride is part and parcel of the nihilism that overtakes us in the most perverse stage of the moralization of bad conscience. It is the nail in the coffin of a second innocence.

Before moving ahead with Nietzsche's account of the slave revolt, let us briefly contrast the Christian notion of altruistic love with the concept of love Socrates presents in Plato's *Symposium*. Socrates' account follows a eulogy of Eros by a famous and very beautiful young poet named Agathon. Despite having been awarded a prize for his poetic prowess the previous day, Agathon's eulogy rather unartfully attributes a vast and varied multitude of goods to Eros. After characteristically condemning the poet with faint praise, Socrates refutes him by showing how Agathon's own reasoning suggests Eros is not beautiful and self-sufficient, as Agathon alleged, but is instead ugly and impoverished. He argues one only loves to the extent that one lacks what one loves. A true god would be perfectly complete, by which Socrates means the god would have everything it needs and would therefore be static or un-altering. Such a god would not love, since love implies desire, desire denotes neediness, and neediness is incompatible with perfection, as Socrates presents it (Plato, *Symposium* 199c – 201c).[24] Like the Christian account, this account of love is false. Yet, while both the Socratic account offered in this dialogue and the Christian account err, Christianity sees or at least helps to bring about something true about love that is overlooked or denied by this classical account—namely, love is a manifestation of potency, not paucity (see GM 1.8). This conclusion is based on the prior realization that love and the motion that attends it are not manifestations of impoverishment. As the theory of generation elucidates it, desire attends both vital potency, and hence the supreme good, as well as vital impotence or paucity. Love, however, can be a shape or manifestation solely of super-abundant vitality or overflowing life. The view of desire and love that Socrates articulates here is, by contrast, traceable to the moral-theological prejudice, which cannot endorse or even acknowledge ongoing human evolution.

To clarify this insight regarding love, let us consider further Nietzsche's brief indication that love does not belong to economics and it is no way tied to the nonsensical notion of altruism. He argues it is instead an expression of super-abundant vitality. As such, it is also an expression of tremendous egoism. Because it is a form or shape of overflowing vitality, which is good, love brings its own reward. No recompense is necessary or desired in the act of loving per se. Indeed, love, properly understood, might be the proper name for the experience of the supreme good. So understood, love is the teaching of Nietzsche's *Thus Spoke Zarathustra* (e.g. see Z, "On Old and New Tablets").

Having had this brief glimpse of a bright world that holds the promise of a genuine future, we return to the gloomy territory of moralized bad conscience. Review where we were before our happy moment of respite. Nietzsche argues the image of God on the cross is not merely super-natural, but *anti*-natural. With this change, effected by the meaning of God on the cross, God becomes the holy or ascetic God, the God that is good precisely because it is stripped of human attributes. In the holy God, Nietzsche discerns not love, but the internalized and highly spiritualized cruelty of the ascetic priests (GM 1.15; GM 3.11). This internalized cruelty seizes upon moralized bad conscience as a most terrible means of torturing the community of drives to which it belongs and against which it acts. Having been discovered by the priests' internalized cruelty, this means to torture is then snatched up by the internalized cruelty of sufferers more generally. However, in a most dangerous and perverse paradox, while the internalized instinct for cruelty feels enlivened by exercising itself in this way, the overall vitality of the individual is diminished. Nietzsche fleshes this perverse disintegrative and self-destructive activity of cruelty:

> You will have guessed *what* has really happened here, beneath all this: that will to self-tormenting, that repressed cruelty of the animal-human made inward and scared back into himself … seized on the presupposition of religion so as to drive his self-torture to its most gruesome pitch of severity and rigor. Guilt before *God*: this thought becomes an instrument of torture to him. He apprehends in "God" the ultimate antithesis of his own ineluctable animal instincts; he reinterprets these animal instincts themselves as a form of guilt before God (as hostility, rebellion, insurrection against the world); he stretches himself on the contradiction "God" and "Devil"; he ejects from himself all his denial of himself, of his nature, naturalness, and actuality, in the form of an affirmation, as something existent, corporeal, real, as God, as the holiness of God, as God the Judge, as God the Hangman, as the beyond, as eternity, as torment without end, as hell, as the immeasurability of punishment and guilt.
>
> In this psychical cruelty there resides a madness of will which is absolutely unexampled: the *will* of man to find himself guilty and reprehensible to a degree that can never be atoned for … his *will* to infect and poison the fundamental ground of things with the problem of punishment and guilt

so far as to cut off once and for all his own exit from this labyrinth of "fixed ideas"; his *will* to erect an ideal—that of the "holy God"—and in the face of it to feel the palpable certainty of his own absolute unworthiness. Oh this insane, pathetic beast—man! What ideas he has, what unnaturalness, what paroxysms of nonsense, what *bestiality of thought* erupts as soon as he is prevented just a little from being a *beast in deed!* . . [W]hoever can still bear to hear (but today one no longer has ears for this!) how in this night of torment and absurdity there has resounded the cry of *love*, the cry of the most nostalgic rapture, of redemption through love, will turn away, seized by invincible horror. — There is so much in man that is hideous! — Too long, the earth has been a madhouse! — (GM 2.22. See also GM 2.7; GM 3.16; GM 3.28; D 77; HH 108)[25]

The priests' moralization of bad conscience proves to be a make-work project for them, one that enables them not merely to hang on to their influence, but to extend and strengthen it. Having created this moral interpretation of the psycho-physiological development, they now offer themselves as specially equipped to alleviate the suffering it causes (see GM 3.15; AC 24; AC 46; AC 52). Their claim to expertise is not hollow, for they are indeed ingenious at this work (GM 3.17). However, while they can alleviate the pain of moralized bad conscience, they cannot cure it. As human beings whose self-experience is almost entirely that of sickness, the ascetic priests neither understand, nor fully believe in, the possibility of health or vital potency. They therefore lack the physio-psychological knowledge that is a necessary precursor to the capacity to cure sickness (GM 3.16 - 3.17). In the absence of a cure, they temporarily alleviate the pain of the sickness using two kinds of methods: those that are "innocent" by modern standards, since they do not exacerbate the sickness, and those that are guilty, which worsen it (GM 3.19).

Self-hypnosis, which Nietzsche compares to hibernation in other animals and estivation in plants, is the most effective of the innocent forms:

> This dominating sense of displeasure is combatted, first, by means that reduce the feeling of life in general to its lowest point. If possible, will and desire are abolished altogether; all that produces affects and "blood" is avoided ... no love; no hate; indifference, no revenge; no wealth; no work; one begs; if possible, no women, or as little as possible; in spiritual matters, Pascal's principle *il faut s'abêtir* [*one must make oneself stupid*] is applied. The result, expressed in moral-psychological terms, is "selflessness," "sanc-

tification"; in physiological terms: hypnotization. (GM 3.17. See also HH
126 – 127; HH 132 – 136)[26]

Although hibernation is the most effective of the innocent means, it
also requires more vital potency and independence than most sufferers
possess. Hence, the priests provide three innocent alternatives to it. The
first consists in highly regimented activity, which precludes leisure and
thus the opportunity for sufferers to dwell upon and to experience more
fully what they are. It is because highly regimented busywork offers relief
from self-suffering that sufferers praise, "somewhat dishonestly," "the
blessings of work" (GM 3.18).

The second alternative consists in petty pleasures. The most common
form, which is also the most highly praised, entails giving pleasure to
others by "doing good, giving, relieving, helping, encouraging, consoling,
praising, [and] rewarding" (GM 3.18). The effectiveness of petty pleasure
arises partly from the fact that, like hibernation, it distracts sufferers from
themselves. In addition, it also temporarily affords sufferers the feeling of
increased vitality (GM 3.18).

The third innocent alternative to hibernation consists in belonging to
associations that exist to alleviate suffering. Nietzsche observes that "[w]
hen one looks for the beginnings of Christianity in the Roman world,
one finds associations for mutual aid, associations for the poor, for the
sick, for burial, evolved among the lowest strata of society, in which this
major remedy for depression, petty pleasure produced by mutual help-
fulness, was consciously employed" (GM 3.18). These associations have
no purpose beyond the utilitarian, negatively defined good of alleviating
pain. As such, they are not truly life-promoting; that is, they aim to avoid
a bad, but they offer no direction about the positively defined or content-rich good. They offer no direction for, or impetus to, growth. Their
inherent inadequacy for life can be seen in the fact that, if they were to
succeed at eliminating suffering, they would become redundant (BGE
201). A life-promoting end, by contrast, aims at growth, which is not
only the supreme good, but is also inexhaustible in principle. Nietzsche
illustrates the character of associations by likening the individuals that
comprise them to grains of sand on a beach (HH 45). Like sand grains,
these sufferers are proximate to each other, but their co-habitation is
accidental. They remain fundamentally isolated from each other in their
private end of alleviating their own pain. By contrast, individuals within a

non-utilitarian, life-affirming community are united by the shared project of augmenting the human being. Each individual plays a meaningful
part in this larger project. To use Nietzsche's language, associations that
aim only to alleviate suffering are not ordered like an organism; hence,
they do not "live" (HH 45). By contrast, wherever the noble type rules,
"something new soon arises, a ruling structure that *lives*, in which parts
and functions are delimited and coordinated, in which nothing whatever
finds a place that has not first been assigned a 'meaning' in relation to the
whole" (GM 2.17).

Following his description of the innocent forms of pain relief,
Nietzsche turns to the guilty methods. All involve orgies of feeling; that
is, sudden and violent explosions of one or more passions (see GM 3.19
– 3.20). Any passion can be inflamed to an orgiastic intensity. However,
the passion priests chiefly employ is the sense of guilt, the passion whose
meaning is deeply entangled with the genealogy of the ascetic ideal (GM
3.20). They agitate the sufferer's sense of guilt until the sufferer becomes
hysterical. By inducing this frenzied state, the priests not only distract
the sufferer from his pain, but also enliven for a time his experience of
his will to power. However, this frenzy and sense of empowerment are
unsustainable. The passion soon explodes, and it does so at the cost of the
patient's vitality, bringing it to a lower point than it was prior to the orgy.
Over time and with repeated uses of this guilty method of pain-relief,
the sufferer is exhausted to the point where he comes to have a wraith-
like existence. His vitality is all but exhausted, but he persists in living
nevertheless:

> The old depression, heaviness, and weariness were indeed *overcome* through
> this system of procedures; life again became very interesting: awake, ever-
> lastingly awake, sleepless, glowing, charred, spent and yet not weary—thus
> was the man, "the sinner," initiated into *this* mystery. This ancient mighty
> sorcerer in his struggle with displeasure, the ascetic priest—he had obvi-
> ously won, his kingdom had come: one no longer protested against pain,
> one *thirsted* for pain; "*more* pain! *more* pain!" ... Every painful orgy of feeling,
> everything that shattered, bowled over, crushed, enraptured, transported;
> the secrets of the torture chamber, the inventiveness of hell itself—all were
> henceforth discovered, divined, and exploited, all stood in the service of the
> sorcerer, all served henceforward to promote the victory of his ideal, the
> ascetic ideal. — "My kingdom is not of *this* world"—he continued to say, as
> before: but did he still have the right to say it? (GM 3.20)

Cycle back and delve more deeply now into the most brilliant part of the ascetic priests' plan. Earlier, we discussed Nietzsche's observation that a move toward political despotism is always accompanied by a move toward a monotheistic god. The interrelated moves of politics and religion arise from the fact that, fundamentally, they are one and the same. Both articulate claims about what constitutes just authority over a people or over all human beings. Since there cannot be two equally authoritative, incompatible claims to justice, where politics and religion are not explicitly united, one or the other will rule. The one that rules is thereby the real political and religious authority, regardless of whether it is recognized as such. The remaining other—the other that is also both political and religious but is not authoritative—necessarily assumes a subordinate position, implicitly or explicitly. When we discussed these matters earlier, we emphasized the case in which religion, narrowly understood as something distinct from politics, is always reformed to reflect the emergence of political despotism (GM 2.20). See now: since strictly speaking there is no difference between religion and politics, the reverse motion can also occur. A change in religion, narrowly understood as something separate from politics, can yield a reformation in a political regime. This is precisely what happened, for the first time ever, in one most crucial, world-historical case—namely, Christianity.

The ascetic priests take full advantage of the general ignorance about both the inseparability of religion from politics and the efficacy of religion as a form of warfare. They realize that a universal God seems disconnected from politics. By so seeming, this God can pass through safeguards that aim to protect a regime. Once inside the regime, a religion of this sort can subvert the form of the regime, so that it comes to reflect the concept of God that infiltrated it. Nietzsche argues this is precisely what the priestly-aristocrats did with the concept of the Christian God and of Jesus Christ in particular. This tactic was so successful that the ascetic priests' power has spread throughout the world.

You do not see it? As Nietzsche sees it and as we discussed earlier, such blindness is due in part to the fact that this ideology need not appear in its overt form. It can also take forms that are not readily recognizable as Christian but that are so nevertheless, for they emerge from and share in the essential doctrines of reactive morality. By conceiving of a maximum, universal or world God who does not limit his allegiance primarily to a Chosen People, the priests moved beyond the boundaries of a single people to include, in principle, all human beings. What began as rebellion and war within a particular people thereby burgeons into a worldwide assault on the noble type. Moreover, since Christianity need not appear in its overtly religious form, again where religion is narrowly defined so as to be limited to the church, a great many people who are co-opted into this worldwide assault may not even realize they are fundamentally Christian. They may even believe themselves to be atheists.

Nietzsche expects his exposition of this brilliant war plan, so vast in scope and so long-standing, to be met with incredulity. His hypothesis is resisted if for no other reason than that the democratic belief in equality inclines people to balk at the idea that any human being or group of human beings could be so intelligent and foresighted as to conceive of such a plan. Nietzsche responds. This incredulity bespeaks an incapacity of intellect and imagination, which are not even counterarguments to what he sees in history, much less refutations of his hypothesis. He has conceived of such a plan. It is therefore manifestly possible that such a plan can be conceived! Nietzsche seems implicitly to insist his hypothesis is not only plausible, but is also the best analysis of the interrelated genealogies he tracks, for it makes the most sense of the various and complex facts at hand:

> But you do not comprehend this? You are incapable of seeing something that required two thousand years to achieve victory? –There is nothing to wonder at in that: all protracted things are hard to see, to see whole. That, however, is what has happened: from the trunk of that tree of vengefulness and hatred, Jewish hatred—the profoundest and most sublime kind of hatred, capable of creating ideals and reversing values, the like of which has never existed on earth before—there grew something equally incomparable, a *new love*, the profoundest and most sublime kind of love—and from what other trunk could it have grown?
>
> One should not imagine it grew up as the denial of that thirst for revenge, as the opposite of Jewish hatred! No, the reverse is true! That love grew out of it as its crown, as its triumphant crown spreading itself farther and farther into the purest brightness and sunlight, driven as it were into the domain of light and the heights in pursuit of the goals of that hatred—victory, spoil, and seduction—by the same impulse that drove the roots of that hatred deeper and deeper and more and more covetously into all that was profound and evil. This Jesus of Nazareth, this incarnate gospel of love, this "Redeemer" who brought blessedness and victory to the poor, the sick, the sinners—was he not this seduction in its most uncanny

and irresistible form, a seduction and bypath to precisely those *Jewish* values and new ideals? Did Israel not attain the ultimate goal of its sublime vengefulness precisely through the bypath of this "Redeemer," this ostensible opponent and disintegrator of Israel? Was it not part of the secret black art of truly *grand* politics of revenge, of farseeing, subterranean, slowly advancing, and premeditated revenge, that Israel must itself deny the real instrument of its revenge before all the world as a mortal enemy and nail it to the cross, so that "all the world," namely all the opponents of Israel, could unhesitatingly swallow just this bait? And could spiritual subtlety imagine any *more dangerous* bait than this? Anything to equal the enticing, intoxicating, overwhelming, and undermining power of that symbol of the "holy cross," that ghastly paradox of a "God on the cross," that mystery of an unimaginable ultimate cruelty and self-crucifixion of God *for the salvation of man?*

You are still incredulous? Would an appeal to additional authorities be more convincing? Although Nietzsche speaks of the way in which the priests extended their war strategy to a universal scope by means of Christianity, he does not dwell on the way the priests reversed the traditional relationship between politics and religion. For an explicit account of this reversal, we can turn to Rousseau, a philosopher with whom Nietzsche often disagrees, but with whom he shares this crucial conclusion. Rousseau speaks neither of master and slave morality nor of the war between the priestly and warrior-aristocrats. He does, however, argue that the Christians who were politically oppressed by the Romans ultimately triumphed over these oppressors by means of their morality. He agrees both that Christianity was the first religion to be used as ideological warfare and that Christianity established a political despotism by means of the concept of a universal, monotheistic God:

> The question may be asked why under paganism, when each State had its cult and its Gods, there were no wars of religion. I reply that it was for this very reason that each State, having its own cult as well as its government, did not distinguish between its Gods and its laws. Political war was also theological. ... The God of one people had no rights over other peoples. The Gods of the pagans were not jealous Gods. ... But when the Jews, subjected to the kings of Babylon and later to the kings of Syria, wanted to remain obstinate in not acknowledging any other God than theirs, this refusal, regarded as rebellion against the victor, brought on them the persecutions of which we read in their history, and of which there are no other examples prior to Christianity. ... Finally, the Romans, having spread their cult and their Gods along with their empire, and having themselves adopted the

Gods of the vanquished by granting legal status in the City to them all, the peoples of that vast empire would insensibly come to find themselves having multitudes of Gods and of cults, which were approximately the same everywhere. And this is how paganism in the known world finally became a single, identical religion.

It was under these circumstances that Jesus came to establish a spiritual kingdom on earth. By separating the theological system from the political system, he brought about the end of the unity of the state, and caused the internal divisions that never ceased to stir up Christian peoples.²⁷ Now since this new idea of an otherworldly kingdom could never be understood by the pagans, they always regarded the Christians as true rebels who, beneath a hypocritical submissiveness, were only awaiting the moment to become independent and the masters, and to usurp adroitly the authority they pretended to respect out of weakness. This was the cause of the persecutions.

What the pagans feared happened. Then everything took on a different appearance, the humble Christians changed their language, and soon this supposedly otherworldly kingdom was seen to become, under a visible leader, the most violent despotism in this world.²⁸

The difference between Rousseau's account and Nietzsche's hypothesis does not pertain to the employment of Christianity as ideological warfare. Rather, as we noted earlier, Nietzsche thinks this tactic of altering politics by means of religion, rather than the reverse, is first employed in the context of a war between the ruling factions within the Jewish people. The employment of this warfare upon the Romans is therefore secondary to this internecine battle.

Nietzsche goes on to remark that this strategic use of narrowly defined religion has been a surpassingly successful means of overthrowing the political rule of the noble type across the globe: "What is certain, at least, is that *sub hoc signo [under this sign]* Israel, with its vengefulness and revaluation of all values, has hitherto triumphed again and again over all other ideals, over all *nobler* ideals— " (GM 1.8). He ends the eighth section of the first essay of *The Genealogy* with this grim pronouncement.

Immediately following this judgment, he begins section nine, the middle section of the first essay. It begins with an interruption by a so-called "free spirit," a moniker that here signifies someone who thinks he is free from all deeply held commitments and from the authority of the church in particular (GM 1.9; see also BGE 44). Adopting the voice of this free spirit, Nietzsche allows this character to interrupt the first essay for almost the whole of this middle section. The character begins by repeating Nietzsche's conclusions concerning the victory of the slave revolt in what seems to be an exasperated tone. He objects at the very least to Nietzsche's terminology, and in particular to his references to noble or master and slave types and their respective moralities:

"But why are you talking about *nobler* ideals! Let us stick to the facts: the people have won—or 'the slaves' or 'the mob' or 'the herd' or whatever you like to call them—if this has happened through the Jews, very well! in that case no people ever had a more world-historical mission. 'The masters' have been disposed of; the morality of the common human being has won. One may conceive of this victory as at the same a blood-poisoning (it has mixed the races together)—I shan't contradict; but this intoxication has undoubtedly been *successful*. The 'redemption' of the human race (from 'the masters,' that is) is going forward; everything is visibly becoming Judaized, Christianized, mob-ized (what do the words matter!). The progress of this poison through the entire body of humankind seems irresistible, its pace and tempo may from now on even grow slower, subtler, less audible, more cautious—there is plenty of time.— (GM 1.9)

While contemplating the spread of this poison, he wonders whether the existence of the church is still necessary: "'[D]oes the church today still have any necessary role to play'" in the spread of this poison, or "'could one do without it? *Quaeritur [one asks]*'" (GM 1.9). His use of Latin suggests he thinks education, or at least his education, has made the Church unnecessary. He likely regards it as an embarrassing hold-over of a dark age. He proceeds to proclaim that he believes in progress, by which he seems to mean precisely the kind of education or enlightenment that he believes has liberated him from the prejudice. He adds that the spread of the poison belongs to such progress and then confesses he loves the poison. Why? He does not explain. Perhaps he loves it because he thinks it liberated him from his devotion to the church. Insofar as the church was hierarchical as well as non-rational in its reliance on authority, it carried a lingering scent of noble politics. He seems not to have noticed that these attributes of the church were incidental remnants of a noble culture. The poison he allegedly loves, meanwhile, is the very essence of the church since, at bottom, both are defined by slave morality. In his ignorant shallowness, he speaks with glee of annihilating the church while endorsing the ongoing spread of its poison:

"Ought ... [the church] not become at least a little more refined? — Today it alienates rather than seduces. — Which of us would be a free spirit if the church did not exist? It is the church, and not its poison, that repels us. — Apart from the church, we, too, love the poison— " (GM 1.9)

The free spirit apparently departs following this diatribe. Nietzsche abruptly returns to his own voice and concludes the section: "This is the epilogue of a 'free spirit' to my speech; an honest animal, as he has abundantly revealed, and a democrat, moreover; he had been listening to me till then and could not endure to listen to my silence" (GM 1.9).

Although he calls the free spirit's interjection an "epilogue," this section is only the ninth section in an essay that consists of seventeen (GM 1.9). By characterizing the free spirit's speech as an ending of sorts, Nietzsche indicates that the free spirit aims to stop him from saying anything further. By calling the free spirit's speech an epilogue and then continuing nonetheless, Nietzsche signals that he will initiate a second part or new beginning to the essay, after having brought the first part to a close.

To help us better understand what this new beginning means, let us investigate precisely why the free spirit wanted to end Nietzsche's speech. Regarding the free spirit's intention, Nietzsche observes: "[He] had been listening to me till then and could not endure to listen to my silence" (GM 1.9). Why was the free spirit so eager to end Nietzsche's speech at precisely this point? What did Nietzsche communicate in his silence that was unendurable to this human type? He has already been so revolutionary in his thinking, so brazen, and potentially inflammatory that one might wonder what more could he say such that the free spirit tries only now to stop him from speaking further—or, to be more precise, from communicating in silence.

An analysis of the moment of the free spirit's rude interjection sheds light on this mystery. As noted, he interrupts in a moment of silence, following Nietzsche's observation that the priests have "hitherto triumphed again and again over all other ideals, over all *nobler* ideals" (GM 1.8). Perhaps this free spirit does not like to be reminded that nobler ideals have been defeated. Yet, he goes on to say he loves the poison, and this poison is meant to destroy both noble ideals and the noble human type. The free spirit cannot love the poison without also loving its purpose. Having declared his devotion to slave morality, he emphasizes the poison's unstoppable spread:

"The people have won. ... 'The masters' have been disposed of; the morality of the common human being has won. ... [T]his in-toxication has undoubtedly been successful. The 'redemption' of the human race (from 'the masters' that is) is going forward; everything is visibly ... mob-ized. ... The progress of this poison through the entire body of humankind seems irresistible" (GM 1.9).

The words capture a version of Nietzsche's hypothesis, but the tone differs. In this discrepancy, we see what the free spirit finds unendurable. It is not that he disagrees with the conclusions he mouths. Nor does he want Nietzsche's hypothesis, as he re-mouths it, to be wrong. Rather, he stumbles upon Nietzsche's claim that the slave revolt has been victorious. It is this, or rather it is his insecurity about the decisiveness of Nietzsche's conclusion on this point, that the free spirit finds unendurable. In other words, when Nietzsche observes that slave morality has "hitherto triumphed again and again over all other ideals, over all *nobler* ideals," it is the single word—"hitherto"—that provokes the free spirit to cut him off. This temporal qualification indicates decisively, if discreetly, that Nietzsche does not think the war is necessarily over. Slave morals have previously triumphed, but this is not to say they always will. The future is undetermined. Nietzsche thereby disagrees with the free spirit's hope that the spread of the poison through the whole of humankind is irresistible (GM 1.9). The two opposing sentiments—the free spirit's hope that the war has been won absolutely and Nietzsche's hope that the war is unresolved—battle each other in the moment of Nietzsche's silence. The free spirit's interruption indicates he was broken in this agonistic moment. His insistence that the victory has been decisive is mere whistling in the dark. In truth, he fears the future holds the possibility of a reversal in the war.

The free spirit leaves after his outburst. Nietzsche reassumes his own voice. He reflects on the free spirit's behavior. Then, he informs us he is going to make a new beginning of sorts, one shrouded in silence: "[H]e had been listening to me till then and could not endure to listen to my silence. For at this point I have much to be silent about" (GM 1.9). By telling us he now has "much to be silent about," he subtly alerts us to be on the lookout for what he does *not* say, in addition to what he says.

In the second half of the first essay, Nietzsche speaks of the slave revolt in much broader terms. He no longer focuses so exclusively on the political circumstances that surround the creation of slave morality. Rather, he depicts and analyzes the physio-psychology that underlies it, in all its forms. In what he says and does not say about this physio-psychology lies Nietzsche's strategy for overthrowing the victory of the slave type in its battle against all things noble.

Chapter Four

Warspeak

The subtitle to *On the Genealogy of Morals* is "A Polemic"—that is, "Warspeak." With it, Nietzsche signals his entry into the slave type's secret, psychological battle against noble human beings and everything characteristic of super-abundant vitality. As noted previously, Nietzsche briefs us on the background of this war in the first half of *The Genealogy's* opening essay—"'Good and Evil,' 'Good and Bad.'" The central section of this essay is a kind of fulcrum upon which Nietzsche turns away from his briefing and pivots to fighting in this war. In the second half of the essay, Nietzsche begins his counterattack. We join him as he advances.

Before accompanying him further, ask: What provokes him to enter this war? In the "Preface" to *The Genealogy*, he shares an intimate view of his own soul, which he likens to a lovely, private garden-world. Why does he leave its solitary loveliness for very public warfare as an isolated soldier against a mass movement? Anticipating our question, he offers a preliminary answer. He notes the slave revolt has been so successful that the human being is now in danger of devolving, perhaps irreversibly. Modernity has not yet seen the seriousness and the urgency of this threat. Far from having an accurate account of the degenerating human being, this being is touted as an improvement over the beast-of-prey human because of the very traits that signal diminished vital potency. Indeed, the very "meaning of culture," according to modernity, consists in taming the beast-of-prey human so that savage, ferocious, and violent drives are bred out of existence (GM I.11).

The allegedly more advanced, modern human is soft, more domesticated, certainly not savage or ferocious. His almost total lack of overt ferocity is especially acclaimed, as though it were the very essence of good character. What lacks ferocity and the hardness that accompanies it is purportedly preferable in all respects to the severe, formidable being, the being with the potential to be dreadful. This predilection for softness over severity and ferocity betrays something of the utilitarian belief that the good is freedom from suffering.

While Nietzsche acknowledges that the human being who harbors savage drives can be terrifying, he chastens us to weigh the pros and cons of these drives more thoughtfully and thoroughly against the standard of life. We must ask whether such drives are conducive to, and perhaps even necessary for, the ongoing growth or enhancement of the human being. In considering this question, Nietzsche comes to realize that these savage drives are inextricably bound up with super-abundant vitality *and vice versa*: super-abundant vitality is inextricably bound up with the savage drives. We want super-abundant vitality because our most life-affirming activity—self-directed growth—depends upon it. We direct our growth by ideals or goals that are content-rich, and such goals can only be created pro-actively, out of super-abundant vitality. A "Yes!" to our most life-affirming activity must therefore also be a "No!" to the modern project to extinguish the savage drives and the noble human type. The savage drives must not be eliminated.

The necessary link between savage drives on the one hand and growth on the other is decisive for our evaluation of the modern project of domestication. It is nevertheless helpful to consider in addition the surprising connection between savage drives and the most humane characteristics, which seem to be eagerly endorsed by modernity. Savagery and humanity are often regarded as opposite characteristics. In fact, however, both have their source in overflowing vitality. They are therefore not opposites. Moreover, they are interdependent, or rather, genuine humaneness only exists to the extent that it is rooted in savagery. Although humaneness is a more civilized manifestation of super-abundant human life and savagery is more primitive, humaneness grows out of savagery and is sustained by it as it becomes increasingly refined. Hence, Nietzsche does not merely argue that the savage drives must not be eliminated.

To illustrate the necessary connection between savagery and humaneness, Nietzsche likens the growth or evolution of the human being to that of the tree. The most delicate, newly formed tree leaves, which thrust themselves ever higher into the air, correspond to the human being's newly spiritualized drives—that is, drives that have most recently evolved so as to become involved with consciousness, with mind (see GS 11; GS 110). It is partly because of their involvement with mind that they are usually regarded as the opposite of our simplest, most primitive drives, which act instinctively or without any significant degree of mind. These most primitive drives are akin to the tree's roots.

While we can speak of a tree as having these distinct parts, we also recognize that this division is somewhat artificial and arbitrary. In truth, all of the parts merge into each other to form the tree as a whole. For the tree to remain healthy as is pushes itself further and further into the rarefied air, its roots—its more primitive genealogical origins—must thrust themselves ever-deeper into the ground, into the past, so to speak (see Z, "On the Tree on the Mountainside"; BGE 257; BGE 295). If the tree's upward augmentation is not counter-balanced by a corresponding increase in the strength of the roots, the tree will become unhealthy and susceptible to destruction.

So too, in the case of the human being, the more ancient, primitive, and savage drives in our physio-psychology must continue to become more profound—that is, more comprehending of our genealogical origins and thus more deeply rooted—if they are to support our ongoing evolution and hence the growth of our most spiritual refinements. Only by extending into and cultivating the entire genealogical spectrum of human health, including our savage drives, can one increase the vigor of, and enhance, the human being.[29] In sum, therefore, the tamer the human being becomes, the weaker he becomes, and the weaker he becomes, the less able he is of evolving into a higher, more enhanced life-form (see Z, "Zarathustra's Speeches"; GS 26; BGE 259; WP 398). In light of his account of the necessary connection for growth between our savage and refined drives, Nietzsche understands the true aim and purpose of culture, not as the elimination of savage drives, but as the cultivation of the *whole* human being, including the savage drives.[30]

Nietzsche makes explicit both the need for cultivating savage drives and the discomfort one might feel in the face of this fact by portraying Dionysus contemplating how he might enhance us. As the god reflects on this question, Nietzsche reflects on the god:

[I]f it were permitted to follow human custom in attributing to ...

[Dionysus] many solemn pomp-and-virtue names, I should have to give abundant praise to his explorer and discoverer courage, his daring honesty, truthfulness, and love of wisdom. But such a god has no use whatever for all such venerable junk and pomp. "Keep that," he would say, "for yourself and your likes and whoever has need of it! I—have no reason for covering my nakedness."

One guesses: this type of deity and philosopher is perhaps lacking in shame?

Thus he once said: "Under certain circumstances I love what is human"—and with this he alluded to Ariadne who was present—"the human being is to my mind an agreeable, courageous, inventive, animal that has no equal on earth; it finds its way in any labyrinth. I am well disposed towards him: I often reflect how I might yet advance him and make him stronger, more evil, and more profound than he is."

"Stronger, more evil, and more profound?" I asked, startled. "Yes," he said once more; "stronger, more evil, and more profound; also more beautiful"—and at that the tempter god smiled with his halcyon smile as though he had just paid an enchanting compliment. Here we also see: what this divinity lacks is not only a sense of shame—and there are also other good reasons for conjecturing that in several respects all of the gods could learn from us humans. We humans are—more humane.— (BGE 295; see also Z, "On The Higher Men," 5)

His arguments against the extermination of great health and the beast-of-prey human being who embodies it are informed by his understanding of the activity that is life, but this knowledge is not the sole or even the primary reason for his decision to wade into war. Nietzsche is not a martyr for truth (BGE 25). Nor does he harbor an unegoistic concern for the species (see GM 3.7). Ask again: Why does he leave his secret garden-world to go to war—as a *commander*, no less?

In the second intimate moment Nietzsche shares in *The Genealogy*, he tells us he wades into this war because the pervasive sight of the degenerating human being threatens to transform *him* into a nihilist:

[T]his is how things are: the diminution and leveling of ... *the human being* constitutes *our* greatest danger, for the sight of him makes us weary.— We can see nothing today that wants to grow greater, we suspect things will continue to go down, down, to become thinner, more good-natured, more prudent, more comfortable, more mediocre, more indifferent, more Chinese, more Christian—there is no doubt that the human being is getting "better" all the time. ... [T]ogether with the fear of the human being we have also lost our love of him, our reverence for him, our hopes for him, even the will to him. The sight of man now makes us weary—what is nihilism today if it is not *that?*— We are weary *of the human being.* (GM 1.12; see also BGE 203; GM 3.14; Z, "On the Rabble"; AC 7; EH, "Why I Am a Destiny," especially 6)

Nietzsche speaks here of nihilism "today." By so doing, he indicates this concept has a genealogy, so that the meaning it has now is not the same as the meaning it had in the past. More specifically, today it no longer denotes the belief that there is no such thing as truth, understood as a correspondence to, or a reflection of, a supposedly transcendent realm of eternal, unaltering, and absolute being. Rather, nihilism today denotes disbelief in the human potential to be or grow into new, enhanced and more vital forms of itself. It is disbelief in the possibility of a *genuine future* for the human being.

We may call this disbelief in a genuine future the nihilistic passion. This passion is complex. One of its components is a particular kind of pity, which Nietzsche associates with vital impotence and Christianity. This pity is an expression of one's belief that those whom one pities cannot surmount their unchoiceworthy condition. They can neither take charge of their own growth nor can they grow as a result of any natural influence that is external to them. Such pity can be directed toward specific individuals or groups of people. It can also be an attitude toward the human being per se.

Given this disbelief in growth, those who have this kind of pity act at best merely to alleviate suffering. They aim only at a negatively defined concept of the good because they do not believe, or do not believe strongly enough, in a positively defined goal for growth. By setting their sights solely on a negative goal, they may wittingly or unwittingly thwart and sacrifice possibilities for a genuine future (AC 7).

The other component of modern nihilism is nausea at what the human being currently is. In sum, therefore, nihilism today consists of the combination of enervating pity plus nausea. Nietzsche describes this complex passion as follows:

What is to be feared, what has a more calamitous effect than any other calamity, is that man should inspire not profound fear but profound *nausea*; also not great fear but great *pity*. Suppose these two were one day to unite, they would inevitably beget one of the un-canniest monsters: the "last will" of man, his will to nothingness, nihilism. And indeed a great deal points to this union. Whoever can smell not only with his nose but also with his eyes and ears, scents almost everywhere he goes today something like the air of madhouses and hospitals—I am speaking, of course, of the cultural domain, of every kind of "Europe" on this earth. The *sick* are man's greatest danger; *not* the evil; *not* the "beasts of prey." Those who are failures from the start, downtrodden, crushed—it is they, the *weakest*, who must undermine life among humans, who call into question and poison most dangerously our trust in life, in the human being, and in ourselves. Where does one not encounter that veiled glance that burdens one with a profound sadness, that inward-turned glance of the born failure that betrays how such a human being speaks to himself—that glance that is a sigh! "If only I were someone else," sighs this glance: "but there is no hope of that. I am who I am: how could I ever get free of myself? And yet—I *am sick of myself!*" (GM 3.14; see also Z, "On the Rabble"; EH, "Why I Am So Wise," 8)

Nietzsche enters the war primarily because the ferocity of his self-love is roused to fight against his succumbing to this nihilism, but it would be incorrect to think his self-love is selfish or narrowly self-concerned. Rather, he experiences himself not only as an individual, but also as a species-being. Stated succinctly, he feels and understands himself as a human individual (see BGE 199; BGE 4; GS 1; TI, "Skirmishes of an Untimely Man," 19 - 20). His overflowing self-love is therefore also a love for the human being.

He explains that, because of eons of breeding, our human physio-psychology necessarily incorporates something of the desire to promote and secure the thriving life of the human being per se. The most vitally potent human beings, whose instincts and primitive drives are most deeply rooted and most vigorous, feel this desire most strongly, but it exists to some degree in all humans as our deepest, best-preserved instinct (GS 1). This species-instinct must not be confused with the herd-instinct.

The species-instinct loves the thriving human being. When it is sufficiently potent, it seeks to promote thriving life in the human being per se. The herd-instinct, by contrast, does not aim directly at growth. It aims at mere self-preservation. It has this uninspiring aim because it lacks the vital potency for grander goals. If it had more vitality, its efforts would no longer be limited to mere self-preservation. This is to say that, if the herd-instinct had more vitality, it would cease to be the herd-instinct.

As someone with great love for the human being, Nietzsche attempts to enhance what we are, but, to be clear, his attempt is not unegoistic nor could it be. As an individual, he wants to experience his will to power maximally. As a powerful species-being, he knows he will attain this goal if he enhances the human being per se. Stated generally and more strongly, if one has tremendous will to power, one necessarily seeks to express this super-abundant vitality in the act of augmenting the human being, for such action is the highest, most fulfilling expression of human life (e.g. see Z, "On Old and New Tablets," 3; GS 337). To this general claim, we must add that such enhancement only occurs by way of the enhancement of individuals (see BGE 257). We add this in an effort to avoid the misleading impression that the concept of the species has a self-subsisting reality. It is an abstraction drawn from individuals that have roughly the same genealogies.

Having revealed something of his personal reasons for entering the war, Nietzsche becomes even more intimate. He offers a heart-rending observation about the terrible and repeated hardships one can endure, provided one continues to believe in the possibility of human growth:

> How much one is able to endure: distress, want, bad weather, sickness, toil, solitude. Fundamentally one can cope with everything else, born as one is to a subterranean life of struggle; one emerges again and again into the light, one experiences again and again one's golden hour of victory—and then one stands forth as one was born, unbreakable, tensed, ready for new, even harder, remoter things, like a bow that distress only serves to draw tauter. (GM 1.12; see also BGE "Preface"; GS "Preface," 3; Z, "Prologue," 3 - 5)

This hope that the human being will continue to be a bridge or a precarious tightrope on which he moves toward something more vital than what he currently is must have some basis in reality if it is to be sustained. It must be fed by at least an occasional glimpse of a human being who embodies super-abundant vitality, someone who can grow and from whom this enhancement can circulate, so that it is eventually incorporated into other human beings and hence into the human being per se. Aware that he is in danger of losing this hope, and thereby becoming a nihilist, Nietzsche himself wishes for even a momentary sighting of such a person:

> [G]rant me from time to time—if there are divine goddesses in the realm beyond good and evil—grant me the sight, but one glance of something perfect, wholly achieved, happy, mighty, triumphant, something still capable of arousing fear! Of a human being who justifies the human, of a complementary and redeeming lucky hit on the part of the human being for the

sake of which one may still *believe in the human!* (GM 1.12; see also BGE 207)

Rather than waiting passively for his wish to be granted, Nietzsche fights to secure a genuine future for himself and the human being. Such action demonstrates that he is the kind of person he wishes to behold. He seeks a second self. Against this backdrop of personal struggle and courage, we join Nietzsche on the battlefield.

His counter-attack strategy comes into focus in section ten of "'Good and Evil,' 'Good and Bad'"—the first section of the second half of the essay. Here, Nietzsche subtly yet clearly indicates he will fight fire with fire: slave morality is a psychological weapon; he fights it with superior psychology. More specifically, he fights slave morality by an acute analysis of physio-psychology that produces it. This analysis reveals crucial contradictions in slave morality that shatter its claim to authority.

In keeping with this strategy, he introduces and analyzes a previously unidentified passion—*ressentiment*. Nietzsche retains the French word to denote this passion, which is not to say he retains its French meaning.[31] Its fuller meaning will become clear as we move through Nietzsche's account of it. As a starting point, we understand it as the product of the suppressed desire for revenge, where we do not impute to revenge any necessary or direct connection with justice. Someone who suffers from a bad day at work can alleviate this pain by kicking the wall, knowing that the wall is not the cause of his suffering.

Ressentiment can be experienced by any human being, regardless of how strong or weak he is. If it appears in the noble human being, however, it typically does not amount to anything significantly different from simple revenge. It "consummates and exhausts itself in an immediate reaction" (GM 1.10). By contrast, in one who is impotent to express his desire for revenge immediately in an outwardly directed act, the passion builds up in this person's physio-psychology. Eventually, it becomes involved with the mind. If it lingers long enough in the internal realm of the mind, it becomes creative. More specifically, while *ressentiment* does not become powerful enough to create something content-rich, it can become sufficiently powerful to say "No!" to its object. Such a "No!" to noble morality is precisely how slave morality is made. Thus, Nietzsche refines his hypothesis that the slave revolt originates with the priestly-aristocrats in their struggle for political power against the co-ruling warrior-aristocrats. It is the priests' *ressentiment* that generates the slave values, which constitute the origin of this revolt.

Given their similar genealogies, it should come as no surprise that *ressentiment's* creations share an identifying characteristic: they are all forms of "imaginary revenge" (GM 1.10). These revenge fantasies help to compensate the impotent individual for being "denied the true reaction," deeds in the external realm (GM 1.10). Nietzsche makes the additional observation that *ressentiment's* revenge-fantasies bespeak the slavish valuator's need to turn his "value-positing eye" away from himself. This reactionary valuator tries to avoid looking at himself because he is aware of what he is, and he does not like what he is. He therefore tries to distract himself from himself, and he tries to lie to himself about what he is. This fundamental lie to oneself about oneself is "the essence of *ressentiment*" (GM 1.10). Paradoxically, therefore, *ressentiment's* creativity is less about revenge than about upholding this foundational lie in the soul.

This dislike of oneself—*not* a concern for justice—accounts for the slavish human being's deep-seated, spiritualized hatred for the vitally potent human being: the noble human being reminds the slavish human being of what he is not and what he is. To obscure this knowledge, *ressentiment* distorts the image of the noble human being to the point where this object becomes an unreal thing, "a caricature and monster" that does not belong to the world (GM 1.10). Having fabricated an absurd enemy, the slavish valuator flatters himself that he is the opposite of this enemy. Whereas his enemy sides with the devil, with pure evil, he walks with God, with pure goodness. Indeed, he goes so far in his lying as to tell himself and others that he is not weak, but potent. Or rather, he attributes power to God, and then claims that God loves only him and those like him. Those whom God loves will enjoy potency in a post-death-life, if not now.

Given that the slavish human being does not act in ways that evince potency, he must argue that he has this power, but he chooses not to express it. He makes this choice, he must claim, because it is good. Thus, vital impotence is rebranded as moral strength.

Thinking over the slavish human being who lies to himself and others in this way about his moral freedom, Nietzsche says:

> This type of man *needs* to believe in a neutral independent "subject," prompted by an instinct for self-preservation and self-affirmation in which

every lie is sanctified. The subject (or to use a more popular expression, the *soul*) has perhaps been believed in hitherto more firmly than anything else on earth because it makes possible to the majority of mortals, the weak and oppressed of every kind, the sublime self-deception that interprets weakness as freedom, and their being thus-and-thus as a *merit*. (GM 1.13. See also GM 1.14; GM 3.14)

The notion that vital potency could express itself in acts that evince impotence depends upon two foundational ideas. First, it depends upon the idea that there is a separation between an actor and his action. Second, in order to credit to the actor with moral strength one must assert that there is such a thing as free will: the actor must have the free choice to act either morally or wickedly (GM 1.13; BGE 21). Without this freedom, the slavish human being cannot claim that he is good for acting weakly. In addition, without this freedom, sin—the freely chosen evil act—is impossible.

The doctrine of free will originates in a simpler doctrine that offers an account of the will without attributing freedom to it. This simpler doctrine posits that the will, which here is equated with mind, is distinct from the desires, which are associated with the body. Moreover, in this account, the mind is typically held to be the proper ruler of the body. It can rule the body or the appetites because it stands apart from the desires, it can judge them as good or bad, and it has the power to act or not act upon the desires according to its judgment of them.

This conception of the mind as something distinct from the body can develop into the notion that the mind is not only distinct from the body, but also separate from it. In turn, the idea that the mind is separate from the body may invite the idea that, although the body is corruptible and dies, the mind or soul may live on after death, perhaps even eternally.

That this doctrine of the will can develop along these lines does not mean it must develop into the belief in an immortal soul. For example, at least for pedagogical reasons, Plato's Socrates and Aristotle regard the mind, psyche, or soul as distinct from the body or the appetites. They also seem to think the mind can and should rule the body. Yet, a close reading of their works suggests neither philosopher insists that the soul outlives the body in any shape that adequately fulfills our desire for immortality. Furthermore, to the extent that they seem to think the mind can rule the body, their accounts of this relationship between mind and body do not amount to the doctrine free will. They argue that human beings *neces-*

sarily do what they know or believe to be good for themselves. Hence, we are *unfree* to do what we know or believe is bad for us. One who acts in manner that harms himself can only do so out of ignorance or error.

To move beyond this doctrine of the will to the doctrine of free will, slave morality must proclaim that human beings, or at least those human beings who live after our fall from Paradise, always have adequate knowledge of good and evil. Unlike the classical philosophers, therefore, slave morality posits that, despite knowing good and evil, we are not necessarily ruled by this knowledge. Our fallen nature may tempt us to act wickedly, and we may freely choose to follow our wicked nature. If we make this wicked choice, we are guilty of sin.

Contrary to the doctrines of the free and the unfree will, Nietzsche argues that there is no entity that stands apart from the action associated with it. The entity *is* the action and nothing besides:

> A quantum of force is equivalent to a quantum of drive, will, effect—more, it is nothing other than precisely this very driving, willing, effecting, and only owing to the seduction of language (and of the fundamental errors of reason that are petrified in it) which conceives and misconceives all effects as conditioned by something that causes effects, by a "subject," can it appear otherwise. (GM 1.13; see also BGE 21)

Languages that separate nouns from verbs mislead us by giving us the false impression that there are things that exist apart from actions. Regarding what we are as human individuals, they mislead us into thinking that we are essentially an unchanging, unified "I" that is distinct from our acts. Languages in which the actor is incorporated into the verb form are more representative of reality than those that separate nouns from verbs.

Speaking of the abstract concept of the "I" and of those who accept this abstraction as though it were adequate to reality, Nietzsche says:

> There are still harmless self-observers who believe that there are "immediate certainties"; for example, "I think," or as the superstition of Schopenhauer put it, "I will"; as though knowledge here got hold of its object purely and nakedly as "the thing in itself," without any falsification on the part of either the subject or the object. ... Let the people suppose that knowledge means knowing things entirely; the philosopher must say to himself: When I analyze the process that is expressed in the sentence, "I think," I find a whole series of daring assertions that would be difficult, perhaps impossible, to prove; for example, that it is *I* who think, that there

must necessarily be something that thinks, that thinking is an activity and operation on the part of a being who is thought of as a cause, that there is an "ego," and, finally, that it is already determined what is to be designated by thinking—that I know what thinking is. ... Whoever ventures to answer these metaphysical questions at once by an appeal to a sort of intuitive perception, like the person who says, "I think, and know that this, at least, is true, actual, and certain"—will encounter a smile and two question marks from a philosopher nowadays. "Sir," the philosopher will perhaps give him to understand, "it is improbable that you are not mistaken; but why insist on the truth?" (BGE 16; see also BGE 17 – 19; TI, "The Four Great Errors")

Having introduced us to the theme of lying and to the depth, quantity, and pervasiveness of the lies the belong to slave morality, Nietzsche unsheathes the full force of his counter-attack on slave morality in the fourteenth section of the first essay of *The Genealogy*. This attack is introduced in the form of a story that depicts how ideals are manufactured in a workshop of mendacity. The narrative style has distinct advantages. To begin, it enables Nietzsche to condense the genealogy of slave morality, which covers thousands of years, into a single scene. Additionally, it helps him move the reader viscerally in addition to appealing to the reader's intellect. The story is also memorable, which makes it a highly effective conduit for an attack upon slave morality.

The tale begins with Nietzsche addressing an audience, including the reader, directly, as a teacher: "Would anyone like to take a look into the secret of *how ideals are made* on earth? Who has the courage?" (GM 1.14). There is at least one volunteer for the lesson: Mr. Rash and Curious. We are to learn along with this student. To the extent that we do so, we may be this student.

What are we to make of Nietzsche's choice of this student's name? In particular, what are we to make of Nietzsche's characterization of his student as rash? Rashness is typically understood as excessive confidence in the face of danger, and such excess is not usually regarded as good. Rather, it is held to be imprudent, an effect of ignorance, which is bad. Rashness seems to stand in contradistinction to courage, understood as the right comportment of the passions in the face of a danger that one recognizes as terrible. Thus, we have an explanation of the student's name. He is someone who is about to undertake a dangerous act with a confidence that is excessive because it is ignorant of the danger at hand. But this account is inconsistent with Nietzsche's interest in this student and with his philosophy more generally. Nietzsche is the philosopher who understands philosophy as an attempt, an experiment, a terribly thrilling risk. An alternative account of the name is required.

We suggest that Nietzsche calls this student rash, not because he wants to emphasize a problem with the student's interest in learning how slavish ideals are made. Rather, he aims to indicate succinctly that rashness is necessary to anyone who embarks upon a genuine investigation of a serious issue, such as morality. It is necessary because life is radically undetermined; hence, one cannot know beforehand what the effects of an investigation of a serious matter will be. The knowledge one gains might be harmful or deadly (see GS 107; GS 110). We should say more about this radical indeterminacy so that we better understand why rashness, understood as a kind of ferocious audacity, is necessary for learning about serious matters and hence for philosophy.

Contrary to the traditional, teleological account of the human being, human life is not something bound by a fixed human nature. All that is given to us is our genealogy. It tethers us like a ribbon to our past. By so doing, it determines something of our future possibilities, but the future itself is unknown and unlimited. To live it fully, at the edges of what a human being can be, requires one to leap into the unknown and unbound future. This leap is guided by a goal, but one cannot know what goals are attainable except by attaining them. One only truly knows what is possible after it has been actualized. That is, there is no self-subsisting potential that is waiting to be discovered and can tell us what can be actualized. We can now see more fully why Nietzsche describes philosophy as the continuous transformation of all that one is into "light and flame" (GS "Preface," 3; see also GS 26). The upper edge of human life, which the philosopher embodies, consists of the attempt to make more robust the most rarified and most vital version of the human shape.

In keeping with this account of rashness, we infer that the student does not learn because he believes knowledge is good. That opinion belongs to the moral-theological prejudice. In the Nietzschean spirit, he learns because learning makes him feel most alive. He will continue to pursue learning above all else so long as this activity maximizes his experience of his will to power (GS 110).

To support this conclusion that a certain kind of rashness is necessary for learning and hence for philosophy, we turn to Nietzsche's explicit statement that one needs both ferocious courage and curiosity if one wants to explore the most serious questions:

> When I imagine a perfect reader, he always turns into a monster of courage and curiosity; moreover, supple, cunning; a born adventurer and discoverer. In the end, I could not say better to whom alone I am speaking at bottom than Zarathustra said: to whom alone will he relate his riddle?
>
> "To you, the bold searchers, researchers, and whoever embarks with cunning sails on terrible seas—to you, drunk with riddles, glad of the twilight, whose soul flutes lure astray to every whirlpool, because you do not want to grope along a thread with cowardly hand; and where you can guess, you hate to *deduce*." (EH, "Why I Write Such Great Books," 3).

The lesson begins. The teacher guides Mr. Rash and Curious to a crack in the wall of a dim workshop of ideals. He directs him to wait until his eyes become accustomed to the darkness before reporting what he sees in the "false iridescent light" (GM 1.14). The student duly recounts the numerous ways in which he sees vital impotence "'being lied into something meritorious'" (GM 1.14). In the student's words, "'impotence that does not requite'" is obscured by its characterization as "'goodness of heart'" (GM 1.14). "'[A]nxious lowliness'" is falsely depicted as humility (GM 1.14). Subjection "'to those one hates'" is called obedience, not to those one hates, but to God, "'of whom they say he commands this subjection'" (GM 1.14). The necessary "'inoffensiveness of the weak man,'" the cowardice that causes his "'lingering at the door,'" his need to wait and to flatter are recast as patience and even "'virtue itself'" (GM 1.14). The weak person's "'inability for revenge is called unwillingness to revenge, perhaps even forgiveness'" or "'love of one's enemies'" (GM 1.14). The student remarks that this last teaching is always delivered anxiously, with profuse sweating on the part of those who espouse it (GM 1.14).

Unprompted by the teacher, Mr. Rash and Curious briefly shifts his attention from the mendacious re-presentation of weakness to the physio-psychologies of the human beings who fabricate these lies. He claims "it is clear" that they are miserable, but they lie to themselves and to others about this truth. We can reasonably infer that this lie must be edited or augmented whenever its mendaciousness becomes too apparent for it to be effective either as a consolation for the slave type or as a weapon against the noble type. Its effectiveness also requires that it develop in tandem with the genealogy of the human being. Only by so doing will it remain meaningful.

The student relates the development of the lie as follows. In the beginning, the story portrays suffering as a sign of being specially chosen by God, for "'one beats the dog one loves best'" (GM 1.14). Later, this story becomes more sophisticated. Misery, it says, has a God-given purpose for the human being. It is either a test or an education. Either way, it is a manifestation of God's love. When this account becomes ineffective, the story projects the human being's sense of the sanctity of the debtor-creditor relationship into the cosmic order. Thus, sufferers can tell themselves their misery is a form of payment to God: "'[P]erhaps … something that will one day be made good and recompensed with interest, with huge payments of gold, no! Of happiness'" (GM 1.14).

Like earlier versions of the tale, the effectiveness of this version of the deception eventually flags. It is renovated again, this time by interlacing it with the moral-theological prejudice. This interlacing yields the most elaborate and fantastic story the world has ever seen. The story turns life entirely upon her head: the powerful are impoverished in every way, and the impotent are empowered in all things. The authors in the workshop fabricate an eternal life for the soul in a transcendent realm behind the world. In this post-death-life in this otherworld, they and their followers will exist everlastingly, as good—perhaps even purely good—beings. They will be forever happy, by which they mean that they will be free of suffering. Meanwhile, the post-death-lives of their enemies will be utterly, eternally, and hopelessly wretched. With eyes set upon this story of the future, the vitally impotent conclude that "'they [themselves] are not merely better than the mighty, the lords of the earth … but are also 'better off,' or at least they will be better off someday'" (GM 1.14; see also BGE 225).

Why is it not sufficient for the weak to believe that their suffering will cease forever in this afterlife? What does the thought of the everlasting wretchedness of noble human beings add to this fantasy?

The student interrupts our thoughts with his cries: "But enough! Enough! I can't take any more. Bad air! Bad air! This workshop where ideals are manufactured—it seems to me it stinks of so many lies" (GM 1.14). He experiences this version of the lie aesthetically, as a bad smell he can hardly endure. The teacher insists that his student not leave this post until he has witnessed what he calls the slave type's masterpiece. Only by

seeing it will the student come to realize that *ressentiment* is the source
of their lies:

> –No! Wait a moment! You have said nothing yet of the masterpiece of these
> black musicians, who make whiteness, milk, and innocence of every black-
> ness—haven't you noticed their perfection of refinement, their boldest,
> subtlest, most ingenious, most mendacious artistic stroke? Attend to them!
> ... –[W]hat have they made of revenge and hatred? Have you heard these
> words uttered? If you trusted simply to their words, would you suspect you
> were among men of *ressentiment?* ... (GM 1.14)

Through Mr. Rash and Curious' eyes, we also witness this masterpiece:

> [What these human beings] desire they call, not retaliation, but the "tri-
> umph of justice"; what they hate is not their enemy, no! they hate "injus-
> tice," they hate "godlessness"; what they believe in and hope for is not the
> hope of revenge, the intoxication of sweet revenge (–"sweeter than honey"
> Homer called it), but the victory of God, of the *just* God, over the godless;
> what there is left for them to love on earth is not their brothers in hatred
> but their "brothers in love," as they put it, all the good and just on earth."
> (GM 1.14; see also GM 1.8)

The teacher pushes onward: "—And what do they call that which
serves to console them for all the suffering of life—their phantasmagoria
of anticipated future bliss?" The student responds: "They call that 'the
Last Judgment,' the coming of their kingdom, of the Kingdom of God'"
(GM 1.14). Justice and a kingdom—it is apparent from their account of
heavenly rewards that these are the things the slave type most wants.
With this last, crucial revelation, the teacher ends the lesson by repeating
the student's earlier cry: "–Enough! Enough!"

The meaning of the teacher's exclamation initially seems ambigu-
ous. Does it mean that he, like his student, can no longer endure the
smell of such lies? Perhaps something of his disgust is expressed in his
exclamation, but it is not intended primarily as a pronouncement on the
repulsiveness of the mendaciousness he has exposed. Rather, with this
cry, Nietzsche signals the crux of his counterattack. Can we discern it?
Let us review some details to test ourselves.

In one front of his counterattack, Nietzsche sheds light on the logical
contradiction in the masterpiece of mendaciousness. This version of the
story alleges on the one hand that noble human beings will be punished
eternally in a post-death-life for being what they are and for enjoying
the goods that they have on earth. On the other hand, this mendacious

tale proclaims that those who follow slave morality will be rewarded everlastingly in a post-death-life with the very attributes and trappings of political power that are characteristic of the noble human type prior to the success of the slave revolt. Either vital potency and the trappings of political power that belong to it in a genuine aristocracy are good or they are evil. They cannot be both, or at least they cannot be both in a morality that claims good and evil are unchanging and absolute opposites. Slave morality is guilty of precisely this logical self-contradiction.

This logical self-contradiction is the fault of *ressentiment*, the passion that authors the story. Is *ressentiment* a self-contradictory passion? In the second front of Nietzsche's attack, he shows us that this is the case. More precisely, he shows us that envy is at the core of *ressentiment*, and envy is self-contradictory.

Today, envy is often and perhaps even typically regarded as a synonym for jealousy. Alternatively, the definitions of envy and jealousy are reversed, so that jealousy is likened to a malicious, green-eyed monster, whereas envy is held to be a benign manifestation of appreciation for its object. What accounts for this confusion? It may be due to a genuine overlap between the two passions. Both pertain to an object that is believed or known to be good. Both describe a passion for something that the one does not possess or does not possess securely. Yet, the two passions are different. As we shall see, jealousy belongs to vital potency whereas envy belongs to impotence. Given this distinction, perhaps the erosion of the difference between the passions reflects the increasing success of slave morality.

Whatever the cause of the confusion, Nietzsche is not especially helpful in dispelling it. Despite being very clear about the difference between the character of these two passions, he is not always precise about the terms he uses to denote each of them. Sometimes, as in *Homer's Contest*, he uses the words envy (*Neid*) and jealousy (*Eifersucht*) interchangeably, to signify the same passion. In the context of his investigation of *ressentiment*, he does not use either word. He simply describes *ressentiment*, together with the slave values and the revenge fantasies that it generates. From his description, we can identify the passion, but he leaves it to us to identify it with a word.

To place ourselves in a better position to distinguish accurately between the two passions, we turn to Aristotle, who depicts both jealousy and envy with remarkable clarity. Of jealousy, which may also be translated as emulation, Aristotle says:

> Jealousy [ὁ ζέλος / zelos] is pain caused by seeing the presence, in persons whose nature is like our own, of good things that are highly valued and are possible for ourselves to acquire; but it is felt not because others have these goods, but because we have not got them ourselves. ... Jealousy makes us take steps to secure the good things in question. ... [It] must therefore tend to be felt by persons who believe themselves to deserve certain good things that they have not got. [[For no one aspires to things which appear impossible."]] (Aristotle, *The Rhetoric* 1388a 29 – 1388b 5).

Aristotle does not depict the pain of jealousy as something objectionable. On the contrary, this pain is "a good feeling felt by good persons" (Aristotle, *The Rhetoric* 1387b 22 – 1388a 8). A healthy or excellent human being ought to desire the good, which is to say that he ought to experience, and he ought to want to experience, this pain in the face of goods that he lacks. Jealousy rouses him to improve himself. At least for Nietzsche, we may infer that one should always want to feel jealous of something, for the presence of this passion is indicative of goods still to be attained. The ongoing feeling of jealousy therefore holds the promise of ongoing growth.

Like jealousy, envy (ὁ φθόνος / phthonos) is also pain at the sight of good things (Aristotle, *The Rhetoric* 1387b 22 – 1388a 8). However, whereas jealousy is a good feeling insofar as it motivates us to improve ourselves, envy is "a bad feeling felt by bad persons." The envious person recognizes the good things as good, but his envy does not incline him to try to secure these things for himself. Instead, it motivates us to "take steps to stop our neighbor from having them" (Aristotle, *The Rhetoric* 1388a 29 – 1388b 1).[32] In more Nietzschean language, although the envious person is not moved to improve himself, he nevertheless does seek to express his will to power in some kind of relationship with the object of his desire. He finds this relationship in the effort to destroy it. Thus, we see that envy is a simultaneous love and hatred of the same object (see WS 29).

Contrary to what common opinion might have us believe today, the malicious intention to harm the object of desire is not intrinsic to jealousy, as it is to envy. The jealous person might harm those whom he regards as competitors for the good he seeks if he thinks this good is limited or that its goodness will be unacceptably diminished by sharing it. However, the harm that accrues from such circumstances is incidental to the passion. For example, a lover who wants to be loved exclusively by his beloved might harm someone who competes with him for his beloved's affections. However, if two or more people were jealous of a good they did not regard as limited, such as knowledge, the impetus for harming the others would be removed. Indeed, to the extent that they have the same taste regarding a significant good, they would likely have goodwill toward each other and would have a good chance of being friends if their characters were also sufficiently compatible to share a life together. Regarding their learning, they might work together to secure this good for themselves as individuals and perhaps also as true friends.

Max Scheler, the scholar who has written what is perhaps the most authoritative work on Nietzsche's treatment of *ressentiment*, argues that envy only comes into existence if and when one comes to believe that the person who has the good that one covets is responsible for one's deprivation of it. This account invites us to conclude that envy involves a concern for justice. The envious person wants to right a wrong, to take back something that he believes has been taken from him:

> 'Envy' ... is due to a feeling of impotence which we feel when another person owns a good we covet. But this tension between desire and non-fulfillment does not lead to envy until it flares up into hatred against the owner, until the latter is falsely considered to be the *cause* of our privation. Our factual inability to acquire a good is wrongly interpreted as a positive action against our desire. ... Both the experience of impotence and the causal delusion are essential preconditions of envy. (Scheler 1961, 52)

Aristotle's accounts of envy and justice make it quite clear that these things are unrelated. Envy has no concern for justice per se, which is not to say that the envious person might not wish to appear to be just. As Aristotle defines it, justice in the highest sense is a kind of proportion by which each individual receives what is appropriate for him (Aristotle, *Nicomachean Ethics* 1108b 1-8; 1131a - 1131c; 1137a - 1138b 35). One who is seriously concerned about acting justly must therefore undertake the difficult task of trying to understand adequately the relevant aspects of the individuals in a given case. Only by so doing is one sufficiently able to determine what portion of the good in question is appropriate for each individual. Since the envious person does not undertake such investigations, we can deduce that he has no serious interest in justice. Any claim to justice that the envious human being makes is false to the extent that it is motived by, or inflected with, envy.

Once we have been informed or reminded of the difference between jealousy and envy, we begin to notice how prevalent it is and the extent to which it is addressed in great works of literature and philosophy. For example, Plato's Socrates claims envy—not justice—is the real motive for the charges were brought against him in the trial that costs him his life (Plato, *The Apology of Socrates*, 18d; see also Plato, *Meno* 93c - d; Plato, *Menexenus* 242a).[33] Iago, the anti-hero in Shakespeare's *Othello*, affords a clear and extended illustration of the envious person. While the main target of Iago's envy is Othello's good or beautiful soul, he articulates his envy most explicitly in terms of Cassio's physical beauty, which serves in the play as a parallel for Othello's soul. Iago acknowledges Cassio's beauty, but rather than appreciating it or trying to make himself more beautiful in some way, Iago claims it diminishes him: "[Cassio] has a daily beauty in his life that makes me ugly" (Shakespeare, *Othello*, 5.1.18 - 19). In keeping with envy, Iago seeks to destroy beauty while also loving it. Although he also claims to suspect both Othello and Cassio of having cuckolded him, he takes no steps to determine whether his suspicious are valid. Hence, we conclude that his claim is a hollow justification for his actions. It is a lie told to conceal his actual motive from others and perhaps also from himself (Shakespeare, *Othello*, 1.1.284 – 310).

Returning to Nietzsche, we can now see that his depiction of *ressentiment* in the masterpiece of mendaciousness accords with the descriptions of envy offered by Aristorle, by Plato's Socrates, and by Shakespeare's depiction of it via Iago. Envy is intrinsic to *ressentiment*. In his portrayal of *ressentiment*, Nietzsche is intent upon exposing the falsity of any connection one might make between it and justice. Indeed, he argues that the effort to make this false association belongs to the war of lies directed against the noble type:

> Here a word in repudiation of attempts that have lately been made to seek the origin of justice in ... *ressentiment*. To the psychologists first of all, presuming they would like to study *ressentiment* close up for once, I would say: this plant blooms best today among anarchists and anti-Semites—where it has always bloomed, in hidden places, like the violet, though with a different odor. And as like must always produce like, it causes us no surprise to see a repetition in such circles of attempts often made before ... to sanctify *revenge* under the name of *justice*—as if justice were at bottom merely a further development of the feeling of being aggrieved—and to rehabilitate not only revenge but all reactive affects in general. To the latter as such I would be the last to raise any objection: in respect to the entire biological

problem (in relation to which the value of these affects has hitherto been underrated) it even seems to me to constitute a service. All I draw attention to is the circumstance that it is the spirit of *ressentiment* itself out of which this new nuance of scientific fairness (for the benefit of hatred, envy, jealousy, mistrust, rancor, and revenge) proceeds. For this "scientific fairness" immediately ceases and gives way to accents of deadly enmity and prejudice once it is a question of dealing with another group of affects, affects that, it seems to me, are of even greater biological value than those reactive affects and consequently deserve even more to be scientifically evaluated and esteemed: namely, the truly active affects, such as lust for power, avarice, and the like. ... [T]he *last* sphere to be conquered by the spirit of justice is the sphere of the reactive feelings! When it really happens that the just man remains just even toward those who have harmed him (and not merely cold, temperate, remote, indifferent: being just is always a *positive* attitude), when the exalted, clear objectivity, as penetrating as it is mild, of the eye of justice and judging is not dimmed even under the assault of personal injury, derision, and calumny, this is a piece of perfection and supreme mastery on earth—something it would be prudent not to expect or to *believe* in too readily. On the average, a small dose of aggression, malice, or insinuation certainly suffices to drive the blood into the eyes—and fairness out of the eyes—of even the most upright people. The active, aggressive, arrogant man is still a hundred steps closer to justice than the reactive man; for he has absolutely no need to take a false and prejudiced view of the object before him in the way the reactive man does and is bound to do. For that reason, the aggressive man, as the stronger, nobler, more courageous, has in fact also had at all times a *freer* eye, a *better* conscience on his side: conversely, one can see who has the invention of the "bad conscience" on his conscience— the man of *ressentiment*!

Finally, one only has to look at history: in which sphere has the entire administration of law hitherto been at home—also the need for law? In the sphere of reactive human beings, perhaps? By no means: rather in that of the active, strong, spontaneous, aggressive. From a historical point of view, law represents on earth ... the struggle against the reactive feelings, the war conducted against them on the part of the active and aggressive powers who employed some of their strength to impose measure and bounds on the excesses of the reactive pathos and to compel it to come to terms. (GM 2.11; see also GM 2.8; GM 2.10; BGE 259)

Nietzsche understands justice, not as something given to us by nature, but as a concept created by human beings. As an original, content-rich concept, it must have been generated by a pro-action, which is to say it must have been created by the noble type. We can flesh out this origin, locating it in two instincts: the noble type's characteristic instinct for rank and its instinctive reverence for things it judges to be of high rank (see BGE 263; BGE 260). The instinct for rank tells the noble human being when he is the presence of someone who, like himself, has the potency for self-determined actions. Analogously to the way the noble human being instinctively reveres this potency in himself and deems it good, he also reveres it in other super-abundantly vital beings. These two instincts cause noble human beings to adopt in their inter-actions with each other what Nietzsche calls good manners "in a certain rough sense" (BGE 259; see also GM 2.8). These manners can blossom into true love and friendship. Thus, law is not necessary in these circumstances. The noble type's powerful and well-ruled instincts are sufficient for them to live together.

The noble type generates justice, as law, when it founds the first state. This founding unites noble human beings with human beings who are not their equals in power and who do not have the inherent self-rule and well-developed instinct for rank that characterize the noble type (see BGE 263; BGE 265). Under these conditions, the noble type creates law as a means of making human beings who cannot rule themselves behave in a manner that is consistent with the regime's goals, as determined by the noble type (GM 2.8; GM 2.11). Law serves a kind of stand-in for the good manners that noble human beings exercise amongst themselves.

The realization that justice must originate in a pro-action—that it simply cannot be the product of a reaction—is crucial to understanding the significance of *ressentiment's* claims to justice in its most masterful lie. To recap, this lie expresses the slave type's wish to have at least the *appearance* of justice. But envy is intrinsic to *ressentiment,* and envy is not concerned with justice. Thus, although this masterful lie might initially seem to express a genuine concern for justice, we are now in a position to realize that justice per se is not the slave type's true desire. Rather, what it truly wants—what it *loves*—is the capacity for pro-action. This love explains why the slave type grants itself the power and the political trappings that belong to those noble human beings who found the first state. The second part of *ressentiment's* lie, according to which the noble type, the embodiment of super-abundant vitality, will be eternally punished in an afterlife, expresses the other component of envy—namely, its hatred for that which it loves.

Intent upon fortifying these revelations about *ressentiment's* masterpiece, Nietzsche proceeds to lead us directly to hell for a firsthand look at this fantasy. On our descent, he pauses briefly to correct Dante's sign above the gates to the inferno. He notes that the poet made a "crude" psychological "blunder" when he "placed above the gateway of his hell the inscription, 'I too was created by eternal love'" (GM 1.15; see also WP 1030). Nietzsche corrects the inscription so that it confesses: "'I too was created by eternal hate'" (GM 1.15).

We pass beneath these gates into the vitriolic *ressentiment*-fantasy of Tertullian, a Church Father. This fantasy appears in a passage that Nietzsche excerpts from Tertullian's *De Spectaculis*. In this book, Tertullian exhorts Christians to avoid spectacles, especially blood sports such as gladiatorial contests. He begins relatively continently, arguing that spectacles are ungodly and that the enjoyment of them is unseemly:

> It is a good thing when the guilty are punished. Who will deny this but the guilty? Yet it is not becoming for the guiltless to take pleasure in the punishment of another; rather, it befits the guiltless to grieve that a man, like himself, has become so guilty that he is treated with such cruelty. (Tertullian 1959, 19.2)

Ten short chapters later, his self-control begins to waver. He now argues that blood lust can be indulged in the context of Christ's crucifixion:

> If you [Christians] think that you are to pass this span of life in delights, why are you so ungrateful as not to be satisfied with so many and so exquisite pleasures given you by God? ... To trample underfoot the gods of the heathens, to drive out demons, to effect cures, to seek revelations, to live unto God—these are the pleasures, these are the spectacles of the Christians, holy, everlasting, and free of charge. ... Do you have desire for blood, too? You have the blood of Christ. (Tertullian 1959, 29.1 – 5)

The very next chapter contains the passage Nietzsche excerpts. Now, the suffering of the damned is not merely tolerated, it is embraced with delight. And who are the damned? Tertullian identifies them as the politically powerful, the wise, natural philosophers, and poets. Tertullian's hateful glee is so flagrant by this point that we need no help from Nietzsche in identifying it as a manifestation of envy:

> How vast a spectacle then bursts upon the eye! What there excites my admiration? What my derision? Which sight gives me joy? Which rouses me to exultation? —as I see so many illustrious monarchs, whose reception into the heavens was publicly announced, groaning now in the lowest

darkness with great Jove himself, and those, too, who bore witness of their exultation; governors of provinces, too, who persecuted the Christian name, in fires fiercer than those with which in the days of their pride they raged against the followers of Christ. What world's wise men besides, the very philosophers, in fact, who taught their followers that God had no concern for aught that is sublunary, and were wont to assure them that either they had no souls, or that they would never return to the bodies that at death they had left, now covered with shame before the poor deluded ones, as one fire consumes them! Poets also, trembling not before the judgment-seat of Rhadamathus or Minos, but of the unexpected Christ! I shall have a better opportunity then of hearing the tragedians, louder-voiced in their own calamity; of viewing the play-actors, much more 'dissolute' in the dissolving flame; of looking upon the charioteer, all glowing in his chariot of fire; of beholding the wrestlers, not in their gymnasia, but tossing in the fiery billows; unless even then I shall not care to attend to such ministers of sin, in my eager wish rather to fix a gaze *insatiable* on those whose fury vented itself against the Lord. 'This,' I shall say, 'this is that carpenter's or hireling's son, that Sabbath-breaker, that Samaritan and devil-possessed! (Tertullian 1959, 104 – 107; Nietzsche provides the quotation in GM 3.15)

Nietzsche claims Tertullian's passion is typical of the leaders of slave morality. To the extent that his expression of envy is unusually shocking, it is so only because he allows it to speak in a "stronger key" than most. To support this claim, Nietzsche poses the question of what constitutes the "bliss of this Paradise," and then leaves Thomas Aquinas to answer it in his own words:

> We might ... guess [what constitutes this bliss], but it is better to have it expressly described for us by an authority not to be underestimated in such matters, Thomas Aquinas, the great teacher and saint. *"Beati in regno coelesti,"* he says, meek as a lamb, *"videbunt poenas damnatorum, **ut beatitudo illis magis complaceat"**["The blessed in the kingdom of heaven will see the pun-ishments of the damned, **in order that their bliss be more delightful for them"**].* (GM 1.15)

Why is Nietzsche so intent upon exposing envy's central role in slave morality's masterpiece? How might this exposure advance Nietzsche's counterattack in the slave type's psychological warfare against all things noble?

Recall our earlier observation that the genealogy of slave moral-ity must correspond to a significant degree with the genealogy of the human being if it is to retain its meaning for us. The human being has become more rational over the course of its evolution, and slave morality has been altered to reflect and to promote this increase in rationality. However, reason cannot abide incoherence. Hence, however much slave morality has been altered so as to make it more attractive to reason, reason cannot be satisfied with it once it discovers that slave morality is self-contradictory.

We do not mean to suggest that Nietzsche thinks all believers in slave morality will cease to believe upon learning of its incoherence. Nietzsche is acutely cognizant of the fact that reason does not yet have this degree of authority over us. What we are suggesting is that Nietzsche has appropriated the slave type's mode of psychological warfare, and he is employing it against this type. More specifically, while reason might not immediately overthrow the influence of slave morality in the slave type's physio-psychology, Nietzsche's exposure of slave morality's incoherence promotes discord within the slavish human being's physio-psychology.

Like all drives, *ressentiment* will strive to advance the power it wields. When it becomes involved with the mind, it will pursue this power by way of its revenge fantasies. So too, reason will strive to advance the power it has by virtue of its facility at detecting contradictions. But we can now see that *ressentiment* and reason are at odds with each other. *Ressentiment* is fundamentally incoherent, as is its most masterful fantasy. Indeed, although we followed Nietzsche in his analysis of *ressentiment's* best fantasy, we can deduce that all of *ressentiment's* fantasies must be incoherent: they cannot escape this fundamental characteristic of their maker. Nietzsche has directed reason's attention to these incoherencies. Thus, we expect *ressentiment* and reason will now go to war against each other within the slavish human being.

Nietzsche's exposure of envy at the core of slave morality also serves as the basis of his answer to the charge that, regardless of his intentions, his genealogical work promotes nihilism because it concludes there is no such thing as the human good. Before seeing how he answers this charge, we must first better understand the charge itself.

Nietzsche's genealogy of morality unearths two opposing concepts of the good. This discovery proves one of two things. If this opposition cannot be resolved by any kind of shared, authoritative standard, then Nietzsche's work would support nihilism. Absent a universal good for the human being, we have no meaningful way of directing our growth. Morality is merely relative, a matter of personal opinion, nothing serious. Anyone who is clear-sighted and who has an intellectual conscience becomes a nihilist.[34]

Alternatively, Nietzsche's discovery of two opposite concepts of the good could mean that one of the two accounts is true. If this is the case, the good is not relative. However, to come to this conclusion we would have to determine which of the two accounts is true. Even those who want to defend Nietzsche against the charge that his work promotes nihilism typically collapse when faced with this demand. They either regretfully conclude that Nietzsche does not meet this demand, or they have the vague impression that he does meet it, but they cannot say how he does so.

Nietzsche himself remains confidently on his feet in the face of this challenge. He points to envy as his defense. The role that envy plays in *ressentiment's* mendacious masterpiece is Nietzsche's proof that the slave type secretly agrees with the noble type's concept of the good. Far from supporting nihilism's advance, therefore, Nietzsche's genealogical work tackles nihilism by revealing the human *consensus* regarding the good.

But hold on! A new challenge now comes upon us in the form of a question: Can there be such a thing as the supreme good, given that noble morality has a genealogy and hence its content is historical? Nietzsche answers this question with a resounding and well-grounded "Yes!" But he does not stop to help us understand him. While leaping from mountaintop to mountaintop, he merely hints at what the supreme good is. He offers one such hint in his account of the paramount desire and pursuit of all animals, including the human animal:

> Every animal—therefore *la bête philosophe, too*—instinctively strives for an optimum of favorable conditions under which it can expend all its strength and achieve its maximal feeling of power; every animal abhors, just as instinctively and with a subtlety of discernment that is "higher than all reason," every kind of intrusion or hindrance that obstructs or could obstruct this path to the optimum. (I am *not* speaking here of its path to happiness, but its path to power, to action, to the most powerful activity, and in most cases actually its path to unhappiness). (GM 3.7; see also Z, "On Self-Overcoming")

This hint becomes more substantial when it is considered in conjunction with his clear-eyed account of what life is:

> [B]eware of superficiality and get to the bottom of the matter, resisting all sentimental weakness: life is essentially appropriation, injury, overpower-

ing of what is alien and weaker; suppression, hardness, imposition of one's own forms, incorporation and at least, at its mildest, exploitation—but why should one always use those words in which a slanderous intent has been imprinted for ages? (BGE 259)

In light of these two statements, we can elucidate Nietzsche's understanding of the supreme good as follows. On the one hand, all living beings want to experience the maximum expression of their vitality. On the other hand, more vitality is always better than less. The desire for more vitality is consistent with the activity that is life. The more vital a being is, the better able it is to appropriate and reform what is alien so as to extend itself. This self-augmentation by appropriation and reformation is growth. Since all living beings want to experience their will to power maximally, and since more life is always better than less, we can deduce that the supreme good for all living beings is maximum super-abundant vitality. Because super-abundant vitality necessarily expands or grows, we may also describe the supreme good as maximum expansion or growth.

Whenever the supreme good is encountered, it is concrete, particular, and historical. However, the historical good is only good because it is an articulation of super-abundant vitality. This means super-abundant vitality is not the same as the historical good—it is not the same as its shape or its content. If it were, it could not establish the goodness of the historical good. What we see in the relationship between the supreme and historical goods, therefore, is a complex whole in which there are two distinct but inseparable components.

In this complex whole Nietzsche discovers a life-affirming route between two concepts to which most and perhaps all prior philosophers have fallen prey in their efforts to describe the good: namely, pure being and pure becoming. When these concepts are separated from each other, neither is reflective of life nor useful for growth. The flux of becoming cannot provide us with a goal by which we can direct our growth, and the permanence of being cannot accommodate the motion of growth. Nietzsche's clear-sightedness regarding why these two concepts must be conjoined and how they are united gives us hope that there may be a new kind of warrior, a warrior in the realm of the mind, fighting on the side of thriving life. With this warrior, "[l]ife and I and you and all of us … may become interesting to ourselves once again" (GS 1).

Chapter Five

Mind Matters

Despite the lesson in the workshop of ideals, the warrior-philosopher is hobbled by his ongoing faith in the moral-theological prejudice or, more succinctly, the ascetic ideal. According to this ideal, the mind is separate from and superior to the body, which is associated with allegedly base animal passion. Because the warrior-philosophers continue to hang onto this notion, they believe their thinking properly belongs solely to the interior realm of mind, and they disdain action in the exterior world. Moving further into the intellectual arena of the slave war against all that is noble, Nietzsche attacks the slavish interpretation of mind by illuminating the union of thought and action. He shows us that "the greatest thoughts are the greatest events" (BGE 285; see also Z, "The Stillest Hour").

In keeping with his understanding of philosophy, Nietzsche elucidates what the mind or thinking is by tracking its genealogy. So shall we. Loop back in our investigation to the three epochs of human evolution as they are reflected in the three meanings of the original concept of the good. As we re-cover this ground, be especially attentive to the development of mind.

During the physio-psychological epoch defined by the first meaning of the noble concept of the good, super-abundant vitality manifests in its human shape most potently and significantly in the very act of creating this concept *ex nihilo*. Spontaneous creation is not unique to these first valuators. It is repeated each time a noble valuator proactively generates a meaning of the good, which augments the pre-existing concept. Nevertheless, the creation of the first meaning is especially significant, for this single act lays the foundation for the creation of all subsequent meanings of the historical good. This first act of valuation is therefore the origin of the human being's most characteristic and vitalizing act—namely, self-creation (GM 2.1 – 2.3; GM 2.16 – 2.17). It is the de-mythologized origin—the real "In the beginning"—of the creature we call human. Nietzsche's Zarathustra describes the momentousness of value-creation in these divine terms:

> "Verily, human beings gave themselves all their good and evil. Verily, they did not take it, they did not find it, nor did it come to them as a voice from heaven. Only the human being placed values in things to preserve himself—he alone created a meaning for things, a human meaning. Therefore, he calls himself 'human being,' which means: the esteemer.
>
> "To esteem is to create: hear this, you creators! Esteeming itself is of all esteemed things the most estimable treasure. Through esteeming alone is there value: and without esteeming, the nut of existence would be hollow. Hear this, you creators!" (Z, "On the Thousand and One Goals")

The project of human enhancement—of making the human being more vital—starts with the noble type's articulation of what goodness is. However, this act alone is insufficient for the human being to take charge of his evolution. To enhance the human being, one must rule him sufficiently to reshape him, and the most obvious way in which this rule is enacted is by means of a political regime. Whether it is recognized consciously and is explicitly acknowledged, or whether it is unconscious or implicit, the formation of the human being is the essence of politics.[35] Every regime is organized according to a notion of the good that serves as the basis for laws and mores. Thus, the notion of the good directs the actions of everyone within the regime and, by so doing, alters the human being's physio-psychology. To the creation of the first meaning of the original concept of the good we must therefore add the noble type's imposition of the first political order upon less well-ordered, relatively impotent human beings, together with the ruling power these noble human beings wield in this aristocracy and in every subsequent, genuine aristocracy, wherein the ruling class is comprised predominantly of the noble human type.

Nietzsche offers an account of how this physio-psychological enhancement occurs (BGE 257; BGE 258). Once the noble type has generated a content-rich concept of the good and has organized an aristocracy on the basis of this concept, the hierarchical political structure has an effect on the ruling aristocrats themselves that is especially significant for human enhancement. It sharpens their sense of the differences between themselves and those whom they rule. This heightened awareness of difference may involve some exaggeration of these dissimilarities, and it is almost certainly accompanied by a significant degree of ignorance about similarities between themselves and people in the lower political classes. Accuracy, however, is not of primary importance; growth is. As the aristocrat's sense of difference is honed by his persistent experience of the hierarchical political structure, he develops what Nietzsche characterizes as "that other, more mysterious pathos," which craves

> an ever-new widening of distances within the soul itself, the development of ever higher, rarer, more remote, further-stretching, more comprehensive states—in brief, simply the enhancement of the type 'human being,' the continual 'self-overcoming of the human being,' to use a moral formula in a supra-moral sense. (BGE 257)

This "more mysterious pathos" is related to the aristocrat's pathos of distance and its attendant capacity to rank human beings, but it is not the same as this pathos. It would therefore be a mistake to assume this mysterious pathos moves the aristocrat to rank his drives according the same notion of the good by which they order the aristocratic regime. Rather, Nietzsche tells us this mysterious pathos denotes the aristocrat's heightened interest in distinguishing between different drives within his soul. In other words, whereas previously the noble human being was inclined to experience himself as simple—that is, undifferentiated or lacking distinct psychic parts—he now becomes aware of different drives or passions within himself. As a direct result of noticing these distinctions, the aristocrat's experience of his drives or passions becomes subtler, more acute, and more intense. He thereby becomes even more conscious of his manifoldness. Metaphorically speaking, an increase in a human being's conscious awareness of differences stretches his physio-psychology, whereas similarities draw it together and thus increase its integrity:

> Greater complexity, sharp differentiation, the contiguity of developed organs and functions with the disappearance of the intermediate members—if that is perfection, then there is a will to power in the organic process by virtue of which dominant, shaping, commanding forces continually extend the bounds of their power and continually simplify within these bounds: the imperative grows.
>
> "Spirit" is only a means and tool in the service of higher life, of the

enhancement of life; and as for the good, as Plato (and after him Christianity) understood it, it seems to me to be actually a life-endangering, life-calumniating, life-denying principle. (WP 644)

We may liken the noble aristocrat's heightened awareness of distinctions or differences both within and without himself to an alteration in visual acuity. Prior to experiencing the mysterious pathos, it is as if the noble human being sees the boundaries or shapes of entities relatively indistinctly and monochromatically. Now, he sees shapes more sharply and in a spectrum of color.

Fleshing out his account of the how the noble aristocrats enhance their form, Nietzsche describes the kind of distinctions the noble aristocrats make regarding their own souls. He begins by observing that the noble valuators who rule in healthy aristocracies dominate other human beings because of their tremendously superior vital potency or strength of soul. Expanding upon this claim, he attributes their potency directly to the fact that they are "more whole human beings (which also means at every level, 'more whole beasts')" (BGE 257).[36] In other words, their strength arises from the fact that their physio-psychologies comprehend into a fecund whole more of our human genealogy than the physio-psychologies of weaker human beings. By linking their greater strength of soul to the genealogical completeness and integrity of their physio-psychologies, and by doing so in the context of a discussion about the mysterious pathos that initiates the noble aristocrats' hunger for their own psychic development, Nietzsche indicates their growth results especially from their increased clarity about the differences between their savage and civilized drives. The heightening of the contrast between these drives makes each more of what it is (BGE 257; see also WP 684; HC).

We know the creation of the first state also alters the physio-psychologies of the vanquished human beings. It causes their savage drives, which previously expressed themselves outwardly, to reverse direction and thus to internalize. What these internalized drives create is dependent upon the creation of the state. Nevertheless, their creation is arguably more astounding than the creation of the first state. They create "the womb of all ideal and imaginative phenomena" or what we now call the soul, mind, or consciousness:

> One should guard against thinking lightly of this phenomenon [of internalization] merely on account of its initial painfulness and ugliness.

For fundamentally it is the same active force that is at work on a grander scale in those artists of violence and organizers who build states, and that here, internally, on a smaller and pettier scale, directed backward, in the "labyrinth of the breast," to use Goethe's expression, creates for itself a bad conscience and builds for itself negative ideals—namely, the *instinct for freedom* (in my language: the will to power); only here the material upon which the form-giving and ravishing nature of this force vents itself is the human being himself, his whole ancient animal self—and *not*, as in the greater and more obvious phenomenon, some *other* human being, *other* human beings. This secret self-ravishment, this artists' cruelty, this delight in imposing forms upon oneself as a hard, recalcitrant, suffering material and in burning a will, a critique, a contradiction, a contempt, a No into it, this uncanny, dreadfully joyous labor of a soul voluntarily at odds with itself that makes itself suffer out of joy in making suffer—eventually this entire *active* "bad conscience"—you will have guessed it—as the womb of all ideal and imaginative phenomena, also brought to light an abundance of strange *new* beauty and affirmation, and perhaps beauty itself. After all, what would be "beautiful" if the contradiction had not first become conscious of itself, if the ugly had not first said to itself: "I am ugly"? (GM 2.18)

Having depicted the internalized drives as expressions of the will to power or life and thus as good, Nietzsche complicates the picture. He shifts his focus away from these drives, considered independently, to the community of drives that constitute this human individual. Their inward action diminishes the overall vitality of this individual by transforming him into a being who is at odds with himself. He is unable to wage this internal war in a manner that invigorates him. Hence, he disintegrates and thereby degenerates (GM 2.18).

Although the development of consciousness or mind is terribly painful and enervating, at least initially, Nietzsche warns us against concluding precipitously that internalization is altogether bad (GM 1.5; GM 2.7; GM 2.17). What is at stake in evaluating it is whether it conduces to growth (e.g. see GM 2.7; GM 3.28). With this standard before him, Nietzsche speaks highly of internalization, not because it is good per se or when considered out of context, but because he sees in it the promise of tremendous human growth, the like of which the world has never seen. Specifically, the development of mind introduces the possibility that we might come to direct our evolution consciously or mindfully and perhaps indefinitely.

One way we might do this is by employing the tension internalization creates between different drives within the soul as a kind of springboard for growth (Z, "On Child and Marriage"). More specifically, we can leverage our moral values by employing a life-promoting perspective to see or interpret in a new way what previously seemed merely ugly within ourselves so that its beauty is made manifest. By reading and writing this new narrative, one resurrects and redeems what was ugly. The vitality released by this resurrection of one or more drives from ugliness to beauty reorders one's physio-psychology. One thereby re-generates oneself.

This process of self-redemption and subsequent self-overcoming is captured in the concept of the overman, the being who repeatedly leverages the tension within himself so as to supersede himself. By means of the character Zarathustra, Nietzsche likens this self-propelled growth to climbing upon one's own head (Z, "Zarathustra's Speeches," 3 – 4; Z, "The Convalescent"). The possibility of this overman is born in the context of the coming together of the first state on the one hand and internalization on the other. In other words, it is conceived by the union of the will to power in its noble and slavish shapes:

> [T]he existence on earth of an animal soul turned against itself, taking sides against itself, was something so new, profound, unheard of, enigmatic, contradictory, and *pregnant with a future* that the aspect of the earth was essentially altered. Indeed, divine spectators were needed to do justice to the spectacle that thus began and the end of which is not yet in sight—a spectacle too subtle, too marvelous, too paradoxical to be played senselessly unobserved on some ludicrous planet! From now on, the human being is included among the most unexpected and exciting lucky throws in the dice game of Heraclitus' "great child," be he called Zeus or chance; the human being gives rise to an interest, a tension, a hope, almost a certainty, as if with him something were announcing and preparing itself, as if the human being were not a goal but only a way, an episode, a bridge, a great promise.— (GM 2.16; see also WP 966)

Nietzsche illustrates how he can judge the internalization of drives as bad and good by likening internalization to pregnancy. Insofar as pregnancy weakens the mother, at least temporarily, it is bad, a "sickness," to use Nietzsche's language (GM 2.16). Yet, it is also the most obvious example of generative phenomena (GM 2.16). Serious parents hope their child will supersede what they are and thereby enable them to continue participating in generation or growth. They can hold this hope even while knowing the risks they incur, as individuals and as lovers, in having a child. Nietzsche evaluates internalization from a perspective comparable to that of a parent, especially a mother (e.g. see GM 3.8; GS 72). He gestates hopes for the possibility that we might consciously or mindfully direct our growth, and he is willing to shoulder the sickness and risks that attend internalization for the sake of these hopes. Exciting as this possibility is, Nietzsche only hints at it at this point in his treatment of internalization. We therefore put it aside and return to our primary investigation here: namely, tracking the genealogy of the noble concept of the good with a view to its involvement with the development of mind.

In the second stage of this concept's genealogy, it takes what Nietzsche describes as a "subjective turn" (GM 1.5). From our earlier discussion, we know this turn means the concept of the good has become involved with mind. In the context of our interest in tracking the genealogy of mind, we now note it signifies that the noble valuators who generate this second meaning are more conscious than their predecessors: they have a nascent sense of self-perception. This consciousness is traceable to an increase in their physio-psychological complexity. To see this development more fully, let us elaborate on the comparative lack of consciousness in the noble valuators who generate the first meaning of the good.

Insofar as the first moral valuators come to differentiate more acutely between their different drives or passions, they must be aware of them in some way. However, they do not experience them to any meaningful degree engaging with each other as distinct entities; that is, in a manner analogous to the way one human being can perceive another. While they come to experience themselves as manifold, they are not aware of themselves as complex wholes, as beings comprised of multiple wills that co-exist in a community (see BGE 19). Because they lack significant awareness of this multiplicity, they experience themselves as psychically simple rather than complex.

So long as noble human beings both experience themselves as simple and have significant associations only with those like themselves, they will not designate themselves as good, for the concept of the good is a contrast, which is absent under these conditions. The necessary contrast is available in two ways. One way is when the noble valuator encounters someone whom he recognizes as having an experience of world that is significantly different from his own. A second way is available when the noble valuator is complex enough to act consciously as both the judge and the object of his own judgment. Since these noble human beings of the first era of valuation lack this complexity, only the first option is available to them: they must confront the human being whom they recognize as the "other."

We know that the noble human type's characteristic and foundational experience is of his own vital potency. He knows himself as one who satisfies his desires readily and fully. The "other" for the noble human being must therefore be someone whom he recognizes as vitally impotent. Only when he confronts this other is he stimulated to name himself as the good, the real, or the true, in contradistinction to the vitally impotent human being whom he deems bad (BGE 259).

Against this genealogical backdrop of the first valuators, return to the noble valuators who generate the second meaning of the good. As we noted, they are conscious to a significant degree of their different drives perceiving each other (see WP 504). This consciousness is apparent in the distinction they make between the objective concept of the good and themselves; that is, they regard themselves as good according to a standard they believe is objective and distinct from themselves. With regard to the development of the physio-psychology of the noble type, the distinction they make between themselves and the good is an external expression of the complex relationship between one or more drives within these noble valuators. Unlike their predecessors, they now act on the one hand as judges and, on the other hand, as the objects of their judgment. Because they are conscious of their own multiplicity, they can do what their predecessors cannot: they can perceive their goodness independently of external points of contrast.

It might seem suspicious with regard to fair evaluation that these noble human beings judge themselves to be good according to a meaning they generate. Is their self-judgment reducible to relativism? Is it a mere prejudice in favor of themselves? It is neither. As is the case with the first meaning of the good, the second meaning reflects the human awareness of the supreme good, which is embodied in these noble valuators. While both the first and second meanings share and communicate this awareness, it has developed over time. Whereas in the first definition the awareness is largely unconscious and instinctual, the subjective turn that the concept takes in its second meaning evinces at least a glimmer of conscious recognition by these noble valuators of the fact that, while they embody super-abundant vitality in its human shape, the goodness of overflowing life is distinct, if not separate, from the specific configuration it has in any particular human being. This change in their sense of the supreme good is a manifestation of a further development of consciousness or mind in the noble human type.

The centrality of mind in the self-experience of the second-era valuators also indicates that, like the slavish human beings, they now have an internal realm. How did it develop in them? As we know, Nietzsche hypothesizes that the mind is originally created by drives that internalize when their outward direction is suddenly and violently reversed. While this precipitous, forced reversal is necessary to create the mind initially, there is no reason to think mind cannot be inherited by later generations. In such cases, sudden force need not be directly involved with its creation. Nor is inherited self-consciousness necessarily symptomatic of vital impotence. A being can evolve so that it retains an attribute that required impotence and even damage for its inception, but not for its continuation after its structure has been sufficiently incorporated or hardened in the being's physio-psychology. Do the noble valuators who generate the second meaning of the good inherit mind? Or, like those human beings upon whom they imposed the structure of the aristocratic regime, do they face some sudden violence that forces their drives backward?

If they inherit interiority, it would have to come from the slave type. The ancestors of these second era noble valuators would therefore have to have interbred to a significant degree with the slave type. However, the genealogy of the original concept of the good indicates this intermixing of human types does not occur until the third era in the concept's genealogy, too late to account for interiority in these second era valuators (GM 1.5). Thus, we deduce either vital impotence or vulnerability causes internalization in the noble type. Reasoning through these options, we conclude vital impotence cannot be the cause, because these valuators generate the second meaning of the good proactively, and such valuation necessitates vital potency. Therefore, we must conclude they are vitally potent, but they are nevertheless vulnerable to some kind of an attack that forces their drives to reverse direction and thus to internalize.

How are we to understand the fact that they are somehow both super-abundantly vital and vulnerable to internalization? Some might argue that, paradoxically, the noble aristocrats are so successful at establishing peace within and without the state that they no longer have adequate outlets for their savage drives. Hence, the drives internalize. There are two problems with this hypothesis. First, there is no reason to think these noble aristocrats must establish or honor peaceful conditions with all other states or even with all of their own people. If they want or need to exercise their savage drives, they are free to do so. Second—and this is decisive—the effects of peaceful conditions are not sudden. Peace can undermine savagery, but it does so by the slow drain of vitality that results from having to fend off for a sustained period of time weaker powers that incessantly nibble away one's vitality. Alternatively, and as we noted earlier, prolonged peace affords savage drives the time they typically require in order to become more domesticated or to lose their savage shape altogether (e.g. see BGE 205). In light of these considerations, we eliminate peace as the cause of internalization in the second era noble valuators. Additionally, we can dismiss slavish human beings as a possible direct cause of such sudden violence. Not only is overt action not the slave type's mode of behavior, but they would also fail to overcome the noble type by confronting them directly and violently. One option remains. The noble human beings who lived in this era do face a sudden and violent change in circumstance, but it is covert; it is the slave revolt.

As we have seen, slave morality pronounces manifestations of super-abundant vitality, and hence the noble type, as evil. Despite being super-abundantly vital, these noble human beings are poorly equipped to recognize the slavish accounts of good and evil as lies and thus to dismiss them. In the absence of an adequate defense against the slave type's ideological warfare, the noble type is infiltrated. This infiltration causes them to experience significant self-doubt for the first time in their genealogy. In doubting and questioning themselves, they themselves suddenly and violently reverse the outward, free expression of their undomesticated drives. Self-sabotage, under the influence of slave morality, is the answer to the question of how internalization begins in the noble type (see e.g. BGE 48).

This interpretation wins support from Nietzsche's observations regarding the noble type's relationship to political power. As we noted previously, the noble type constitutes the ruling class in the first epoch of the genealogy of the original concept of the good. By analyzing the various meanings of the good, Nietzsche concludes the noble type no longer occupies the ruling class in the third epoch in the concept's gene-alogy. From these facts, we can infer that the noble human type loses political power during the second era, the era in which this type acquires a significant degree of interiority or mind (GM 1.5). Given Nietzsche's emphasis on the slave type's covert and mendacious psychological war against the noble type, it is reasonable to conclude the slave revolt, and more particularly the self-sabotage it spawns in the noble aristocrats, is also the proximate cause of the noble type's loss of political power. Thus, we see that, at this point in the evolution of the noble type, mind is not accompanied by an overall increase in the noble human being's vitality or strength. On the contrary, it is accompanied by a loss not only of political power, but also and more importantly of vital power, albeit not to the point of impotence.

In the era following the decline of aristocracies, the noble valuators augment the original concept of the good with a third meaning, according to which it especially denotes nobility of soul or mind *(seelischen)* (GM 1.5). The centrality of mind in this third meaning indicates the noble val-uators' physio-psychologies have developed to the point where they now have sophisticated calculative capacities (GM 2.16). Since internalization creates the mind, we infer that the noble type likely develops reason in proportion to the internalization of its drives.

To some extent, we can understand the noble type's calculative capacity as a further development of the capacity for discernment and self-perception that the type develops in the first and second eras of val-uation respectively. We discussed earlier how, as a result of their honed capacity for differentiation and the pathos of distance, the noble aris-tocrats came to discern more clearly the differences between the drives that comprise what they are. This development continues, so that their drives eventually become capable of perceiving each other. At this point, the noble valuators generate the second meaning of the good, which reflects this physio-psychological evolution. In the third era, the noble type moves further along this developmental trajectory. Thus, they evolve to the point where their drives not only perceive each other, but also acquire a significant capacity to speak silently to each other. This silent speaking is reasoning.[37]

Given this development, it is not surprising that this third era corresponds to the epoch in which reason or speech is typically mistaken as a self-subsisting and universal standard of the real or the true. This error is consistent with an emphasis on the goodness of reason, understood as something separate from and superior to perception and the so-called body. It belongs to slave morality. Insofar as it infects the noble human beings of the third era, it both reflects and advances their enervation in comparison with their simpler and healthier ancestors. Moreover, the fact that these noble valuators are vulnerable to this error testifies to the fact that the warrior of the mind is not yet mature. His mind has not yet been sufficiently integrated with the noble type's characteristic strength of soul or super-abundant vitality.

In truth, reason does not transcend its dependence on perception and the body. This is because reasoning or speaking consists of giving accounts of beings in terms of inter-relations between wholes and parts. However, neither wholes nor parts when considered per se—that is, as individual units—are available to reason; they must be perceived to be known. Since reason consists in giving accounts of inter-relations between wholes and parts, and since both wholes and parts are unavailable to reason, reason utilizes names or nouns, which serve as metaphors for the entities that must be perceived. Names enable us to fold wholes and parts into a reasoned account and to speak of them in relation to other beings while nevertheless acknowledging their wholeness and hence their direct unavailability to reason. Fundamentally, names—and most obviously proper names—are substitutions for pointing or directing our perception at someone or something (see GM 3.8; WP 584). This remains true, if less apparently so, of generalizations or categories, which can only be produced by considering together, as a kind of unit, two or more individuals according to some cognized similarity amongst them, and then disregarding for the purpose of the generalization all of the differences between these individuals.

Although the noble valuators of this third era mistakenly believe in the slavish concept according to which reason is something separate from and superior to the body and actions in the external realm, they nevertheless also characteristically glorify the shape that super-abundant vitality has in them. Hence, they do not value all kinds of reasoning as good. Instead, they deem only a certain *quality* of reasoning or mind as good. Specifically, the *noble* mind is good. What is meant by this? What is noble reasoning?

The concept of a noble mind suggests that at least some of the characteristics highlighted in the prior meanings of the original concept of the good persist in this third era meaning. Now, however, a significant number of these characteristics are transfigured by their involvement with mind. To use Nietzsche's language, they are spiritualized. Of special note, ferocious courage, the predominant characteristic of the noble human beings who generate the first meaning of the original concept of the good, is spiritualized in this third era. It is this spiritualized courage in particular that characterizes a noble—hence, good—mind.

Courage is the willingness to face great danger. Since all animal pro-action presupposes such willingness, and since all pro-action is an expression of super-abundant vitality, courage is inseparable from super-abundant vitality in animals, including the human animal. In other words, courage is the foundational shape of vital potency in animals. All other shapes of animal pro-action pre-suppose courage. It is therefore not surprising that the warrior and the warrior's characteristic courage are always celebrated by noble morality. On the other hand, it is not sufficient to say the third meaning of the original concept of the good celebrates courageous thinking merely because the noble morality always celebrates courage, and it simply continues to do so when courage becomes involved with mind. This is insufficient at least partly because Nietzsche does not only draw our attention to this third meaning and its connection with a development in the physio-psychology of the noble type. In addition, he characterizes the third meaning of the good as a ripening and sweetening of the original concept (GM 1.5).[38] Given that this third meaning arises from the valuators' self-experience, this characterization of the concept indicates the physio-psychology of noble type has also become ripe and sweet in some way. What way? Ripe and sweet with respect to what?

Nietzsche's interest in the genealogy of morality and what it means for the future of the human being suggests the ripeness and sweetness to which he refers relates to his particular interests. Regarded in this context, we infer the ripeness and sweetness of the concept and of the noble type consist in the type's newly acquired capacity to fulfill the promise that began with the creation of the first state and the interiority it precipitated—the promise of conscious self-creation. Specifically, the noble type now has this capacity because he brings together in a life-promoting manner the ferocious courage that enables him to create *ex nihilo* in the external realm and the courageous, self-conscious intellect necessary for him to guide mindfully his actions in both the inner and outer worlds.

To make his ripeness more apparent, consider the philosophy that underlies Nietzsche's elimination of the slavish prejudice according to which reasoning is relegated to the interior realm of mind and properly precludes actions in the external realm and that denies in particular the notion there could be such a thing as a genuinely philosophic commander.

As we know, in his cosmic hypothesis of the will to power, Nietzsche considers the idea that everything might be explicable by one thing—the will to power (BGE 36). As he moves away from his cosmic hypothesis and toward the realm of the will to power, understood as the vitality that constitutes what we typically recognize as life-forms, he often speaks of the will to power in terms of drives. In other words, he divides the undifferentiated will to power that belongs to the cosmic hypothesis into discreet entities. Thus, we can think of drives as particular shapes of the will to power; that is, of the will to expand or grow maximally (see WP 480 – 487; WP 625):

> All "purposes," "aims," "meaning" are only modes of expression and metamorphoses of one will that is inherent in all events: the will to power. To have purposes, aims, intentions, *willing* in general, is the same thing as willing to be stronger, willing to grow—and, in addition, willing the means to this.
>
> The most universal and basic instinct in all doing and willing has for precisely this reason remained the least known and most hidden, because *in praxi* we always follow its commandments, because we *are* this commandment—
>
> All valuations are only consequences and narrow perspectives in the service of this one will: valuation itself is only this will to power.
>
> A critique of being from the point of view of any one of these values is something absurd and erroneous. Even supposing that a process of decline begins in this way, this process still stands in the service of this will.
>
> To appraise being itself! But this appraisal itself is still this being! — and if we say no, we still do what we *are*.
>
> One must comprehend the absurdity of this posture of judging exis-

tence, and then try to understand what is really involved in it. It is symptomatic. (WP 675; see also WP 702; WP 728; BGE 36)

Reflecting further in his notebooks upon what a drive is or might be,
Nietzsche concludes the most primitive drive lacks intelligence: it makes
no calculations of any kind, including calculations of utility. It simply
and necessarily expresses itself maximally at all times unless and until its
action is counter-balanced or overpowered by one or more other drives:

> As every drive lacks intelligence, the viewpoint of "utility" cannot
> exist for it. Every drive, in as much as it is active, sacrifices force and other
> drives: finally it is checked; otherwise it would destroy everything through
> its excessiveness. Therefore: the "un-egoistic," self-sacrificing, imprudent, is
> nothing special—it is common to all the drives—they do not consider the
> advantage of the whole ego (because they do not consider it at all!), they act
> contrary to our advantage, against the ego: and often *for* the ego—innocent
> in both cases! (WP 372)

To be clear, although the most primitive drive is nothing but the will
to expand, the fact that it is a will means it has both motion and direction; both are intrinsic to will. Moreover, a willed or directed motion
requires that the will have some awareness of the difference between
what is inner and outer with respect to itself. In other words, willed
direction cannot occur in the absence of some sense of direction. This
sense is therefore also intrinsic to will since both direction and motion
are intrinsic to it. In hypothesizing about what the most basic element
of the world might be, Nietzsche knows he is anthropomorphizing the
drive. He also knows that this cannot be helped. We necessarily bring
what we are as human beings to our concepts (see GS iii - 112). With
this qualification in mind, he continues his more speculative thinking in
full knowledge that such speculations cannot be confirmed. Nevertheless, such thinking must be done, if only to determine when we move
from this speculative realm into the world of human things, which we
can confirm adequately.

The hypothetical, simplest drive does not experience itself as having
any needs, for it lacks a sophisticated consciousness. That said, according
to the theory of generation, simple drives can evolve. Nietzsche points
to this evolution by describing a drive or will as "the primitive form of
affect" or passion (WP 688). All other, more sophisticated affects arise

from the development of the most basic shape of the will to power and from the interactions between the drives" (WP 688. See also WP 670).

This consideration of what a drive is begins to explain why Nietzsche chooses to speak of the will to power rather than of force, the term employed in physics. Like the concept of the will to power, the notion of a force signifies motion with direction. Like a will, a force also has a certain degree of strength or power, which is determined in relation to other powers. However, the notion of force does not signify any sense on the part of the force of what is inner and outer to itself. A force is not a willed direction; rather, a force's activity is merely mechanical. As something purely mechanical, a force is never pro-active. Nor can it react, strictly speaking. A reaction is stimulated by something external to the reactor, but the reactor nevertheless exhibits the will or desire to strike back against the entity that is advancing upon it so as to recover the power it has lost or at least to prevent the advancing entity from further encroaching upon it and perhaps even destroying it. It is true that, if the advancing entity is sufficiently superior in strength to prevent the reactor from expanding or growing, the reactor can appear as though it is neither moving nor willing. However, this is mere appearance. If the balance of power shifted, the entity that previously seemed will-less would advance. This indicates the reactor is always working or willing to expand; it will be pro-active when and if it is able. The mechanistic account of motion and of any entity, no matter how primitive, cannot account for pro-actions and reactions. Thus, it cannot account for motion, including the motion we readily observe. Since it is inadequate to the facts, it is insupportable:

> "Attraction" and "repulsion" in a purely mechanistic sense are complete fictions: a word. We cannot think of an attraction divorced from an intention. —The will to take possession of a thing or to defend oneself against it and repel it—that, we "understand": that would be an interpretation of which we could make use.
>
> In short: the psychological necessity for a belief in causality lies in the inconceivability of an event divorced from intent; by which naturally nothing is said concerning truth or untruth (the justification of such a belief)! The belief in *causae* falls with the belief in *téle [action at a distance]* (against Spinoza and his causalism). (WP 627)

In lieu of the inadequate mechanistic theory of forces, Nietzsche notes our experience and conception of action depend upon the notion of will or desire, which is inherently directed. Hence, he rejects the concept of force in favor of the will to power:

> The victorious concept "force," by means of which our physicists have created God and the world, still needs to be completed: an inner will must be ascribed to it, which I designate as "will to power," i.e., as an insatiable desire to manifest power; or as the employment and exercise of power, as a creative drive, etc. Physicists cannot eradicate "action at a distance" from their principles; nor can they eradicate a repellent force (or an attracting one). There is nothing for it: one is obliged to understand all motion, all "appearances," all "laws," only as symptoms of an inner event and to employ the human being as an analogy to this end. In the case of an animal, it is possible to trace all its drives to the will to power; likewise, all the functions of organic life to this one source. (WP 619; see also WP 617 – WP 627; WP 634; WP 639; WP 481; WP 670; WP 688; BGE 14; BGE 36)

The mechanical interpretation of beings is false and therefore objectionable, but Nietzsche rejects it primarily because it is enervating (e.g. see BGE 4; WP 480; WP 507). By failing to acknowledge or by outright denying that living beings have a will to grow, the mechanical interpretation undermines our hope and efforts to be meaningfully involved in our own ongoing growth and in the ongoing evolution of the species. To the extent that these interpretations have this enervating effect, they are properly understood as modern expressions of slave morals and hence of the ideological war against the noble human type. In contrast to the mechanistic theory of beings, Nietzsche's theory of generation—that is, the morphology of the will to power—both describes phenomena more adequately than the mechanistic account, and it invigorates the human being.

Against this overview of Nietzsche's judgement that wills are superior to forces as an explanation of phenomena, consider how the will to power evolves to produce both the so-called physical and the so-called spiritual or mental characteristics of the human being. By reflecting upon how the more complex shape that is mind or thinking arises from a transfiguration of the will to power in its simpler shapes, such as the body and passions, we see clearly the incoherence of accepting the theory of evolution on the one hand and, on the other, adopting an interpretation of the human being that separates mind from body and thus the interior realm from actions in the external world.

Interactions between strong and weak wills determine which drives dominate and impose their form on other drives. These interactions produce or help to produce durable communities of drives, some of which persist long enough to develop into the complex forms we recognize as living beings. Continue along the genealogy of the will to power from simpler to more complex shapes of it. Eventually, this continuum of development brings us to the non-rational animal. To emphasize in what ways this creature is distinct from simpler life-forms, we can speak of this creature in terms of the activity that is peculiarly developed for the first time in it. Thus, we call it the passionate or passionating animal.

The passionate animal's complexity is due in part to the fact that it is comprised of a community of drives that is not only larger than that of the simpler entities, but also consists of more different kinds of drives than a simpler being (see BGE 36). In addition to these structural complexities, a greater number of the individual drives that comprise the community that is the passionate animal are more evolved than the drives that comprise simpler beings. For example, while all drives must have some degree of awareness, since they must have a sense of inner and outer, this awareness can develop. Indeed, according to the theory of generation, every drive and therefore every community of drives is continually degenerating or growing. Whatever appears to be static is acting against another power in an unstable equilibrium. To remind us of the matter at hand, this means only these three options exist for mind, too. Mind is never simply static; it is never perfect, if by perfection we mean a stable stasis. Not even death produces this alleged perfection.

At the low end of the continuum of awareness, a drive or simpler creature seizes on whatever it can, however it can, in its effort to appropriate other entities and thus to satisfy its will to express itself or expand fully. In contrast to relatively simple shapes of the will to power, the passionate animal has an extraordinarily acute perception of itself in relation to other beings. As a result of this high degree of awareness, the passionate animal does not typically experience its will to power amorphously, as an undetermined will to expand or grow. Rather, it aims to appropriate specific things according to the particular desire or meaning such things have for the animal at a given time. For example, a polar bear can recognize a dog as both a potential meal and a potential playmate. It will interact with a dog in either way, depending on what the bear desires most.

Our consideration of what the theory of generation tells us of the complexity of a passionate animal and the way this animal's will to power manifests in contrast with that of simpler beings enables us to deduce what the most aware entity to date is. Such a being is comprised of the greatest number of the most highly evolved drives acting in consort with each other with the highest degree of consciousness that has developed so far. This conscious activity pertains to the realm that is external or outward to the community of drives that constitutes this being, and it applies inwardly, within the community itself. The rational animal—the human being—is this creature (see GM 2.16). Just as the passionate animal emerges from a less aware and less complex predecessor, so too the rational emerges out of a less aware version of itself. More specifically, it emerges out of the passionate animal.

That the rational animal is more complex than the passionate animal is not an especially controversial claim, which is not to say the opinion is typically adopted thoughtfully. If we are not content to assume this conclusion without examining it, we can establish its grounds by reasoning through the implications of Nietzsche's observations about the relationship between passion and reason. Let us first review the philosophical backdrop against which Nietzsche introduces his concept of the rational animal.

Almost all other philosophers claim their conclusions are objectively true because they are unsullied by their passions (BGE 6; see also BGE 191). This claim typically involves the belief that reason is not only distinct but is also separate from passion and hence from the body, which harbors the passions in some way. By thinking of reason in this way, however, one removes the impetus for it to be at work. That is, our experience of reasoning is that it only occurs in conjunction with a motive, and this motive only comes from one or more passions (e.g. see GM 3.12). Reason should therefore be understood, not as something separate from passion, rather as a distinct kind of passionating. That reasoning is a sort of passionating is both a more scientifically elegant explanation than the traditional hypothesis, since it simplifies the explanation of reason, and it is truer to our experience of reasoning. Nietzsche's understanding of evolution as the morphology of the will to power supports our conclusion. Recall, he argues that reason does not belong to any single drive or passion. Rather, reasoning is akin to a conversation between drives or passions within the community of drives that constitutes a being. He states this conception concisely and explicitly in *Beyond Good and Evil*: "thinking is merely a relation of ... drives to each other" (BGE 36). He expands upon it in *Gay Science*:

> *The meaning of knowing.*— *Non ridere, non lugere, neque detestari, sed intelligere!* Says Spinoza as simply and sublimely as is his wont. Yet in the last analysis, what else is this *intelligere* than the form in which we come to feel the other three at once? One result of the different and mutually opposed desires to laugh, lament, and curse? Before knowledge is possible, each of these instincts must first have presented its one-sided view of the thing or event; after this comes the fight of these one-sided views, and occasionally this results in a mean, one grows calm, one finds all three sides right, and there is a kind of justice and a contract; for by virtue of justice and a contract all these instincts can maintain their existence and assert their rights against each other. Since only the last scenes of reconciliation and the final accounting at the end of this long process rise to our conscious-ness, we suppose that *intelligere* must be something conciliatory, just, and good—something that stands essentially opposed to the instincts, while it is actually nothing but a *certain behavior of the instincts toward one another*.
>
> For the longest time, conscious thought was considered thought itself. Only now does the truth dawn on us that by far the greatest part of our spirit's activity remains unconscious and unfelt. But I suppose these instincts that are here contending against one another understand very well how to make themselves felt by, and how to hurt, *one another*. This may well be the source of that sudden and violent exhaustion that afflicts all thinkers (it is the exhaustion on a battlefield). Indeed, there may be occasions of concealed *heroism* in our warring depths, but certainly nothing divine that eternally rests in itself, as Spinoza supposed. *Conscious* thinking, especially that of the philosopher, is the least vigorous and therefore also the relatively mildest and calmest form of thinking; and thus precisely philosophers are most apt to be led astray about the nature of knowledge. (GS 333; see also GS 179)

Immediately following this section, Nietzsche fleshes out his account of rational thinking by likening understanding to a love affair between multiple drives or passions, complete with the fecund agon or strife—the desire for another *as an opponent*—that is proper to true love:

> *One must learn to love.*— This is what happens to us in music: First one has to *learn to hear* a figure and melody at all, to detect and distinguish it, to isolate it and delimit it as a separate life. Then it requires some exertion and good will to *tolerate* it in spite of its strangeness, to be patient with its appearance and expression, and kindhearted about its oddity. Finally, there

comes a moment when we are *used* to it, when we wait for it, when we sense that we should miss it if it were missing; and now it continues to compel and enchant us relentlessly until we have become its humble and enraptured lovers who desire nothing better from the world than it and only it.

But that is what happens not only in music. That is how we have *learned to love* all things that we now love. In the end we are always rewarded for our good will, our patience, fairmindedness, and gentleness with what is strange; gradually, it sheds its veils and turns out to be a new and indescribable beauty. That is its *thanks* for our hospitality. Even those who love themselves have learned it in this way; for there is no other way. Love, too, has to be learned. (GS 334)

Unlike the traditional account of reasoning, which does not connect mind organically to the passions or to the genealogy of the human being, Nietzsche's account enables us to see something of how the rational animal is a more complex form of the passionate animal. That is, since reasoning cannot even occur without simultaneous passionating, it certainly cannot come to be in the absence of passions.[39] Thus, the rational animal must develop after and out of the passionate animal. Furthermore, since reasoning presupposes simultaneous passionating, the rational animal's physio-psychology must incorporate the simpler animal's passionating while also moving beyond it, to reasoning. Indeed, to say a being incorporates the distinctive power of a pre-existing form while also augmenting this form with a new power is what it means to say the latter entity is more complex than the former. What is commonly called reasoning is therefore more accurately called reasonable-passionating or passionating-reason.

The transfiguration or rarefication of passionating into reasoning precludes the possibility that reason is separate from the passions and the body. Mind and body; the spiritual and the physical; reason and passion; internally and externally oriented actions—none of these things are separate strictly speaking since all are shapes of the will to power. For the same reason, we cannot rank according to the moral-theological prejudice mind over body or thoughts over actions in the external world. Rather, all shapes of action are ranked according to how much of the activity that is human life or human being—for human living and being are one and the same—are involved in each. By this standard, so long as passionating-reasoning is the shape of super-abundant vitality rather than vital paucity, it is better to both passionate and reason than to passionate solely. In other words, an expression of super-abundant vitality in the exterior world is greater—it is more of what it is to be—when it is accompanied by a super-abundantly vital act in the interior realm. Potency in two ways is better than potency in one, and potency in one way is better than potency in none!

Although the passionating-rational animal is more complex than the passionating animal, this does not mean reason necessarily increases our vitality. Remember, reasoning developed in response to an overall *decrease* in the human being's will to power, and it has so far typically been employed by vitally impotent human beings for merely utilitarian purposes. Reason and neediness have gone hand in hand, even in the case of the philosopher, who has traditionally regarded philosophy as the very product of paucity. To the extent that reason compensates for vital paucity, it is accompanied by frustration and disgruntlement with what one is. This disgruntlement must make its way into all philosophy that emerges from vital paucity.

Nevertheless, as we noted at the beginning of our discussion, Nietzsche realizes a new kind of philosophy is now available to the warrior-philosopher if he can overcome his attachment to the ascetic ideal. Nietzsche calls the activity of the warrior-philosopher gay science [*Die fröliche Wissenschaft*]. Thus, he recalls the name of the Provençal troubadours of the 11th and 13th centuries and, more generally, "the Provençal concept of *gaya scienza*—that unity of singer, knight, and free spirit that distinguishes the wonderful early culture of the Provençals from all equivocal cultures" (EH, "The Gay Science"; see also BGE 260).[40] In his words: "'Gay Science': that signifies the saturnalia of a spirit who has patiently resisted a terrible, long pressure—patiently, severely, coldly, without submitting, but also without hope—and who is now all at once attacked by hope, the hope for health, and the *intoxication* of convalescence" (GS, "Preface," 1). He continues:

> For a psychologist there are few questions that are as attractive as that concerning the relation of health and philosophy. ... For assuming that one is a person, one necessarily also has the philosophy that belongs to that person; but there is a big difference. In some it is their deprivations that philosophize; in others, their riches and strengths. The former *need* their philosophy, whether it be as a prop, a sedative, medicine, redemption, elevation, or self-alienation. For the latter it is merely a beautiful luxury—in the best cases, the voluptuousness of a triumphant gratitude that eventually

still has to inscribe itself in cosmic letters on the heaven of concepts. (GS, "Preface," 2)

As its name suggests, gay science is characterized by joyful exuberance and love, including and especially self-love.

The most intimate and potent effect of the noble human being's acquisition of reason is his ability to think about what he is as an individual and as a rational life-form. Of special note, this animal's acquisition of reason means he can consider his passions in terms of an expected future time. As we have noted, the passionate animal is distinguished from simpler entities by the fact that the passionate animal desires specific things at particular times. In any given circumstance the animal's action is shaped by what passion or group of passions dominates at that given moment in time, or at least without significant regard for future time and future possibilities. For example, a dog might eat an entire bowl of pasta that has been left unattended only to follow up this binge by vomiting the pasta. In the passionating-rational animal, we call this kind of behavior poor impulse control, by which we mean that the human being has not taken adequate account of whether he truly wants the possible and even likely future outcome of his current actions. Typically, such failures are explained as either overly strong passions, insufficient reasoning skills, or both. Given Nietzsche's genealogical account of the relationship between the passions and reason, we say the human being who characteristically has poor impulse control has passions that have not adequately evolved to the point where they engage in silent speech with each other. That is, it is not as though such a person has something called reason, but he does not usually employ it. Reason is not a self-subsisting faculty. Rather, if a person has passions that have the capacity to speak with each other, they will typically do so. In other words, silent speaking or reasoning is the manner or way of the passions in a passionating-rational animal that is mature. Indeed, we do not expect the rational animal merely to consider future consequences of his current action or possible action. Rather, the mature rational animal's considerations include a consideration of principles. He guides his behavior by an account of the supreme good. Thus, he moves beyond a narrow consideration of self-interest.

That this manner of acting belongs to the rational animal is not to say the mature form of this animal is commonplace. Rather, many human beings are especially inclined not to consider the consequences of their actions, and even fewer hold themselves strictly to considerations of the good. Rather, they act more like passionating animals, using reason only insincerely, as a way of defending non-rational behavior. For example, the Athenians voted by a small margin to kill Socrates when he was charged with impiety by some of his envious enemies. The next day, they reportedly deeply regretted their decision, but they apparently could not reverse it by law. The only recourse they had, therefore, was to encourage Socrates to escape, which would require him to break the law. Thus, the Athenian people, who were highly civilized in comparison to any people who have lived so far in human history, nevertheless clearly show themselves to be both without good judgement and without a deep attachment to justice when their passions are inflamed, in this case as a result of being manipulated by the unscrupulous amongst them. In a more mature form of the rational animal, this reversion to something more like the passionate animal's behavior would not occur or would not occur as easily.

By the genealogical account of the human being, we conclude the passions' involvement with reasoning is not only proper to what it is to be a rational animal, but also that passionating-reason is also vivifying in the mature form of this animal. One of, if not the, most significant ways in which this activity is vivifying is that it allows the rational animal to command his own growth mindfully. By this, we do not mean simply that he can think about how to lead a stimulating life. This is of course true, but it is also nothing new. We mean something quite new in the realm of philosophy and quite literal. When a rational animal thinks, this activity does not actualize some pre-determined potential or final end. Rather, thinking alters our physio-psychology. "Learning changes us; it does what all nourishment does which also does not merely 'preserve'—as physiologists know" (BGE 231). This is what it means to say the greatest thoughts are the greatest events: rational life-forms can be enhanced by something as apparently immaterial as their thinking. By thinking persistently and vividly about what he is at his best and about what he might become, the warrior-philosopher evolves into this superior shadow of himself. Thus, he acts as his own progenitor and offspring. In other words, unlike any prior time, in this era of the human being's genealogy, eternal living becomes a real possibility. That is, far from being

a vague wish, such eternality is now a rationally based and philosophi-
cally considered possibility.

Nietzsche beautifully and compelling depicts this process of thinking oneself into a more robust form of one's higher or more alive self in
a sometimes-silent interaction between Zarathustra and what Zarathustra calls "the stillest hour." The conversation is a life-affirming version
of Jesus' temptation in the garden of Gethsemane. Unlike Jesus, when
Zarathustra is tempted to an alternate future he ultimately takes it:

> [The stillest hour] spoke to me again without voice: "What matters
> their mockery? You are one who has forgotten how to obey: now you shall
> command. Do you not know who is most needed by all? He that com-
> mands great things. To do great things is difficult. This is what is most
> unforgivable in you: you have the power, and you do not want to rule." And
> I [Zarathustra] answered: "I lack the lion's voice for commanding."
>
> Then it spoke to me again as a whisper: "It is the stillest words that
> bring on the storm. Thoughts that come on doves' feet guide the world. O
> Zarathustra, you shall go as a shadow of that which must come: thus you
> will command and, commanding, lead the way." And I answered: "I am
> ashamed."
>
> Then it spoke to me again without voice: "You must yet become as a
> child and without shame. The pride of youth is still upon you; you have
> become young late; but whoever would become as a child must overcome
> his youth too." And I reflected for a long time and trembled. But at last I
> said what I had said at first: "I do not want to."
>
> Then laughter surrounded me. Alas, how this laughter tore my entrails
> and slit open my heart! And it spoke to me for the last time: "O Zarathus-
> tra, your fruit is ripe, but you are not ripe for your fruit. Thus you must
> return to your solitude again; for you must yet become mellow." (Z, "The
> Stillest Hour"; see also GS 58; GS 232)

Chase the idea depicted in this interaction! Become mellow and
again young, like the warrior-philosopher. Conceive a being more vital
than any human life-form that has ever existed. Do so with as much
vividness and clarity as we can muster, for we cannot create a new shape
if we cannot envision it adequately. The image is just ahead of where
the human being is. Or rather, it is just barely where we are in our
physio-psychological evolution: it is the most rarified development in
the current shape of the most advanced human being. Thinking about
this new life-form in a sustained and serious way will move us farther
into the physio-psychology of this imagined entity. The so-called mind
becomes the so-called body, too.

Chapter Six

The Warrior's Riddle

Thinking changes what you are. Reading and writing change not only what
you are, but also what other people are.

Only as creators!— This has given me the greatest trouble and still does: to
realize that what things *are called* is incomparably more important than
what they are. The reputation, name, and appearance, the usual measure
and weight of a thing, what it counts for—originally almost always wrong
and arbitrary, thrown over things like a dress and altogether foreign to their
nature and even to their skin—all this grows from generation unto generation, merely because people believe in it, until it gradually grows to be
part of the thing and turns into its very body. What at first was appearance
becomes in the end, almost invariably, the essence and is effective as such.
How foolish it would be to suppose that one only needs to point out this
origin and this misty shroud of delusion in order to destroy the world that
counts for real, so-called destroy the world that counts for real, so-called
"reality." We can destroy only as creators. —But let us not forget this either:
it is enough to create new names and estimations and probabilities in order
to create in the long run new "things." (GS 58)

***

The third essay of *On The Genealogy of Morals* is a riddle whose unraveling
or guiding ribbon is presented immediately by the mysterious meaning
behind Nietzsche's choice to augment the essay's title with a prefixed
quotation. The title introduces the essay's major explicit theme: "What is
the Meaning of Ascetic Ideals?" Given that the ascetic ideal is one and
the same as the moral-theological prejudice, we can restate this question
in language more familiar to our investigation: What is the value for life
of the moral-theological prejudice? The content of the prefixed quota-

tion is as follows: "Unconcerned, mocking, violent—thus wisdom wants us: she is a woman and always loves only a warrior" (Z, "On Reading and Writing"). How does the titular question belong with this quotation? To resolve this query fully, we must consider the relationship of the titular question not only to the prefixed quotation, but also to the content of the entire section from which this quotation is excerpted; namely, the section of *Thus Spoke Zarathutra* entitled, "On Reading and Writing." Thus, our guiding riddle in its fuller form poses the question: How are particular kinds of reading or interpretation and writing related to the value for life of the moral-theological prejudice? The resolution of this riddle reveals Nietzsche's final blow against the war upon all things noble as well as his leap forward into a life-affirming future—a new kind of promised land—for the human being. Moreover, the unriddling required to see such things is a test, a training, and a calling into being of the latest shape of the noble human type: the artist-philosopher.

That we are correct to regard the riddle as a test and teaching of how to read or interpret and write well is supported by what Nietzsche says in the "Preface" to *The Genealogy* of his choice to begin the third essay as he does:

> [P]eople find difficulty with the aphoristic form: this arises from the fact that today this form is not taken seriously enough. An aphorism, properly stamped and molded, has not been "deciphered" when it has simply been read; rather, one has then to begin its exegesis, for which is required an art of exegesis. I have offered in the third essay of the present book an example of what I regard as "exegesis" in such a case—an aphorism is prefixed to this essay, the essay itself is a commentary on it. (GM, "Preface," 8)

To this evidence, add what Nietzsche says in *Ecce Homo* of his intentionally tricky style in *The Genealogy of Morals*:

> Regarding expression, intention, and the art of surprise, the three inquiries that constitute the *Genealogy* are perhaps un-cannier than anything else written so far. Dionysus is, as is known, also the god of darkness.
>
> Every time a beginning that is calculated to mislead: cool, scientific, even ironic, deliberately foreground, deliberately holding off. Gradually more unrest; sporadic; very disagreeable truths are heard grumbling in the distance—until eventually a *tempo feroce* is attained in which everything rushes ahead in tremendous tension. In the end, in the midst of perfectly gruesome detonations, a new truth becomes visible every time among thick clouds. (EH, "Genealogy of Morals: A Polemic")

Alterted to Nietzsche's esotericism by the author himself, we begin, sharply atuned to details.

Nietzsche starts the first section by repeating the titular query. With a delightful display of succinctness, he answers it in this same first section. He commences with a list of seven different human types for whom the ascetic ideal has meaning, together with the value this ideal has for each type. In the order they appear, the seven types are: artists, philosophers, scholars, women, the "physiologically deformed and deranged (the *majority* of mortals)," priests, and saints:

> In the case of artists, ... [ascetic ideals] mean nothing or too many things; in the case of philosophers and scholars something like a sense and instinct for the most favorable preconditions of higher spirituality; in the case of women at best one more seductive charm ... [I]n the case of the physiologically deformed and deranged (the *majority* of mortals) an attempt to see themselves as "too good" for this world ... their chief struggle against slow pain and boredom; in the case of priests ... their best instrument to power, also the "supreme" license for power; in the case of saints, finally, a pretext for hibernation ... their form of madness. (GM 3.1)

For each of these human types, the ascetic ideal has a specific and different value for life. In no case is its value derived from the transcendent world of absolute or pure, unchanging, being. To the extent any of these human beings believe or proclaim that its value consists in transcendence of the actual world, they misunderstand themselves, they are lying, or both. In lieu of the believed or proclaimed value of this transcendence, Nietzsche discovers that all of these human beings venerate the ascetic ideal because they find in it a means to maximizing the expression of their will to power or life. The recognition of this commonality is insightful, but since all living entities act to maximize the expression of their will to power, this answer is too general to resolve the question of the value of the ascetic ideal specifically. Why is the *ascetic ideal* in particular a means—perhaps the most important means—for these human beings to maximize the expression of their vitality?

To answer this question, consider what unspoken meaning of this ideal unifies the different human types on the list. Nietzsche implicitly responds to this question: "*That* the ascetic ideal has meant so many things to the human being ... is an expression of the basic fact of the human will, its *horror vacui: it needs a goal*—and it will rather will *nothingness* than not will" (GM 3.1). In part, his answer means that, because we are shapes of the will to expand or grow maximally, we cannot but will so long as we are. To be is to will, and to will is to will expansion or growth. In other words, to be is to will power. Therefore, faced with the option of either willing our own degeneration or not willing, we necessarily must will our devolution and destruction. This will to nothingness—to a negation of a genuine future—is nihilism. To be clear and at the risk of repetition, remember, nihilism is neither the absence of a will, nor is it disbelief in the moral-theological prejudice, including its ascetic notion of truth. Since this prejudice actually spawns nihilism, it is incoherent to define nihilism as disbelief in truth, so understood. Rather, nihilism is disbelief in a genuine future; that is, of the possibility of growth. It manifests here in the paradoxically suicidal way the human being has come to express his will to life.

This answer, however, does not adequately comprehend Nietzsche's remarkably concise response in the first section. Perhaps to ensure that a promising reader does not conclude he has mastered the third essay with a partial interpretation of its first section, Nietzsche asks a pointed, cautionary question: "Am I understood?" (GM 3.1). He augments this question with a second: "Have I been understood?" (GM 3.1). This second question is not a repetition of the first. Whereas the first is posed in the present tense and is thus limited to the immediate context in which he offers his succinct answer to the titular question, in the second question Nietzsche uses the perfect verb tense: "Have I been understood?" (GM 3.1). He thereby refers not only to the present, but also to the past. Posed in this form, his question suggests that at least the prior two essays in *The Genealogy* offer the same answer to the question of the meaning of the ascetic ideal that he provides in the first section of the third essay. Indeed, it suggests all of his philosophic works thus far offer this same answer in various forms to this same question. Hence, with the second question Nietzsche is asking whether his account of the human being as he has presented it up to this point in the genealogy of his philosophy has been understood. In the voice of an unusually candid—and thus perhaps also an unusually courageous—reader and would-be student, he offers a single answer to both questions: *"Not at all, my dear sir!"* (GM 3.1).

Faced with this response, Nietzsche graciously decides to begin again and to recap his teaching: "—Then let us start again from the beginning" (GM 3.1). That he says he will restate rather than reconstitute the answer he provides in the third essay's first section indicates he judges its content to be completely adequate. If we are right to suspect his question—"Have I been understood?"—refers to his works thus far, then this single section, properly interpreted also comprehends with diamond-like density all of his philosophy to date. In light of what he indicates about the comprehensiveness of the first section and his conclusion that his reader's comprehension of it thus far is wholly insufficient, we are now quite ready to begin anew, alongside Nietzsche and guided by the riddle he gives us. To keep sight of our way forward, we will restate this conclusion in terms of this riddle; that is, the full meaning of the combination of the titular question and the prefixed quotation. Since the first section is comprehensive, it should unriddle our guide, but the interpretation we have thus far of this first section fails to do so. Hence, our interpretation is incomplete.

Having appropriated the reader's voice as a means of telling him in no uncertain terms that he has not understood what Nietzsche has told him, Nietzsche ends the first section and indicates he will elucidate this first answer in the second and subsequent sections of the third essay. The second section thereby becomes a new first section.[41] In his expanded answer, Nietzsche does not spend equal time on each of the human types he initially lists. Rather, the lion's share of his explicit treatment of the types is spent on the artist, the scholar, the philosopher, the priest, modern scientists—a category he divides into scholars and philosophers of a sort—and historiographers. Little time is spent on the majority of human beings and saints. He treats the majority in his analysis of the priest, and the saint is dismissed with hardly more than a phrase indicating he is of no concern to philosophers (GM 3.8). A saint is also treated in passing as an example of one who uses the ascetic ideal as a means to hypnosis, which he seeks as a means of alleviating suffering (GM 3.17). The discussion of women is similarly scanty. What they are "at best" with regard to the meaning of ascetic ideals—namely, seducers—is not discussed at all, or at least not explicitly. Rather, Nietzsche speaks overtly only of the majority of women. Since the best are by definition the exceptional few, the majority cannot include those women whose employment of the ascetic ideal is best. While remaining silent about these seducers, Nietzsche folds the bulk of women into his account of the priest's dealings with the mass of men, whom he depicts as either "sufferers of the lower classes" or "work-slaves or prisoners" (GM 3.18). He adds women to this context with the passing, parenthetical account of why it is legitimate to do so: most women are simultaneously *both* work-slaves *and* prisoners (GM 3.18).

What is the meaning of Nietzsche's silence about those women who use the ascetic ideal for seduction? It is not credible that his seeming inattention to them is an oversight. He is a writer whose skill is arguably unsurpassed, and he chooses to include women as a category in the first section, which he clearly crafts to be both sufficient and succinct. Since he aims at concisely articulating in a single section an answer he judges to be completely adequate, he would not have included women if they were unnecessary to this answer. Moreover, since he presents the second and subsequent sections, not as a reconstitution or paring down of the first answer, but as a more accessible restatement of the first, we expect "the best" among women for whom the ascetic ideal has value to be addressed somehow in this restatement. Since they are not addressed explicitly, we are provoked to suspect they are addressed implicitly, silently, or esoterically.

Silent speaking about these seducers accords with Nietzsche's teaching on the type, woman. He aligns woman per se or the feminine with the principle of becoming in contrast to the principle of being, which he associates with man or the masculine. This alliance between woman and becoming reflects the fact that, within the larger category of the human being, woman has a pre-eminently supple soul. She is akin to an excellent actor in that she can fill a multitude of diverse roles. However, whereas an actor remains distinct and to some degree separate from the role he plays, woman *is* the "role," which is to say she does not act at all, strictly speaking. In her creativity, she bears some similarity to the artist. Yet, just as the actor is not his role and to this extent is unlike woman, so too the artist is not his artifact. Woman, by contrast, is simultaneously the artist of herself and artifact of her artistry. Nothing of her, as woman, stands apart from her various self-effected transfigurations. In sum, woman is maximally self-creating becoming within the type or shared, general shape that is the human being.

By the standard of the moral-theological prejudice, woman's mutability is suspicious. Since there is nothing true or permanent about her, considered as woman rather than as a human being, she is *essentially* a liar and is therefore a fundamental opponent of the ascetic notion of truth. For this reason, she is guiltier by nature than man. Nietzsche grants woman is not merely a liar, but indeed a superlative liar. However, since he rejects the proclaimed authority of the moral-theological prejudice, when he speaks of woman or indeed of anyone as a liar according to the ascetic standard, his speech is ironic. He uses the traditional moral language, but without conceding the legitimacy of its traditional moral meaning. Thus, whereas the ascetic characterization "Liar!" is intended to be derogatory, in Nietzsche's mouth it is not necessarily so. He rightly reasons that if human beings are required to speak truth as the moral-theological prejudice understands it—so-called objective truth, which allegedly wholly transcends perspective and interpretation—then every human being is necessarily a liar. In truth, all human beings, like all living beings more generally, have a perspective that is determined and bounded by their fluid physio-psychologies. Supra-perspectival objectivity or a kind of seeing and knowing that transcends a being's physio-psychology is nonsense. The relevant difference between the masculine and the feminine, therefore, is not and cannot be that the latter is essentially a liar and the former is not. It is rather the difference Nietzsche highlights: insofar as they are man and woman—rather than the more authoritative category, human being, to which both also belong—they express their will to power differently. This supra-moral understanding of truth and lying, and hence of the masculine and the feminine, does not mean truth should not concern us. It means the pursuit of truth, truth-telling, lying, indeed all acts are properly evaluated in terms of vitality and, ultimately, in terms of the supreme good.[42]

Nietzsche's correction to the ascetic concepts of truth and lying adds to our portfolio on our guiding riddle by helping us better understand the relationship between wisdom and the warrior-philosopher, as encapsulated by the prefixed quotation. While it is correct to associate wisdom and truth, wisdom is not the sum of all objectively determined truths, for such truths do not exist. Rather, truth is more like the shape that facts have in relation to each other, as they are unconsciously and consciously interpreted and discerned by an individual type of being. Wisdom is knowledge of truth, as discerned by every individual human being and perhaps all living beings, together with knowledge of the relations between these discernments. More succinctly, wisdom is knowledge of the activity that is life.

In accordance with this notion of wisdom, Nietzsche personifies wisdom and characterizes her relationship to the warrior-philosopher as passionate rather than ascetic, since asceticism falsely presupposes a metaphysical or other-worldly, non– or supra-perspectival realm. She *loves* the warrior, and *only* the warrior. Since Nietzsche presents wisdom as a woman and the warrior as a man, and since he speaks of wisdom's love for the warrior, we reasonably infer wisdom's love is neither bloodless or dryly intellectual, nor is it unegoistic. These inferences are supported by what Nietzsche says of wisdom, again personified, in *Thus Spoke Zarathustra*. There, Zarathustra describes her as his ferocious beloved:

> [Y]ou will be frightened, my friends, by my wild wisdom; and perhaps you will flee from it, together with my enemies. Would that I knew how to lure you back with shepherds' flutes! Would that my lioness, wisdom, might learn how to roar tenderly! And many things have we learned together.
>
> My wild wisdom became pregnant on lonely mountains; on rough stones she gave birth to her young, her youngest. Now she runs foolishly through the harsh desert and seeks and seeks gentle turf—my old wild wisdom. Upon your hearts' gentle turf, my friends, upon your love would she bed her most dearly beloved. (Z, "The Child with the Mirror"; see also Z, "The Dancing Song")

She is sensual, spiritual, and she is fiercely egoistic or *self*-loving, too.

Consider Nietzsche's depiction of wisdom's beloved. As a war-rior-*philosopher*, he must love wisdom in return. Yet, we are struck by the fact that Nietzsche does not characterize him as either a philosopher or a philosopher-warrior. He leaves us to conclude from his account of the genealogy of the human being that this warrior is also philosophic. By denying us the expected characterization, "philosopher," Nietzsche undermines and corrects the traditional, ascetic interpretation of the philosopher. By speaking of the warrior rather than of the philosopher, Nietzsche may also give a silent nod to the fact that the genuine philos-opher, rather than the ascetic notion of this human type, loves life more than wisdom (see Z, "The Dancing Song").[43]

We fairly infer from the warrior's love for wisdom, such as it is, that he seeks to stoke the flame of her love. To do so, he must not speak the bitter nothings of asceticism. He must instead continue his warrior ways: he must be a ferocious fighter, an intrepid explorer, and he must climb to the highest peaks of spirit that he can reach, as an audacious attempter in both his inwardly and outwardly directed acts. The precise shape these acts take at this point in the philosopher's genealogy and that of the human being is still obscure. However, we can conclude that, whatever this shape may be, it will not prohibit lying. That said, if the philosopher is coherent in his pursuit of the supreme good, he will not aim to undermine either his own or the human being's thriving life. When he tells lies, he will aim to tell only life-affirming or beautiful lies.

A second striking feature of Nietzsche's restated answer to the titular question is his explicit and extended treatment of historiographers, a category of human beings he does not name in his first answer. As we noted in the case of woman, the fact that the first answer is completely sufficient plus the fact that the second and subsequent sections flesh it out suggest that historiographers, or at least a sub-category of historiographers for whom the ascetic ideal has meaning, may be folded into one or more of the human types listed in the first answer. Which one or ones? Add this question, along with our thoughts about the feminine and the apparent absence of "the best" woman in the restatement, to our portfolio on the guiding riddle. Move into the recap.

Nietzsche re-starts by re-stating the opening question on the meaning of ascetic ideals. He begins to answer it at greater length in the case of artists by way of the operatic composer Richard Wagner, whom Nietzsche presents as a typical artist. Recall, in his succinct answer, Nietzsche said ascetic ideals "mean nothing or too many things" to artists (GM 3.2). We expect him to reach this same conclusion in his more accessible answer. His approaches it obliquely, by way of Wagner's interpretation of chastity. Throughout most of his life, Nietzsche tells us, Wagner honored chastity truly, which is to say he did not interpret it ascetically. Only in his old age did he adopt an ascetic view of sensuality. Nietzsche characterizes this change as a leap by the artist into the opposite of what he had been previously. With this observation, Nietzsche shifts his focus from a direct approach to the meaning of ascetic ideals in the case of artists to the question of what it means when an artist makes such a leap. Proceeding by way of this question, Nietzsche remarks:

> [There is] no necessary antithesis between chastity and sensuality; every good marriage, every genuine love affair, transcends this antithesis. Wagner would have done well, I think, to have brought this pleasant fact home once

more to his Germans by means of a bold and beautiful Luther comedy. (GM 3.2)

Even for those human beings for whom "this antithesis between chastity and sensuality really exists, there is no need for it to be a tragic antithesis" (GM 3.2). All "well-constituted, joyful mortals" will instead experience the tension generated by the "unstable equilibrium" between these antipodes as an invigorating seduction to life (GM 3.2).

Those who honor both sensuality and chastity stand in contrast to human beings whom Nietzsche characterizes as "swine who have come to grief and are finally induced to worship chastity" as the antithesis of what they are (GM 3.2). In their worship, we detect the telltale sign of slavishness: their concept of the good is defined only negatively. As we know, this happens because the valuators in question are too impotent to wield their antipodes healthfully or beautifully. Thus, they demonize sensuality and deify sexual abstinence, in keeping with the moral-theological prejudice. It was this ugly antithesis that Wagner "set to music and put upon the stage" in old age (GM 3.2).

Although Wagner seemed in this art to advocate such swinishness, Nietzsche is careful to note Wagner himself was no swine. He was therefore not compelled by his own physio-psychology either to adopt the ugly, ascetic antithesis between chastity and sensuality himself or to produce artifacts endorsing it. To the contrary, Nietzsche says that for most of his life Wagner aimed with all of his vitality at *the highest spiritualization and sensualization* of his art" (GM 3.3). In other words, prior to leaping into his opposite, and regardless of whether he would have articulated his project this way, Wagner aimed in his art at promoting the evolution of the human being. After he made his leap, this project to advance evolution through his artifacts reversed. Since Wagner did not always promote devolution, we ask again: Why did he leave his life-promoting path and project by leaping into his opposite?

Focusing on Wagner's *Parsifal*, the last of Wagner's completed operas, Nietzsche notes that, despite the ugliness of its moral subject matter and of its main character, even it could have been life-affirming. Perhaps with a touch of wistfulness, he describes on the one hand what the main character of *Parsifal* is and what Wagner intended it to be. On the other hand, he sketches what the artifact could have been. More importantly for our effort to unravel our guiding riddle, his sketch also describes what Parsifal *could still become, given a beautiful—that is to say, life-promoting—reading or interpretation:*

> [What was that] male (yet so unmanly) "country simpleton" … [to Wagner], that poor devil and nature boy Parsifal, whom he finally made into a Catholic by such captious means—what? was this Parsifal meant *seriously?* For one might be tempted to suppose the Wagnerian *Parsifal* was intended as a joke, as a kind of epilogue and satyr play with which the tragedian Wagner wanted to take leave of us, also of himself, above all of *tragedy* in a fitting manner worthy of himself, namely with an extravagance of wanton parody of the tragic itself, of the whole gruesome earthly gravity and earthly misery of his previous works, of the *crudest form*, overcome at long last, of the anti-nature of the ascetic ideal. This, to repeat, would have been worthy of a great tragedian who, like every artist, arrives at the ultimate pinnacle of his greatness only when he comes to see himself and his art *beneath* him—when he knows how to *laugh* at himself.
>
> Is Wagner's *Parsifal* his secret laughter of superiority at himself, the triumph of his ultimate artist's freedom and artist's transcendence? One could wish that it were, to repeat again; for what would a seriously-intended Parsifal be? Must one really see in him (as someone put it to me) "the product of an insane hatred of knowledge, spirit, and sensuality"? A curse upon the senses and the spirit in a *single* breath of hatred? An apostacy and return to morbid Christian and obscurantist ideals? (GM 3.3)

With this wish, Nietzsche links tragedy and comedy, indicating the latter can emerge out of the former. We may call the product of this evolution simply a comedy, especially if we want to emphasize the fact that the comedic writer can rise to spiritual heights wherein he no longer experiences anything as tragic and can create an artifact that reflects this state and reproduces it in at least some spectators. So understood, comedy is what Nietzsche presents as a *real*—that is, *this*-worldly—form of transcendence. Nietzsche's creation, Zarathustra, speaks of this comedic height and perspective, which he claims to have reached partly because of his tremendous courage and somewhat mad love of life. This description appears in the section of *Thus Spoke Zarathustra* from which the quotation prefixed to the third essay of *The Genealogy* is excerpted—"On Reading and Writing":

> Aphorisms should be peaks—and those who are addressed, tall and lofty. The air thin and pure, danger near, and the spirit full of gay … [mischief]: these go well together. I want to have goblins around me, for I am courageous. Courage that puts ghosts to flight creates goblins for itself: courage wants to laugh.

I no longer feel as you do: this cloud that I see beneath me, this blackness and gravity at which I laugh—this is your thundercloud.

You look up when you feel the need for elevation. And I look down because I am elevated. Who among you can laugh and be elevated at the same time? Whoever climbs the highest mountains laughs at all tragic plays and tragic seriousness.

Brave, unconcerned, mocking, violent—thus wisdom wants us: she is a woman and always loves only a warrior.

You say to me, "Life is hard to bear." But why would you have your pride in the morning and your resignation in the evening? Life is hard to bear; but do not act so tenderly! We are all of us fair beasts of burden, male and female asses. What do we have in common with the rosebud, which trembles because a drop of dew lies on it? (Z, "On Reading and Writing"; see also: BGE 29; GM 3.3)

If we want to acknowledge the origin and genealogy of such a comedy and thus also preserve the fact that the artifact was tragic prior to its transfiguration by a reading or interpretation that comes from an elevated perspective, we may call it a tragicomedy. We may also choose this designation if the artifact arouses in the artist or its spectators both pain and pleasure, sometimes simultaneously. Homer's Odyssey may be an example of such an artifact. This combination also seems to be illustrated within the pages of Homer's poem. The character Odysseus at least seems to experience sadness and joy simultaneously when he listens to the Phaeacian, Demodokos, sing of the Trojan horse.[44]

Nietzsche tells us the transfiguration of tragedy into comedy occurs when an artist "arrives at the ultimate pinnacle of his greatness" (GM 3.3). This upward motion transpires when the artist "comes to see himself and his art *beneath* him—when he knows how to *laugh* at himself" (GM 3.3; see also Z, "On Reading and Writing"). To say the same thing differently, the artist and his artifact become comic when the artist gains the distance from himself and his art that is necessary to obtain an unusually comprehensive perspective upon both. This comprehensiveness enables one to see all things in their rightful place, which is to say it yields a comic perspective. This comprehensive, comic perspective constitutes a self-surmounting or growth, which is expressed in the artist's mischievous or teasing laughter at his prior gravity and in gay laughter at his newly attained freedom to become something higher, more vital.

Having described the transfiguration of tragedy into comedy, Nietzsche leaves open at this juncture the question of whether Wagner himself became ascetic when he leapt into his opposite. If Wagner did devolve into asceticism, or if he betrayed what he was as an artist by celebrating the ascetic ideal, then his life would describe a fall from a height, which would be tragic. Without revealing the case of Wagner here, Nietzsche instead judges Wagner's artifacts. From an examination of both the artist's complete and incomplete works, he concludes Wagner certainly seemed intent upon teaching, by way of his works, that sensuality is wicked (GM 3.3). *Parsifal* was not an anomaly in this regard:

> [I]n the murky writings of his last years, as unfree as they are perplexed, there are a hundred passages that betray a secret wish and will, a despairing, unsure, unacknowledged will to preach nothing other than reversion, conversion, denial, Christianity, medievalism, and to say to his disciples "it is no good! seek salvation elsewhere!" Even the "blood of the Redeemer" is invoked in one place.— (GM 3.3)

In light of the ambiguity of Wagner's personal position with respect to the ascetic ideal, Nietzsche concludes it is best to "separate an artist from his work, not taking him as seriously as his work," for the artist is only the artifact's "precondition" (GM 3.4). He advises everyone who wishes to enjoy the artifact, especially the aesthetic human being, not only to separate the artist from his artifact, but also in most cases to forget actively the artifact's origin. He thereby appears to indicate the artist is always or is usually an ugly distraction from his completed artifact.[45] By contrast, "vivisectionists of the spirit"—philosophers—are properly undeterred from their characteristic activity by the ugliness entailed in it, including the ugliness of origins and artists (GM 3.4).

Applying his skills as a vivisectionist, Nietzsche reveals that the artist, like a pregnant mother, must assume something of his artifact's shape while creating it, for it is only by way of this similarity that the artist can gestate the artifact out of himself. Perhaps this process of gestation requires a degree of physio-psychological disintegration in the artist that renders him ugly regardless of whether his vision of his completed artifact is ugly or beautiful. Or perhaps the artist's ugliness only occurs when he envisions and intends to create an ugly artifact. However this may be, in the case of *Parsifal* both the artist's vision of, and intention for, the final artifact were ugly. In this intention, Wagner was successful. *Parsifal* is originally ugly. Moreover, while Wagner seemed intent upon making an ugly artifact, but not on making himself ugly or uglier, what

Nietzsche has taught us of physio-psychology tells us it is very likely that the artifact had a reciprocal effect on the artist. It made Wagner in its own image, just as he made the artifact according to his vision of it.

That there is a reciprocal creative relationship between artist and artifact does not mean the artist is the same as his artifact. They differ at least in their primary modes and arenas of existence. Whereas completed artifacts have a relatively fixed or stable existence in the external world, the artist exists primarily within the relatively fluid, internal world of his mind, especially his imagination. The artist's characteristic activity depends upon the primacy of his imagination and the unusual ephemerality of his way of being. It is because he is so ephemeral, imaginative or "unreal" that he can repeatedly imagine an artifact; thrust it out of his mind, into the external world; and then detach from it so as to begin creating anew.

> The fact is that *if* ... [the artist] were ... [his artifact], he would not represent, conceive, and express it: a Homer would not have created an Achilles nor a Goethe a Faust if Homer had been an Achilles or Goethe a Faust. Whoever is completely and wholly an artist is to all eternity separated from the "real," the actual. (GM 3.4)[46]

While the artist properly exists primarily in the realm of imagination, his "eternal unreality," the "falsity of his innermost existence," may nevertheless be wearisome at times (GM 3.4). It is a strain to have to create oneself and one's world consciously and relatively continuously, as one must do when one exists primarily in the realm of imagination. This is not to say actions in the external world do not involve constant interpretation. They must, since we filter everything through what we are as individual human beings. However, we are not conscious of vast amounts of this interpretative work. Much of the external world seems given to us. To repeat, this is not the case for the "unreal" human being in his "unreal" world. The artist's weariness arises precisely because he is more conscious of his constant creativity.

As one who dwells in his vivid imagination, the artist is ill-suited to a robust, primary existence in the external world. However, Nietzsche does not highlight a vivid imagination as the thing that renders the artist incapable of fighting the ascetic ideal. Rather, he associates the artist's incapacity for this battle with the artist's lack of courage. More specifically, the artist does not have the courage for independent acts in the external realm. "Standing alone is contrary" to the artist's "deepest instincts" (GM 3.5). Moved by these instincts, the artist always seeks protection and a prop in an accepted authority, be it morality, philosophy, or religion. He secures the support of such authorities by acting unfailingly as the "valet" of one or more of them (GM 3.4).

By associating the artist's primary existence in his imagination with a lack of courage for external acts, Nietzsche recalls to us his hypothesis that the inner realm of the mind, including the imagination, was created by internalized drives that were too weak to express themselves outwardly. This reminder of the origin of mind together with Nietzsche's observation that the artist's lacks the courage necessary for independent acts in the external realm suggest the artist's creativity is still to a significant degree the product of weakness. Indeed, the artist's acts in general seem still to be wedded to weakness. This is not to say that imagination-dwellers must always lack the courage to stand alone in the external realm. Nietzsche leaves open the possibility that there could be an imaginative human being who has the vital potency for radical independence. What he says only indicates that, if such a human being were to exist, he would not be the artist, or at least he would not be the artist whom Nietzsche describes here.

The archetypal artist, Wagner, found his prop in Schopenhauer's philosophy, which was ascetic. Hence, Wagner was not truly committed to asceticism. Rather, he expressed asceticism in his artifacts at least partly because he was Schopenhauer's valet. With this explanation of the artist's leap into the ascetic ideal, in opposition to what seemed to be his initial project of life-promotion, Nietzsche returns us to his first answer to the question of the meaning of ascetic ideals in the case of artists. For the artist, the ascetic ideal means "nothing or too many things"; *"nothing whatever!"* (GM 3.1; GM 3.5). The ascetic ideal means nothing to the artist because, in truth, no ideals have meaning for the artist. The artist cannot and does not want to take hold of any ideal, because doing so involves a commitment, which in turn involves standing alone. As we have now seen, the artist's deepest instincts avoid this independence. Stated in a manner that will prove useful for resolving our guiding riddle, the artist is, by his very physio-psychology, *free of all ideology, including the moral-theological prejudice.* He has what we might call a Teflon spirit when it comes to ideals; nothing sticks to him.

Having answered the question of the meaning of ascetic ideals for artists, Nietzsche advances, again by what seems to be a rather circuitous route, to expand his answer to the question of the value of the ascetic ideal for philosophers. He begins by way of Arthur Schopenhauer, who stands as the model modern philosopher, the warrior-philosopher. Unlike the artist, the warrior-philosopher has the "knightly courage" to stand independently. Indeed, his capacity for solitude is so marvelous that he is even able to live without the concept of God. Why, then, does he still hang on to the ascetic ideal? This is a "more serious" question than the meaning of the ascetic ideal for artists, who harbor no ideals:

> [W]hat does it mean when a genuine philosopher pays homage to the ascetic ideal, a genuinely independent spirit like Schopenhauer, a man and knight of steely eye who had the courage to be himself, who knew how to stand alone without first waiting for heralds and signs from above? (GM 3.5)

Although Nietzsche shifts his focus from the meaning of the ascetic ideal for the artist to the "more serious" question of its meaning for a genuine philosopher, he continues to speak of the artist in conjunction with the philosopher, thereby further developing his observation that these two human types are linked (GM 3.5). They are associated not only or even primarily by the fact that the artist seeks out the philosopher for protection and as a prop. Nietzsche now links them more substantially by their shared aesthetic comportment toward beauty. This portion of his discussion therefore complements his discussion of the ugliness of both *Parsifal* and of Wagner, at least while the artist was creating ascetic artifacts.

The connection between these two kinds of human beings via aesthetics belies the separation Nietzsche seemed to make earlier between the aesthetic human being, whom he advised to avoid looking into origins, and the philosopher who, as a vivisectionist of the spirit, rightly excavates them. To understand Nietzsche's teaching on the inter-relationship between art and philosophy, track the narrative that leads to this point. Recall, Wagner did not endorse an ascetic interpretation of sensuality until his old age. When he reached old age, it was still not the ascetic ideal per se that seduced him to leap into his opposite. Instead, he leapt partly because he found protection and a prop in the moral-theological prejudice, which assumed a modern expression in Schopenhauer's philosophy. However, Wagner's dependence does not explain why he attached himself to Schopenhauer's philosophy in particular. It is not as though there was a shortage of authorities espousing the ascetic ideal. Why Schopenhauer's version of it? Nietzsche locates the answer to this question in Schopenhauer's interpretation of music, understood strictly as music unaccompanied by words and hence something as distinct from all lyrics, including the operatic libretto.

According to Schopenhauer's philosophy, music is the sovereign art. It is completely separate from all other arts; it is "the independent art as such" (GM 3.5). It is so because, unlike all other arts, it in no way incorporates "images of phenomenality" (GM 3.5). Instead, it alone speaks purely "the language of the will itself, directly out of the 'abyss' as its most authentic, elemental, non-derivative revelation" (GM 3.5). The fact that Schopenhauer separates music from all arts and elevates it above them on the grounds that it does not partake of phenomena, of *our* world, but is instead an unmixed expression of a more authoritative, otherworldly realm identifies his philosophy as metaphysical or ascetic and thus ultimately nihilistic. It therefore opposes the interpretation of music Wagner held or seemed to hold before he leapt into his opposite.

In the period of his life prior to his leap, Wagner regarded music as akin to woman and drama as akin to man. As he understood the sexes, woman requires man as a goal that orients and thereby organizes or directs her fluidity. Since the man is the goal, man is primary; he leads. So too, drama is primary to music and leads or directs it. The primacy of the man or drama does not devalue woman or music. Just as woman needs man, man requires woman as the medium of his expression. Drama requires music for the same reason: it is impoverished by the absence of music, for it fails to communicate and thus achieve its goal as well as it could if it were expressed along with music. The union of man and woman, and thus of drama and music, is therefore more potent than either music or drama alone. Regardless of whether we agree with Wagner's conception of the proper relationship between man and woman or drama and music, his interpretation is not metaphysical or ascetic.

Wagner abandoned this life-affirming notion of music in favor of Schopenhauer's philosophy, not because he thought Schopenhauer's philosophy of music was true or truer than the view of music and drama Wagner had before he leapt into his opposite. Rather, he saw in

Schopenhauer's philosophy a means to the greater expression of his own will to power and *ultimately*, as a way of leaving his "eternal unreality" so as to become "real" (GM 3.5). By Schopenhauer's interpretation of music, the musician—Wagner—would surmount even the priest in his power over the people, for whereas the priest speaks in words, the will is the fundamental metaphysical reality, and it speaks, not in words, but in wordless music. The musician is therefore closer to the fundamental truth of things than the priest.

Having sketched Schopenhauer's philosophy of music and the grounds for Wagner's choice of Schopenhauer in particular as his prop, Nietzsche digs deeper into Schopenhauer's metaphysical interpretation of music. At the first level of this excavation, Nietzsche reveals that Schopenhauer adopted Kant's "version of the aesthetic problem" (GM 3.5). According to Nietzsche, "Kant thought he was honoring art when among the predicates of beauty he emphasized and gave prominence to those which establish the honor of knowledge: impersonality and universality" (GM 3.6). He indicates Kant is incorrect to think these predicates actually do honor knowledge, let alone beauty. However, he puts aside that criticism in favor of following through with his critique of Kant's aesthetics. Because Kant over-valued so-called pure reason, he concluded beauty is that "which gives us pleasure without interest" (GM 3.5). The problem with this interpretation is, first, that it is gleaned only from the perspective of the spectator—the recipient of an act—not that of the *creator*, the artist, or the *participant* in beauty. In addition, Nietzsche thinks Kant did not have sufficient "*personal* experience," even as a mere spectator of beauty, to describe adequately what this experience truly is (GM 3.6). Kant mistakenly tried to handle the *concept* of beauty without having handled sufficiently the *sensual shape* of beauty, the experience of which is necessarily particular and personal.

Nietzsche fears all philosophers, not excluding the warrior-philosopher Schopenhauer, share this insufficient experience of beauty with Kant. Hence, they also share something of Kant's "fat worm of error" (GM 3.6). We must note, however, that whereas all philosophers prior to Nietzsche may be insufficiently experienced with beauty, the cause of Kant's error with regard to beauty is more intrinsic to him. *Kant is bloodless—deficient in passion.* His bloodlessness is relevant here because philosophy depends upon strong passions that are almost monstrously, madly dedicated to philosophizing. Since Kant is deficient in passion, Nietzsche concludes Kant is not a philosopher, strictly speaking (BGE 210; EH, "The Untimely Ones," 3). He is merely a scholar—a workman or tool in the hands of a genuine philosopher. As a scholar, albeit one of very high capacity, Kant is not to be conflated with the example of Schopenhauer. Rather, Nietzsche implicitly draws a contrast between them that will prove to be meaningful for the resolution of our guiding riddle.

Partly to offset Kant's short-comings and partly to highlight the contrast between the scholar and the warrior-philosopher, Nietzsche contrasts Kant's account of beauty with that of Stendhal, a writer who is a red-blooded, "genuine spectator and artist" (GM 3.6). Contrary to Kant's claim that our appreciation of beauty is disinterested, Stendhal recognizes it as highly interested and egoistic or personal. As he sees it, "the beautiful promises *happiness*" (GM 3.6). Nietzsche punctuates the contrast between this account of beauty and that offered by Kant: "[T]o … [Stendhal] the fact seems to be precisely that the beautiful *arouses the will* ("interestedness")" (GM 3.6). Nietzsche reveals which account he judges to be correct by laughing at those who espouse Kantian aestheticism. Their apologies for this impersonal or unegoistic account betray them, for they point in precisely the opposite direction of what these apologists intend to say:

> If our aestheticians never weary of asserting in Kant's favor that, under the spell of beauty, once can *even* view undraped female statues "without interest," one may laugh a little at their expense: the experiences of *artists* on this ticklish point are more "interesting," and Pygmalion was in any event not necessarily an "unaesthetic man." Let us think the more highly of the innocence of our aestheticians that is reflected in such arguments; let us, for example, credit it to the honor of Kant that he should expatiate on the peculiar properties of the sense of touch with the naïveté of a country parson! (GM 3.5)

Having laid out these two opposing interpretations of beauty, Nietzsche locates Schopenhauer between the sensual artist, Stendhal, and the bloodless scholar, Kant. He observes that Schopenhauer is much closer to the arts than Kant, and he is at least as sensual as Stendhal, although less "happily constituted" (GM 3.6). With this observation, Nietzsche indirectly recalls the impression he gave earlier that the aesthetic human being and the philosopher are distinct human types whose different interests are mutually exclusive and thus preclude the union of an aesthetic sensibility and a philosophic spirit in the same individual. His placement of the modern philosopher, the warrior-philosopher, between Stendhal and Kant indicates the aesthetic sense or passion and its rational compliment—sensibility or aesthetic discernment—exist on a continuum and can co-exist in the same human being.

The conclusion that sense and sensibility can exist together in an individual is supported by our earlier investigation of the evolution of the passions into passionating-reason. We learned that passionating can occur in the absence of reasoning, but reasoning cannot occur without simultaneous passionating, since reason is a more complex expression of the passions. Since *sensibility* or aesthetic discernment is rational, and since reasoning cannot exist without passion, sensibility can only be at work in conjunction with aesthetic passionating—that is, the aesthetic *sense*. Following through this line of thinking, we conclude that, since Schopenhauer is *at least* as sensual as Stendhal, his aesthetic sense is at least as acute as that of the "genuine spectator and artist" (GM 3.6). In addition to having an acute aesthetic sense, Schopenhauer is a philosopher. Hence, he also has a powerful intellect. When combined with a vigorous aesthetic sense, his vigorous intellect can come to take the shape of a highly developed and powerful aesthetic sensibility or discernment. Moreover, by placing the warrior-philosopher between the artist and the intellectual, Nietzsche silently indicates the warrior-philosopher is indeed evolving in the direction of *incorporating the most profound, vigorous sensuality along with the highest spiritualization;* he is evolving into the *artist-philosopher.*[47]

Given that Schopenhauer incorporated a significant degree of both sense and sensibility, we might expect him to have preferred Stendhal's account of beauty over Kant's. This was not the case. Schopenhauer was a proponent of Kantian aesthetics. However, while he "made use of the Kantian version of the aesthetic problem," he did not interpret it as Kant conceived of it and as he intended it to be understood by others. So much for impersonality and universalism! We have in Schopenhauer's treatment of Kant's aesthetics another example of someone re-creating an artifact—a philosophy of aesthetics in this case—by way of an interpretation of it that was not intended by the artifact's original creator.

The difference in the interpretations Kant and Schopenhauer give to the same arrangement of words is traceable to the difference in their sensuality. Unlike Kant, Schopenhauer had a lively sex drive, but he found the agitation it caused him torturous. He wanted relief from it, or so he believed. Kantian aesthetics, as Schopenhauer interpreted it, held the promise of a blissful state of sexual transcendence. Thus, far from regarding beauty as pleasure *without* interest, Schopenhauer adopted Kant's metaphysical aesthetic philosophy for very particular and self-interested reasons.

Nietzsche is quick to add that such torture is not necessarily a cause for gloominess. This observation reminds us of what he said earlier of the opposition between chastity and sensuality that some people genuinely experience in their love affairs: there is no need for this opposition to be tragic. All those who experience this opposition but are "well-constituted, joyful mortals" look upon the "unstable equilibrium" between "'animal and angel'" as a "stimulus to life" (GM 3.2). Nietzsche's account of a life-affirming response to antipodes in the context of inter-personal love is analogous to, if not the same as, the case of Schopenhauer. From Nietzsche's remark that Schopenhauer was not as "happily constituted" as Stendhal, we infer that this philosopher was not the model of a joyful human being. He therefore might not have been able to respond to his antipodes like a joyful mortal. On the other hand, Schopenhauer is surely not a swine; he does not embrace the ascetic ideal because he sees in it only his opposite (GM 3.2). In lieu of either of these options, Nietzsche presents a new alternative. He remarks that some people are invigorated by fighting. Schopenhauer, a warrior-philosopher, was such a one:

> Let us not become gloomy as soon as we hear the word "torture": in this particular case there is plenty to offset and mitigate that word—even something to laugh at. Above all, we should not underestimate the fact that Schopenhauer, who treated sexuality as a personal enemy (including its tool, woman, that *"instrumentum diaboli"*), *needed* enemies in order to keep in good spirits; that he loved bilious, black-green words, that he scolded for the sake of scolding, out of passion; that he would have become ill, become a *pessimist* (for he was not one, however much he desired it), if deprived of his enemies, of Hegel, of women, of sensuality and the whole will to existence, to persistence. Without these, Schopenhauer would *not* have persisted, one may wager on that; he would have run away: but his enemies held him fast, his enemies seduced him ever again to existence; his anger was, just as in the case of the Cynics of antiquity, his balm, his refreshment, his reward, his specific against disgust, his *happiness*. (GM 3.7)

The warrior-philosopher not only thrives by fighting external enemies, he can also be invigorated by fighting himself. Thus, something of the agonistic but life-promoting dynamic that can exist between two people in a love affair can also be incorporated into a single, consciously complex person. Add this information to our portfolio on our guiding riddle.

From Schopenhauer's particular case for adhering to the ascetic ideal, Nietzsche pivots to the meaning of the ascetic ideal for philosophers generally or the philosopher per se. In his very concise, first answer, he combines philosophers with scholars on the grounds that, for both types, the ascetic ideal means "something like a sense and instinct for the most favorable preconditions of higher spirituality" (GM 3.1). When he elaborates on his first answer and speaks of the philosopher alone, he notes a surefire way one can tell who is not a philosopher. All genuine philosophers always had and always will have a peculiar

> irritation at and rancor against sensuality. ... There also exists a peculiar philosophers' prejudice and affection in favor of the whole ascetic ideal; one should not overlook that. Both, to repeat, pertain to the type; if both are lacking in a philosopher, then—one can be sure of it—he is always only a "so-called" philosopher. (GM 3.7)

Nietzsche proceeds to explain that the philosopher is ferociously jealous of his independence and therefore feels some degree of hostility toward anyone and anything that seems to him to threaten his freedom to stand alone. How unlike the artist he is on this point of independence! The philosopher desires and needs independence to attain his maximum experience of life. He feels most alive—*not* necessarily happy—while philosophizing, and philosophizing necessitates independence. It is fundamentally solitary. To be clear, this does not mean it is unloving. To the contrary, true love requires independence or solitude.

The philosopher's ascetic behavior is therefore not what it appears to be. It is not a rejection of sensuality and the human being's generative capacity. Rather, the various forms of the ascetic ideal have value for the philosopher because they reveal ways to independence and hence to philosophy. Of particular note in the context of the discussion of the philosopher's red-bloodedness, ascetic ideals help to isolate and protect the philosopher from what may be most threatening to him; namely, the entanglements and hence the loss of solitude that can come of sensuality in the form of sexual love (see GM 3.8). In lieu of this love, the philosopher is immersed in a profound and severely demanding self-love or self-respect. This self-love aims at philosophizing as the best means of attaining the supreme good. Nietzsche offers an ebullient formulation of this love. In seeming asceticism, he says, the philosopher finds

> an optimum condition for the highest and boldest spirituality and smiles—he does not deny "existence," he rather affirms his existence and only his existence, and this perhaps to the point at which he is not far from harboring the impious wish: *pereat mundus, fiat philosophia, fiat philosophus, **fiam!*** [*Let the world perish, but let there be philosophy, the philosopher, **me!***]. (GM 3.7)

Nietzsche augments this explanation of the meaning of the ascetic ideal in the case of the individual philosopher with an account of what this ideal has meant for the development of the philosophic type. Since Nietzsche is no metaphysician, he does not mean by this that some trans-historical, supra-human spirit guides the evolution of the philosopher per se over the course of generations. Rather, we infer that the proactive evolution of the philosophic type results from the cumulative effects of the philosophic drive that unconsciously and sometimes consciously dominates and commands each individual philosopher to become what he is. Nietzsche describes the workings of this drive in his own life in the "Preface" to *The Genealogy*. He describes it again in the context of explaining the value of the ascetic ideal for the philosophic type:

> A philosopher may be recognized by the fact that he avoids three glittering and loud things: fame, princes, and women—which is not to say they do not come to him. He shuns light that is too bright: that is why he shuns his age and its "day." In this he is like a shadow: the lower his sun sinks the bigger he becomes. As for his "humility," he endures a certain dependence and eclipse, as he endures the darkness: more, he is afraid of being distracted by lightning, he shies away from the unprotected isolation of abandoned trees upon which any bad weather can vent its moods, any mood its bad weather. His "maternal instinct," the secret love of that which is growing in him, directs him toward situations in which he is relieved of the necessity of thinking *of himself*, in the same sense in which the instinct of the *mother* in woman has hitherto generally kept woman in a dependent situation. ... Ultimately they ask for little enough... [T]heir motto is "he who possesses is possessed," *not*, as I must say again and again, from virtue, from a laudable will to contentment and simplicity, but because their supreme lord demands this of them, prudently and inexorably: he is con-

cerned with one thing alone, and assembles and saves up everything—time, energy, love, and interest—only for that one thing. ...

As for the "chastity" of philosophers, finally, this type of spirit clearly has its fruitfulness somewhere else than in children; perhaps it also has the survival of its name elsewhere, its little immortality . ... There is nothing in this of chastity from any kind of ascetic scruple or hatred of the senses, just as it is not chastity when an athlete or jocky abstains from women: it is rather the will of their dominating instinct, at least during periods of great pregnancy. ... [S]ensuality is not ovecome by the appearance of the aesthetic condition, as Schopenhauer believed, but only transfigured and no longer enters consciousness as sexual excitement. (GM 3.8)

The ascetic ideal has also served throughout the philosophic type's genealogy as a cocoon for its gestation into maturity (GM 3.10). The frighteningly severe and seemingly anti-natural mask of asceticism has protected the philosopher against the intrusions and interruptions to his work by other people. At least as importantly, it has protected the pre- and immature philosopher against a clear-sighted knowledge of what he is, of what his true task is. The ascetic ideal has thereby served a purpose for the philosopher that is analogous to the purpose the philosopher has served for the artist; it has been the philosopher's protection and prop. The problem of the ascetic ideal is thus duplicated.

If the philosopher had glimpsed himself and his task too soon, he would have been destroyed by what he saw. More precisely, he would have destroyed himself. Up to the point of becoming the warrior, the philosopher needed to believe the human being was by nature, understood as something teleological or something that moves as though guided by a mind, by God. He was not yet ready to see the true indeterminacy of what we are, for such a sight is most terrible, if also most thrilling. Regarding himself more specifically, the philosopher also needed to think he was more average or typical than he is. Just as he was not ready to see how undetermined the human being and our human future is, he was also not ready to realize how solitary he is and must be, as the only human being that has the genuine capacity to be the vanguard who consciously leads the human being into a genuine future. We say this without suggesting the philosopher will succeed in this role. We mean only that he is equipped to make the attempt, and the attempt is as good as an opportunity as there ever has been or will be. A valiant, good attempt to overcome oneself and the human being is *more* than *adequate*. It is *good;* it is the best way of human life. The alternative, which would be a cowardly and thoughtless surrender to mindlessness, is neither more secure nor good. Indeed, we must be most clear on this point: if the philosopher is destroyed and fails to lead the human being into a genuine future at this point in our genealogy, the human being will *necessarily* devolve. Our genealogy has brought us to a stage of evolution in which we are poised to direct our growth consciously, guided by the philosopher. Any form of turning back or turning aside from this stage of evolution and the task it brings with it would constitute devolution. This remains true in spite of the fact that we have yet to resolve our guiding riddle and its implications sufficiently to have a good idea of how to move ahead or of what "ahead" looks like. Onward!

The warrior-philosopher seems strong enough now to see what he is sufficiently to take up this task. He has become "ripe and sweet" (GM 1.5). However, to say he has the necessary strength to attempt to lead the human being into a future is not to say he has actually seen yet what he must see about himself and his task. In fact, the warrior-philosopher has not seen with sufficient clarity what he is. In truth, he is still in the cocoon of the ascetic ideal. He therefore certainly does not know how to proceed with his mission.

Nietzsche looks on in suspense, watching to see whether the warrior-philosopher will become fully what he is and metamorphose into the latest, youngest form of the philosopher. We have named this new shape the artist-philosopher. We have indicated he unifies in his physio-psychology characteristics of the artist and the intellectual in such a way that he has maximum sensuality and maximum sensibility. Schopenhauer, as the modern form of the philosopher, the warrior-philosopher, had both sense and sensibility. However, like a fighter fighting himself, too, he held the antipodes of sensuality and artistry in the one hand and, in the other, the mental acuity that characterize a thinker like Kant. Thus, we might characterize him as gravely or solemnly happy, like a warrior in battle where he has the edge (BGE 226).

As with the earlier, simpler shapes of the philosopher, we expect the artist-philosopher incorporates the warrior's attributes. Unlike the warrior-philosopher, however, the artist-philosopher is not characterized by gravity or weighty seriousness. Rather, Nietzsche uses a beautiful metaphor of a colorful, flying creature to describe something of the light-heartedness and delightfulness of this latest shape of the philosopher.

Nietzsche's description of the winged creature he hopes will emerge from the cocoon of the ascetic ideal serves as an immediate transition to the meaning of the ascetic ideal for the priest. By moving directly from his concerns about whether the dangerous winged creature will emerge to his analysis of the value of the ascetic ideal for the priest, Nietzsche implicitly indicates the dangerous flying creature's fate is somehow tied up with the priest's use of the ascetic ideal. He begins his analysis of the priest by informing us: "Only now that we behold the *ascetic priest* do we seriously "come to grips with our problem: what is the meaning of the ascetic ideal?—only now does it become 'serious' ['*Ernst*']," weighty, or grave: we are now face to face with the actual *representative of seriousness*" or gravity (GM 3.11). Since the many-colored, dangerous creature flies, and since the priest is the representative of gravity, we infer that the main threat to the emerging winged creature is gravity or a certain grim seriousness, for of course gravity opposes flight. We are not in a position to say more about this at this point, but we must be on the look-out for a further elucidation of this threat as we proceed.

Having introduced the priest as the actual representative of gravity, Nietzsche asks a question and then comments provocatively upon it:

> "What is the meaning of all seriousness?"—this even more fundamental question may perhaps be trembling on our lips at this point: a question at this point: a question for physiologists, of course, but one that we must still avoid for the moment. (GM 3.11)

The meaning of gravity is "more fundamental" than the question of the meaning of the ascetic ideal for the priest. So significant is this more profound issue of gravity that it may even make Nietzsche's lips tremble. With fear? With excitement? He tells us he will not speak further of seriousness or gravity "for the moment" (GM 3.11). Accompanying this tease is a quiet promise to speak of it later, but he does not do so in what remains of the essay. Add this puzzle to our portfolio on our guiding riddle and put it aside "for the moment." We shall come back to it, again.

Nietzsche's silence following his tease returns us to the immediate question of the value of the ascetic ideal for the ascetic priest. We have already discussed some of the ways in which the ascetic ideal has value for the priest's life. We know the priest uses it as a means of gaining influence over the many and as a weapon against all things noble. To the extent that we revisit the priest here, we will do so with a view to resolving our guiding riddle. With this goal in our sights, we divide Nietzsche's treatment of the priest into two basic parts. In the first part, Nietzsche discusses what we might loosely call the priest's good attributes and practices. We say loosely because their goodness is not inherent to what they are or how they are employed. It depends instead upon Nietzsche's ability to read in them ways in which they could augment, rather than thwart, thriving life.

In the part about the "good" things associated with the priest's use of the ascetic ideal, several things immediately strike us. First, the priest is a remarkable reader or interpreter, and he is an incredible writer or spinner of tales. He alone offers a comprehensive interpretation of the entire cosmos, including and especially the whole history of the human being. His reading or interpretation of the human being thereby encompasses everything significant to the human being.

He then goes beyond the human world or cosmos by enveloping this cosmology in a metaphysics "grounded" in an imaginary world *beyond* the cosmos or the human world. With this concoction of a metaphysical order and hence of the moral-theological prejudice, the priest turns life upon her head. In so doing, he tells the most fundamental and all-pervasive of lies.

Nietzsche admires and marvels at the priest's audacious ambition to become master over life itself, by way of the ascetic interpretation of it:

> [A]n ascetic life is a self-contradiction: here rules a *ressentiment* without equal, that of an insatiable instinct and power-will that wants to become master not over something in life but over life itself, over its most profound, powerful, and basic conditions; here physiological well-being is viewed askance, and especially the outward expression of this well-being, beauty and joy; while pleasure is felt and *sought* in ill-constitutedness, decay, pain, mischance, ugliness, voluntary deprivation, self-mortification, self-flagellation, self-sacrifice. All this is in the highest degree paradoxical: we stand before a discord that *wants* to be discordant, that *enjoys* itself in this suffering and even grows more self-confident and triumphant the more its own presupposition, its physiological capacity for life, decreases. "Triumph in ultimate agony": the ascetic ideal has always fought under this hyperbolic sign; in this enigma of seduction, in this image of torment and delight, it recognized its brightest light, its salvation, its ultimate victory. (GM 3.11; see also AC 38)

It is perverse—a sign of degenerating and corrupt life—to find one's triumph in trying to undermine thriving life; one's ego, one's reason (GM 3.12). Nevertheless, Nietzsche sees something he can approve in this effort. He fleshes out this insight, beginning with the observation that the philosopher should "not be ungrateful to such resolute reversals of accustomed perspectives and valuations with which the spirit has, with apparent mischievousness and futility, raged against itself for so long" (GM 3.12). Given that the philosopher per se assumed the guise of the ascetic for so long, fooling even himself with it, it is not surprising that something of this ideal has become blood in him. By raging against himself, he has finally developed the *desire* to assume a different perspective. Nietzsche expects this development is

> preparation of the intellect for its future 'objectivity'—the latter understood not as 'contemplation without interest' (which is a nonsensical absurdity), but as the ability to control one's Pro and Con and to dispose of them, so that one knows how to employ a variety of perspectives and affective interpretations in the service of knowledge. (GM 3.12)

The ability to control one's Pro and Con in order to see differently belongs to the true kind of objectivity. It can contribute to growth, and it belongs to a more evolved human being. Hence, the capacity and the desire to see differently is the second "good" thing we unearth from the question of the meaning of the ascetic ideal for the priest.

The third "good" thing is that the priest is so disgruntled with himself that he is constantly looking to be other than what he is. Partly because of the priest's successful pitch for influence, some degree of self-disgruntlement has become the norm among human beings. The vital weakness or sickness that gives rise to this self-disgruntlement is bad per se. However, Nietzsche links this vital impotence or sickness to growth; that is, by being constantly disgruntled with himself, the priest and those who inherit something of the priest's self-disgruntlement become future-oriented. In a more promising form than that which the priest embodies, this future-directedness conduces to growth. It becomes pregnancy both for the individual and for the species or the human being per se:

> The ascetic priest is the incarnate desire to be different, to be in a different place, and indeed this desire at its greatest extreme, its distinctive fervor and passion; but precisely this power of his desire is the chain that holds him captive so that he becomes a tool for the creation of more favorable conditions for being here and being human—it is precisely this *power* that

enables him to persuade to existence the whole herd of the ill-constituted, disgruntled, underprivileged, unfortunate, and all who suffer of themselves by instinctively going before them as their shepherd. You will see my point: this ascetic priest, this apparent enemy of life, this *denier*—precisely he is among the greatest *conserving* and yes-creating forces of life.... [The human being] is *the* sick animal: how has that come about? Certainly he has also dared more, done more new things, braved more and challenged fate more than all the other animals put together: he, the great experimenter with himself, discontented and insatiable, wrestling with animals, nature, and gods for ultimate domination—he, still unvanquished, eternally directed toward the future, whose own restless energies never leave him in peace, so that his future digs like a spur into the flesh of every present—how should such a courageous and richly endowed animal not also be more imperiled, the most chronically and profoundly sick animals of all sick animals? ... The No he says to life brings to light, as if by magic, an abundance of tender Yeses; even when he *wounds* himself, this master of destruction, of self-destruction—the very wound itself afterward compels him *to live.*— (GM 3.13)

Turning now to the priest's bad uses of the ascetic ideal, Nietzsche highlights the priest's arousal of orgies of feeling in sufferers as a means of temporarily alleviating their pain. The priest is ever-focused on discovering new ways of inducing these orgies and he uses them liberally. We know the chief method he employs is the ascetic moral interpretation of bad conscience so that the pain associated with it is believed to be punishment for one's guilt. We also know Nietzsche condemns the priest's use of orgies of feelings as "guilty" because they induce further degeneration. In the context of our current investigation, we should now add to this account Nietzsche's observation that the priest does not realize he worsens his sufferer's condition by these orgies. Thus, he uses them "with a good conscience," profoundly convinced of their efficacy (GM 3.20).

Nietzsche observes that the priest's pervasive use of orgies of feeling, together with his massive influence in at least the Western world have so weakened the human being's physio-psychology that these orgies are *"the true calamity* in the history of European health" (GM 3.21). The only other things that have had comparable degenerative effects, he says, are alcoholism and syphilis, although this latter cause is a distant third from the first two causes.

Nietzsche connects this degeneration to a general decline in taste

or the aesthetic sense and sensibility. That is, human beings in general
no longer have a clear awareness of what constitutes their growth and
their degeneration. In other words, they have become corrupt. The prime
example he uses to illustrate this decline in taste is books. His use of
books as a means of illustrating this decline also reminds us he remains
focused on the theme of reading and writing. Specifically, he contrasts
the Jewish Bible or Old Testament, which he regards as an unsurpassed
masterpiece of taste and of an education in taste, with the Christian
Bible or New Testament, which he regards as tasteless:

> Even in the midst of Graeco-Roman splendor, which was also a splen-
> dor of books, in the face of an ancient literary world that has not yet eroded
> and been ruined, at a time when one could still read some books for whose
> possession one would nowadays exchange half of some national literatures,
> the simplicity and vanity of Christian agitators—they are called Church
> Fathers—had the temerity to declare: "we, too, have a classical literature,
> *we have no need of that of the Greeks*"; and saying this they pointed proudly
> to books of legends, letters of apostles, and apologetic tracts, rather as the
> English "Salvation Army" today employs similar literature in its struggle
> against Shakespeare and other "pagans."
>
> I do not like the "New Testament," that should be plain; I find it
> almost disturbing that my taste in regard to this most highly esteemed and
> overestimated work should be so singular (I have the taste of two millennia
> *against* me): but there it is! "Here I stand, I cannot do otherwise"—I have
> the courage of my bad taste. The *Old* Testament—that is something else
> again: all honor to the Old Testament! I find in it great human beings, a
> heroic landscape, and something of the very rarest quality in the world,
> the incomparable naïveté of the *strong heart*; what is more, I find a people.
> In the New one, on the other hand, I find nothing but petty sectarianism,
> mere rococo of the soul, mere involutions, nooks, queer things, the air of
> the conventicle, not to forget an occasional whiff of bucolic mawkishness
> that belongs to the epoch (*and* to the Roman province) and is not so much
> Jewish as Hellenistic. Humility and self-importance cheek-by-jowl; a gar-
> rulousness of feeling that almost stupefies; impassioned vehemence, not
> passion; embarrassing gesticulation; it is plain that there is no trace of good
> breeding. How can one make such a fuss about one's little lapses as these
> pious little men do! Who gives a damn! Certainly not God. Finally, they
> even want "the crown of eternal life," these little provincial people; but for
> what? to what purpose? Presumption can go no further. ...
>
> It is easy to see that the ascetic ideal has never and nowhere been a
> school of good taste, even less of good manners—at best it was a school of
> hieratic manners: that is because its very nature includes something that

is the deadly enemy of all good manners—lack of moderation, dislike of moderation; it itself is a *"non plus ultra"* [*"ultimate extreme"*] (GM 3.22)

Nietzsche then links this decline in taste with an increased predilection for what he calls "dishonest" lying rather than "honest" lying. Honest lies are those wherein the liar is candid with himself about what he is doing. To be frank with oneself about one's acts requires strength and good taste. It also means one has what Nietzsche deems a good scientific or intellectual conscience. By contrast, the dishonest liar averts his eyes from what he is, and from what he is doing when he lies. He lacks the strength or good taste to be honest with himself. He is therefore deficient in, or devoid of, and intellectual conscience. Nietzsche observes that modern human beings tend to be dishonest liars, and modern books are rife with them:

> If a psychologist today has *good taste* (others might say, integrity) it consists in resistance to the shamefully moralized way of speaking which has gradually made all modern judgments of men and things slimy. One should not deceive oneself in this matter: the most distinctive feature of modern souls and modern books is not lying but their inveterate *innocence* in moralistic mendaciousness. To have to rediscover this "innocence" everywhere—this constitutes perhaps the most disgusting job among all the precarious tasks a psychologist has to tackle today; it is a part of *our* great danger—it is a path that may lead precisely *us* toward great nausea. … Our educated people of today, our "good people," do not tell lies—that is true; but that is *not* to their credit! A real lie, a genuine, resolute, "honest" lie (on whose value one should consult Plato) would be something far too severe and potent for them: it would demand of them what one *may* not demand of them. That they should open their eyes to themselves, that they should know how to distinguish "true" and "false" in themselves. All they are capable of is a *dishonest* lie; whoever today accounts himself a "good man" is utterly incapable of confronting any matter except with *dishonest mendaciousness*—a mendaciousness that is abysmal but innocent, truehearted, blue-eyed, and virtuous. These "good men"—they are one and all moralized to the very depths and ruined and botched to all eternity as far as honesty is concerned: who among them could endure a single *truth* "about man"? Or, put more palpably: who among them could stand a *true* biography? (GM 3.19)

Nietzsche's distinction between honest and dishonest lies may seem troubling in terms of his own philosophy. One may wonder how he makes what seems to be a moral judgment about different kinds of lies while also promulgating the value of living beyond the moral notions of good and evil. To be beyond good and evil, however, is not to be beyond good and bad or, to say the same thing differently, beyond our inherent judgment that thriving life is good and degenerating life per se is bad or unchoiceworthy. We punctuate his account of honest and dishonest lies this way. Because honest lies and liars are strong, they manifest the promise of growth, which we love. Or they at least do not threaten us with decay. Dishonest lies and liars are manifestations of declining life, which is inherently repulsive to us. There is something of what we might characterize as Nietzsche's aesthetic morality in Joseph Conrad's character Marlow from *Heart of Darkness*. Marlow does not explicitly distinguish between dishonest and honest lies, but his actions support the distinction. He says that lies, by which he ultimately seems to mean dishonest lies, smell of death: "You know I hate, detest, a flavor of mortality in lies—which is exactly what I hate and detest in the world—what I want to forget. It makes me miserable and sick like biting something rotten would do."[48]

The fact that the priest's use of the moral interpretation of bad conscience to arouse exhausting orgies of feeling is by far the greatest cause of this degeneration of the generality of human beings does not mean he remains in control of it. Remember, he does not know the effects of this "guilty" method of pain relief. He employs it with a good or clear conscience, which is to say he does not lie dishonestly when he advocates it. The truth of the matter is that the degeneration or disintegration of the human being has gotten away from him. He has created a situation over which he no longer has control. Nietzsche explains that bad taste and hence dishonest lying is now in the blood of most human beings. It has literally been incorporated.

Nietzsche observes that the disintegration of the human being, with its attendant bad taste, have produced a bizarre situation wherein the divided human being, driven by the moral-theological prejudice or the ascetic ideal, can now experience the maximum expression of his will to power in the activity of one part of him crushing another part of him that is vital to his possibilities for growth. In other words, he can feel most alive by annihilating himself. Thus, the mass of humanity in at least the Western world is now in a self-induced death spiral.

Against this backdrop, Nietzsche reveals the climax of the third essay and perhaps of the book as a whole. He tells us his entire purpose has been to shed light on the most "ultimate and most terrifying aspect of the question concerning the meaning of . . [the ascetic] ideal" (GM 3.23). This terrifying truth is the total absence of an ideal to oppose the ascetic ideal:

> The ascetic ideal expresses a will: *where* is the opposing will that might express an *opposing ideal?* The ascetic ideal has a *goal*—this goal is so universal that all the other interests of human existence seem, when compared with it, petty and narrow; it interprets epochs, nations, and ... [human beings] inexorably with a view to this one goal; it permits no other interpretation, no other goal; it rejects, denies, affirms, and sanctions solely from the point of view of *its* interpretation (and has there ever been a system of interpretation more thoroughly thought through?) it submits to no power, it believes that no power exists on earth that does not first have to receive a meaning, a right to exist, a value , as a tool of the ascetic ideal, as a way and means to *its* goal, to *one* goal.— Where is the match of this closed system of will, goal, and interpretation? Why has it not found its match?— Where is the other "*one* goal"? (GM 3.23)

The upshot of this most calamitous crisis is that our human genealogy is well on its way to becoming a final, devastating tragedy. Where are the noble warriors of the spirit who might oppose this ideal with one that is life-affirming? Are there no such warriors? Are they not equipped to face this enemy? Where, then, is that multi-colored, dangerous winged creature of whom Nietzsche speaks so highly and hopefully? At this point, Nietzsche's silence seems deafening.

Let us pause at the climax of this essay to take stock of the ground we have covered in it so far and of where we must go next. This survey will help us to keep better track of the essay's complexities and of their relevance for our guiding riddle. For clarity and as a helpful mnemonic, let us call the part of the essay preceding the climax the "Who" of the ascetic ideal, since it analyzes various human types for whom the ascetic ideal has meaning. In the case of each human type, we highlighted attributes that will prove helpful in resolving our riddle. We also made note of the pregnant absence of an extended treatment of those women who make the best use of the ascetic ideal: namely, the seducers. The climax itself describes the urgent task that lies before the human being and, more specifically, the artist-philosopher. In keeping with Nietzsche's warspeak, we can regard the climax as an exceptionally concise briefing on the mission moving forward. We will call it the "What" of the task at hand. Succinctly, this mission is to discover or create an ideal that opposes the ascetic ideal. The climax or apex of the essay also affords an overview and perspective upon what lies before us in the remainder of the book. Scanning it, we identify the major sweep or movement of thought as the "How" of the mission. Perhaps Nietzsche gives us less than we might wish in this regard. He tells us how the mission is to be executed indirectly, by exposing how it *cannot* be done. He speaks of our failures to overcome the most urgent and dangerous threat that has ever faced us, and he analyzes those warriors and would-be who are still inadequate to the task. With that, we begin the denouement.

The first people we meet in the realm of "How" fall into three categories. They propose what they regard as plausible fighters against the ascetic ideal, or they present themselves as such warriors, or they are addressed by Nietzsche as people who are likely to be solicited for help in the battle against the ascetic ideal or, more precisely, modern nihilism. The first seeming warrior we meet in this realm of "How" is not a human being at all. Rather, it is modern science. It is thrust at us by its fans, who regard it with a kind of religious devotion that is typically reserved for a god. They say science

> has not merely waged a long and successful fight against this ideal, it has already conquered this ideal in all important respects: all of modern science is supposed to bear witness to that—modern science which, as a genuine philosophy of reality, clearly believes in itself alone, clearly possesses the courage for itself and the will to itself, and has up to now survived well enough without God, the beyond, and the virtues of denial. (GM 3.23)

These cheerleaders of science are reminiscent in their shallowness of the sham free spirit from the first essay of *The Genealogy*. Nietzsche regards them with more than skepticism; he regards them with contempt and perhaps some disgust. His observation about them and the insufficiency of their faith is savagely direct. Of particular note, he tells us they are not scientists, for they are too shallow to contain the "abyss" of the scientific conscience:

> Such noisy agitators' chatter … does not impress me: these trumpeters of reality are bad musicians, their voices obviously do not come from the depths, the abyss of the scientific conscience does not speak through them—for today the scientific conscience is an abyss—the word "science" in the mouths of such trumpeters is simply an indecency, an abuse, and a piece of imprudence. (GM 3.23)

The scientific or intellectual conscience to which Nietzsche refers here recalls and develops what he says of the decline of good taste or integrity. In his book, *The Gay Science*, Nietzsche describes the intellectual conscience as the self-imposed demand for a self-justification—an account before oneself of what one is and of how one lives. We recognize this demand as one that could be made legitimately only by a super-abundantly vital rational animal. Only this kind of person would have both the necessary courage and the rational capacity to ask and respond to such a question sufficiently. This is not to say everyone else is entirely off the hook, so to speak. Nietzsche has an aesthetic response to the human being who has reason, but who lies to himself in order to live as though he were a *non*-rational animal. He is repulsed by the decay that manifests in someone who tells these dishonest lies:

> *The intellectual conscience.* — I keep having the same experience and keep resisting it every time. I do not want to believe it although it is palpable: *the great majority of people lacks an intellectual conscience.* Indeed, it has often seemed to me as if anyone calling for an intellectual conscience were as lonely in the most densely populated cities as if he were in a desert. Everybody looks at you with strange eyes and goes right on handling his scales, calling this good and that evil. Nobody even blushes when you intimate that their weights are underweight; nor do people feel outraged; they merely laugh at your doubts. I mean: *the great majority of people* does not consider it contemptible to believe this or that and to live accordingly, without first having given themselves an account of the final and most certain reasons pro and con, and without even troubling themselves about such reasons afterward: the most gifted men and the noblest women still belong to this "great majority." But what is good-heartedness, refinement, or genius to me, when the person who has these virtues tolerates slack feelings in his faith and judgments and when he does not account the desire for certainty as his inmost craving and deepest distress—as that which separates the higher human beings from the lower. ... [T]o stand in the midst of this *rerum Concordia discors [discordant concord of things]* and of this whole marvelous uncertainty and rich ambiguity of existence *without questioning*, without trembling, without at least hating the person who questions, perhaps even finding him faintly amusing—that is what I feel to be contemptible, and this is the feeling for which I look first in everybody. Some folly keeps persuading me that every human being has this feeling, simply because he is human. This is my type of injustice. (GS 2; see also AC 38)

Having dismissed these advocates of science, Nietzsche gives his own general assessment of scientists or scholars. He tells us "the truth is precisely the opposite" of what the shallow advocates of modern science assert. "[S]cience today has absolutely *no* belief in itself, let alone an ideal above it—and where it still inspires passion, love, ardor, and suffering at all, it is not the opposite of the ascetic ideal but rather the *latest and noblest form of it*" (GM 3.23).

He proceeds to explain this insight by dividing modern scientists into two groups and analyzing each of them. The first sub-category is comprised of people whom Nietzsche identifies as scientific or scholarly laborers. They use science as a hiding place and distraction from their self-suffering. Therefore, for them, scientific or scholarly labor is something like an erudite version of the mechanical activity the ascetic priest prescribes to his sufferers as a means to temporary pain relief. Largely because these scholars do not love this activity, but instead employ it as a self-distraction, they are content in their little nooks of obscure inquiry and information gathering. This work can be useful, and Nietzsche does not seek to ruin the kind of contentment they find in it. However, he does insist it is fantastic to think these human beings have what is necessary to counter the ascetic ideal. "[T]hat one works rigorously in the sciences and that there are contented workers certainly does *not* prove that science as a whole possesses a goal, a will, an ideal, or the passion of a great faith" (GM 3.23).

The second sub-category of science is comprised of a rare few human beings—"the last idealists left among philosophers and scholars" (GM 3.24). These few step up of their own accord to announce their belief that they are the warriors to fight the ascetic ideal. Indeed, they claim they have been dedicating their lives primarily to this fight.

Nietzsche grants something of their claim. They are willing to exhaust their vitality in spiritual battle. "[T]hey are so serious on this point, so passionate about it in word and gesture, that the faith that they are opponents of this ideal seems to be the last remnant of faith they have left" (GM 3.24). On the other hand, their passionate commitment to their faith that they fight the ascetic ideal does not make their faith true. Rather, in the era of the passionating-animal, vehement, enthusiastic faith is so suspect as to be nearly enough to prove the opposite of what is proclaimed.

> We "men of knowledge" have gradually come to mistrust believers of all kinds; our mistrust has gradually brought us to make inferences the reverse

of those of former days: whenever the strength of a faith is very prominently displayed, we infer a certain weakness of demonstrability, even the *improbability* of what is believed. We, too, deny that faith "makes blessed": that is precisely *why* we deny faith *proves* anything—a strong faith that makes blessed raises suspicion against that which is believed; it does not establish "truth," it establishes a certain probability of—*deception*. (GM 3.24)

Nietzsche's suspicion is well-founded, for the truth to which these rare few dedicate themselves and for which they are willing to expend their vitality is itself an ascetic concept. It is truth as defined by the moral-theological prejudice.

Nietzsche again presents his criticism of this human type alongside a genuine acknowledgement of what is impressive in these few. He depicts them as "hard, severe, abstinent, heroic" (GM 3.24). He adds that these "pale atheists, anti-Christians, immoralists ... these last idealists of knowledge" are the "honor of our age" (GM 3.24). Solely in their blood does the intellectual conscience run and thus remain "incarnate today" (GM 3.24). Nevertheless, in their devotion to the ascetic concept of truth, these "free, *very* free" spirits are also the embodiment of the most seductive, secret, and robust form of the ascetic ideal today (GM 3.24).

Recall the way the philosopher has unconsciously lived in the cocoon and mask of his enemy, the ascetic priest. Now, we see more fully how dangerous his lack of self-knowledge and self-consciousness is both to him and to the future of the human being. He is not merely living with the enemy. He is not merely disguising himself as the enemy. Rather, because he is too ignorant of what he is, he is also fighting on the side of the enemy. Unbeknownst to himself, he is thereby advancing his own and the human being's self-inflicted and self-sustained death spiral. In short, the modern philosopher seems to be as close as he can come to the ascetic priest without being the ascetic priest! —Or, is he, in fact, the modern shape of the ascetic priest? His zealous faith in the ascetic concept of truth is certainly fundamentally the same as the ascetic priest's belief in God. Nietzsche seems intent upon raising these questions in our minds. He tells us: "[I]f I have guessed any riddles, I wish that *this* proposition might show it!— They are far from being *free* spirits: for *they still have faith in truth*" (GM 3.24).

You do not see their asceticism? Approach Nietzsche's observation from a different angle. Ask: if the philosopher does not understand his opposition to the ascetic ideal in terms of the value he accords to truth—

understood as something pure, unchanging, supra-perspectival; hence metaphysical, hence ascetic—how would he justify to his intellectual conscience his value and the value of his philosophic activity?

Where does this leave the philosopher? Including himself, some part of himself, or a prior version of himself in this group, Nietzsche reviews how philosophers in general arrived at this crisis point:

> It is still a metaphysical faith that underlies our faith in science—and we men of knowledge of today, we godless human beings and anti-metaphysicians, we too, still derive our flame from the fire ignited by a faith millennia old, the Christian faith, which was also Plato's, that God is truth, that truth is divine.—But what if this belief is becoming more and more unbelievable, if nothing turns out to be divine any longer unless it be error, blindness, lies—if God himself turns out to be our *longest lie?*" (GM 3.25)

The very attributes of the philosopher that Nietzsche praises as genuinely impressive—especially the philosopher's intellectual conscience—will drive him inevitably to the question of the value of truth. Why truth at all? "Why not rather untruth? and uncertainty? even ignorance?" (BGE 1) . Unless the philosopher has an adequate answer to this question, he will direct his vitality explicitly and overtly to self-annihilation. Schopenhauer did this already. He is the harbinger of the general fate of philosophers and of philosophy, unless we get off of our current nihilistic course. Nietzsche sketches this impending fate:

> At this point it is necessary to pause and take careful stock. Science itself henceforth *requires* justification (which is not to say that there is any such justification). Consider on this question both the earliest and most recent philosophers: they are all oblivious of how much the will to truth itself first requires justification; here there is a lacuna in every philosophy—how did this come about? Because the ascetic ideal has hitherto *dominated* all philosophy, because truth was posited as being, as God, as the highest court of appeal—because truth was not *permitted* to be a problem at all. Is this "permitted" understood?—From the moment faith in the God of the ascetic ideal is denied, *a new problem arises*: that of the value of truth.
>
> The will to truth requires a critique—let us thus define our own task— the value of truth must for once be experimentally *called into question*. (GM 3.24)

Returning to a consideration of science in general, Nietzsche expands upon his initial dismissal of scientists as plausible opponents of the ascetic ideal. It seems unlikely that the rare few are included in these general criticisms. He begins with the observation that science is "not nearly self-reliant enough to be" the "natural antagonist of the ascetic ideal" (GM 3.25). Insofar as the scientist cannot stand alone, he is reminiscent of the artist (see GM 3.1; GM 3.5). However, whereas the artist's lack of independence arises from his need for an established authority to serve as a prop and protection, especially against his own physio-psychological insubstantiality in the external world, modern science lacks independence because it does not believe in its own value, and it is incapable of creating values. Thus, it "first requires in every respect an ideal of value, a value-creating power, in the *service* of which it could *believe* in itself" (GM 3.25). Since only the ascetic ideal has existed to date, this is the ideal from which science has taken its value. Since its value comes from the ascetic ideal, it does not truly oppose it. Rather, it "may even be said to represent the driving force" in the ascetic ideal's "inner development" (GM 3.25).[49] Scientific work has cleared away what is exoteric—the exterior flotsam and jetsam surrounding this ideal. By so doing, it has liberated the "life" in this ideal (GM 3.25). Science and the ascetic ideal are also allied by their shared assumption that the value of truth is "inestimable and cannot be questioned" (GM 3.25). Finally, both science and the ascetic ideal are rooted in the same physio-psychological cause: namely, vital impotence. This impotence is the most fundamental linkage between these two. It undergirds all the other connections. Science cannot create values because it is vitally impotent; it lacks self-respect because it is vitally impotent; and science believes in the metaphysical or ascetic notion of truth because it is vitally impotent.

Nietzsche concludes his thoughts with a final shot at those who suggest modern astronomy does not fit into his account of science, since it seems to reveal a universe devoid of God and of the human being's special place in it. To this claim regarding what Nietzsche calls "theological astronomy," he retorts:

> Since Copernicus, … *[a]ll* science … natural as well as unnatural—which is what I call the self-critique of knowledge—has … the object of dissuading the human being from his former respect for himself, as if this had been nothing but a piece of bizarre conceit. One might say that its own pride, its own austere form of stoical ataraxy, consists in sustaining this hard-won self-contempt of the human being as his ultimate and most serious [or grave] claim to self-respect. (GM 3.25)

These considerations lead Nietzsche to dismiss the scientist as a potential spiritual warrior who can oppose the ascetic ideal. Before moving to the next possible candidate for this mission, we circle back to note an oddity that occurs in the midst of Nietzsche's account of the reasons why science has failed and will continue to fail to oppose the ascetic ideal. Just after our observation that the scientist is akin to the artist in his inability to stand alone, Nietzsche says modern science and the ascetic ideal share the same over-estimation of truth. He then makes what seems to be a digression. He notes a field that, unlike science, is "fundamentally opposed" to the ascetic ideal and is its genuine antagonist. This field is art. He characterizes the fundamental, genuine antagonism between science and art by way of two great—possibly the two greatest—writers on each side in this battle: "Plato versus Homer" (GM 3.25). He also tells us he will at some time return to this subject at greater length, but he does not do so in what remains of the third essay of *The Genealogy*. Of course, he may mean he will return to discuss the opposition between science and art in a different work. We do not rule out this reading. However, given that he also promised earlier to return to the question of graveness, apparently in *this* book, plus the fact that he does not engage explicitly in a further discussion of gravity in what remains of the third essay, we must be open to the possibility that he repeats this kind of promise and pattern here again with respect to the war between science and art. Add this possibility to the information we are gathering to resolve our guiding riddle. Add also Nietzsche's observation that art has always been the fundamental and genuine antagonist of science, together with his account of why art and science have so far been opposed. Finally, note Nietzsche's judgment on the artist who places himself in the service of the ascetic ideal. This judgment clearly pertains to Wagner:

> (*Art*—to say it in advance, for I shall some time return to this subject at greater length—art, in which precisely the *lie* is sanctified and the will to deception has a good conscience, is much more fundamentally opposed to the ascetic ideal than is science: this was instinctively sensed by Plato, the greatest enemy of art Europe has yet produced. Plato versus Homer: that is the complete, the genuine antagonism—there the sincerest advocate of the "beyond," the great slanderer of life; here the instinctive deifier, the *golden* nature. To place himself in the service of the ascetic ideal is therefore the most distinctive *corruption* of an artist that is at all possible; unhappily, also one of the most common forms of corruption, for nothing is more easily corrupted than an artist.) (GM 3.25)

By presenting the artist as the genuine opponent of the ascetic ideal, we conclude that the spiritual warrior whom Nietzsche seeks is an artist of some kind. By counterpoising Homer to Plato, Nietzsche indicates this spiritual warrior must not only be an artist, he must be a storyteller, an interpreter of history. More precisely, he must be a *poet* of history—literally a *maker* of history. We therefore refine our description of the new shape of the philosopher from the artist-philosopher to the poet-philosopher.

Since poeticizing history emerges as central to the mission, we might hope to find the spiritual warrior who can oppose the ascetic ideal amongst modern writers of histories or, translating the term literally and without any special technical meaning, modern historiographers. Nietzsche considers them next. He notes that modern historiographers pride themselves on being beyond art and interpretation. They present themselves, not as artists of any kind, but as recorders of only facts. They say and may even believe they are *purely* objective or supra-perspectival. They disdain judgments (GM 3.26). These assertions, which are essentially claims to authority couched in the mask of so-called objectivity, presuppose all perspective seeing is lying, and all lies are shameful. In their moral interpretations and judgments of perspectivism and lying, they reveal their belief in foundational aspects of the moral-theological prejudice. Yet, they reject the teleology associated with older interpretations of the moral-theological prejudice. They thereby reveal themselves to be more nihilistic than the older, less naked version of the ascetic ideal.

Nietzsche divides modern historiographers into two groups. He calls the first historical nihilists. Leo Tolstoy typifies this kind of historian:

> [Modern historiography's] noblest claim nowadays is that it is a mirror; it rejects all teleology; it no longer wishes to "prove" anything; it disdains to play the judge and considers this a sign of good taste—it affirms as little as it denies; it ascertains, it "describes" ... All this is to a high degree ascetic; but at the same time it is to an even higher degree *nihilistic*, let us not deceive ourselves about that! One observes a sad, stern, but resolute glance—an eye that looks far, the way a lonely Artic explorer looks far (so as not to look within, perhaps? So as not to look back? ...) Here is snow; here life has grown silent; the last crows whose cries are audible here are called "wherefore?, "in vain!," *"nada!"*—here nothing will grow or prosper any longer, or at the most Petersburg meta-politics and Tolstoian "pity." (GM 3.26)

The second sub-category of historiographers is comprised of sham "contemplatives." They are "even more 'modern'" (GM 3.26), and even more soul-destroying than the historical nihilists. Not only are they nihilistic, but they also take bad taste to a new low of baseness or ugliness:

> [The] "other type of historian, an even more 'modern' type perhaps, a hedonist and voluptuary who flirts both with life and with the ascetic ideal, who employs the word 'artist' as a glove and has today taken sole lease of the praise of contemplation: Oh! how these sweetish and clever fellows make one long even for ascetics and winter landscapes! No! the devil take this type of "contemplative"! I would even prefer to wander through the gloomy, gray, cold fog with those historical nihilists! Indeed, if I *had* to choose I might even opt for some completely unhistorical, anti-historical person. (GM 3.26)

Whereas there is something respectable in the ascetic ideal—its brilliance, its comprehensive interpretation of the world and the human being, the fact that it preserved the will—these sham contemplatives are in no way admirable. Nietzsche focuses in particular on the fact that, while the other groups of people who are openly or inadvertently proponents of the ascetic ideal at least believe it to some degree, the contemplatives do not. They believe in nothing. Yet, they adopt the language of believers and heroes. They do not do so merely out of shallow, passing vanity (GM 3.27). Their comportment is a symptom of *ennui* that makes all-too-similar to The Last Man, the creature in whom the will to life has devolved and dwindled to its lowest recognizably human shape (GM 3.27. See also Z, "Zarathustra's Speeches"). Here, at the lowest of low points amongst sham contemplatives, we find the "latest speculators in idealism, the anti-Semites" (GM 3.27).

In what seems like a moment of relatively idle musings, Nietzsche briefly wonders how many of these speculators, these buffoons or "comedians" of the Christian-moral ideal, would have to be "exported from Europe today before its air would begin to smell fresh again" (GM 3.26). He adds that, if they were exported, they would "idealize" the planet. He then considers more seriously what is required to overcome them. All that would be necessary, he concludes, would be "the hand, the uninhibited, the very uninhibited hand—" (GM 3.26). Do not be over-hasty when interpreting this remark, which may seem initially to suggest he is advocating violence. To understand him, we must hear him, and to hear him, we must begin by attending to the context of his remark. He

is speaking here of the artistic paucity and nihilism of modern historiographers. The modern historiographer arises in contrast to Homer,
one of, and perhaps the, greatest poets of history. Given these facts, we
understand that Nietzsche is not speaking of a violent hand, but of the
hand of a writer. That is, he concludes the only thing needed to cure the
Western world of these buffoons of the Christian-moral ideal is a poetic
historian with a very free hand. He ends the section with this rather
open-ended suggestion.

The subsequent, penultimate section of the essay, begins with the
cry, repeated earlier in the book on three occasions: "Enough! Enough!"
(GM 3.27). He then tells us he plans to write a history, which we reasonably infer is the kind of history he has in mind as the means of sweeping
aside the effects of the sham contemplative's work:

> Enough! Enough! Let us leave these curiosities and complexities of
> the most modern spirit, which provoke as much laughter as chagrin: *our*
> problem, the problem of the meaning of the ascetic ideal, can dispense with
> them: what has this problem to do with yesterday or today! I shall probe
> these things more thoroughly and severely in another connection (under
> the title "On the History of European Nihilism"; it will be contained in a
> work in progress: *The Will to Power: Attempt at a Revaluation of All Values*).
> (GM 3.26)

He does not write a book with this title. Hence, his announcement here
of a chapter in this book seems to pertain to a piece of writing he envi-
sioned, but never completed. However, as with his earlier announcement
that he will write more about the war between science and art, the fact
that he may have planned to write different works on these subjects does
not preclude the possibility that he is also up to something tricky and is
teasing us here. We already suspected as much when he indicated earlier
that he would take up in *this* book the more fundamental question of
the meaning of graveness, and then nothing of this discussion appears
explicitly thereafter. Nor can we forget that he tells us directly that he is
being tricky in this book. Hence, we once again leave open the possibility
that things are not what they seem in this case, too. To sum up, we now
have three instances where Nietzsche says he will speak further on a
topic, and then does not do so in what remains of the third essay. The
first instance is when he says he will speak again of seriousness; the second is when he says he will discuss further the war between philosophy

and art; the third is when he says he will write a history. Ensure all three observations are in the folio on our guiding riddle.

Having announced his own project for a work on history, he makes another striking statement. He tells us he has been concerned here with only one thing; namely, identifying the comedians of the ascetic ideal as the only "kind of real enemy capable of harming it … —for they arouse mistrust of it" (GM 3.27). He calls the sham contemplatives the buffoons or "comedians" of the Christian-moral ideal. Is he now identifying *them* as the proper warriors against the moral-theological prejudice? Buffoons as effective, if unwitting, aids in the fight *against* the ascetic ideal? But these base comedians are not a helpful means to forestalling nihilism. Their writing advances it in its ugliest form. It is therefore more likely that Nietzsche indicates something about the tone or type of poeticized history that is required to oppose the ascetic ideal: it must be a comedy, albeit of a high order, and it must arouse laughter in its audience on occasion. This conclusion is consistent with what he says explicitly in "On Reading and Writing," the section of *Thus Spoke Zarathustra* to which Nietzsche draws our attention at the beginning of the third essay:

> I would believe only in a god who could dance. And when I saw my devil I found him serious, thorough, profound, and solemn: it was the spirit of gravity—through him all things fall.
>
> Not by wrath does one kill but by laughter. Come, let us kill the spirit of gravity! (Z, "On Reading and Writing")

No laughter is aroused by what Nietzsche says next. He wends his way back to the marvelously succinct answer he gave to the meaning of the ascetic ideal in the first section of the third essay. Recall, there he answers: "*That* the ascetic ideal has meant so many things to the human being … is an expression of the basic fact that the human will, its *horror vacui [horror of a vacuum]*: it needs a goal—and it will rather will nothingness than not will" (GM 3.1). Twenty-seven sections later, he offers essentially the same answer, only now we know that he was implicitly including in his first answer the interaction between the genealogy of the ascetic ideal and that of the human being. The way the ascetic ideal expresses itself over time alters in conjunction with alterations in our human physio-psychology. We alter it; it alters us. We are both artist and artifact of our own ideal. What remains, what we have incorporated, deeply because of the ascetic ideal, is the need for meaning. Over time, as our passions have become more reasonable, our need for a rational or scientific account of human life and of our place in the cosmos has also proportionally increased. Throughout these alterations, nothing but the ascetic ideal has responded to our need for meaning.

> *This* is precisely what the ascetic ideal means: that something was *lacking*, that the human being was surrounded by a fearful *void*—he did not know how to justify, to account for, to affirm himself; he *suffered* from the problem of his meaning. He also suffered otherwise, he was in the animal a sickly animal: but his problem was *not* suffering itself, but that there was no answer to the crying question, *"Why* do I suffer?"
>
> The human being, the bravest of animals and the one most accustomed to suffering, does *not* repudiate suffering as such; he desires it, he even seeks it out, provided he is shown a *meaning* for it, a *purpose* of suffering. The meaninglessness of suffering, *not* suffering itself, was the curse that lay over humankind so far—and the ascetic ideal offered the human being meaning! It was the only meaning offered so far; any meaning is better than none at all. … In it, suffering was *interpreted*. … This interpretation—there is no doubt of it—brought fresh suffering with it, deeper, more inward, more poisonous, more life-destructive suffering: it placed all suffering under the perspective of *guilt*.
>
> But all this notwithstanding—the human being was *saved* thereby, he possessed a meaning, he was henceforth no longer like a leaf in the wind, a plaything of nonsense—the "sense-less"—he could now *will* something; no matter to what end, why, with what he willed: *the will itself was saved.* …
>
> We can no longer conceal from ourselves *what* is expressed by all the willing that has taken its direction from the ascetic ideal: this hatred of the human, and even more of the animal, and more still of the material, this horror of the senses, of reason itself, this fear of happiness and beauty, this longing to get away from all appearance, change, becoming, death, wishing, from longing itself—all this means—let us dare to grasp it—*a will to nothingness*, an aversion to life, a rebellion against the most fundamental presuppositions of life; but it is and remains a *will!* … And, to repeat in conclusion what I said at the beginning: man would rather will *nothingness* than *not* will.— (GM 3.28)

Despite the fact that we need meaning and only the ascetic ideal has so far fulfilled this need, the lifespan of this ideal is now drawing to a close. Schopenhauer, the knight of the steely eye, reached the penultimate stage of the life of this ideal, marked as it was by the question of the meaning of life. But this knight succumbed to this question, and the ideal lived on. The ultimate stage in this ideal's dwindling life will arrive when the ascetic ideal turns upon itself and asks for an account of truth or God: "Why truth or God? What is the value of truth or God?" Nietzsche knows this end is immanent, for he alone has already met this question. He is therefore ahead of this time. Meeting this final question in his solitude, he claims it as his own:

> [H]ere I touch again on my problem, on our problem, my *unknown* friends (for as yet I *know* of no friend): what meaning would *our* whole being possess if it were not this, that in us the will to truth becomes conscious of itself as a *problem?*
>
> As the will to truth thus gains self-consciousness—there can be no doubt of that—morality will gradually perish now: this is the great spectacle in a hundred acts reserved for the next two centuries in Europe—the most terrible, most questionable, and perhaps also the most hopeful of all spectacles.— (GM 3.27)

With the question of the meaning of all will to truth, the moral-theological prejudice must self-destruct, for neither we nor it can backtrack on our evolutionary paths; nor can the ascetic ideal answer this question on its own terms; nor are there any other terms.

But this ultimate question in the lifespan of the ascetic ideal is Nietzsche's question! Does he not have an answer to it? Does he not have a will that can oppose the will that undergirds the ascetic ideal? Where is he now? Is there no savior? No warrior-philosopher adequate to the mission? No poet-philosopher?

The book ends, apparently abandoning us in an accelerating, self-inflicted death spiral that we cannot escape and cannot overcome.

Did you fail? —Or did you resolve the riddle?

Chapter Seven

Psyche Airborne

Nietzsche successfully executes the mission to oppose the ascetic ideal because he does not fight only as a warrior-philosopher but also augments the warrior's mode with action from a height, as a many-colored, dangerous, winged creature: as psyche airborne, the poet-philosopher. Thus, by way of his own acts, as they are available to be seen by a careful reading of his work, Nietzsche fulfils his promise to elucidate further the fundamental opposition and genuine antagonism between the artist with the golden nature and the ascetic philosopher. In the poet-philosopher, this opposition is overcome because his vitally potent embodiment of characteristics from each type enables him to rise above and thus oppose the ascetic ideal with a new will and a new kind of ideal, an ideal that lives. View his success from this height.

See first the airborne spirit himself, the poet-philosopher. Nietzsche describes this shape of the philosopher using the metaphor of a caterpillar's metamorphosis into a butterfly. The metaphor cannot be extended too far, since butterflies are not dangerous. Elsewhere, Nietzsche speaks of himself, the model of the poet-philosopher, as a phoenix (EH, "*Thus Spoke Zarathustra*: A Book for All and None"). In several respects, the fire-bird is a more fitting image for the poet-philosopher than the butterfly. Its fiery nature reflects Nietzsche's description of the philosopher's vitality: "Life—that means for us constantly transforming all that we are into light and flame—also everything that wounds us; we simply can do no other (GS "Preface," 3). The phoenix's mythic capacity to resurrect itself from its own spent ashes is also consistent with how the philosopher wounds and exhausts himself in his characteristic activity, only to resurrect and reignite himself by a new, vitalizing transfiguration of his wounds. His wounds are part of his raw material for his re-birth. Speaking of this cycle of cataclysm and rebirth, Nietzsche says: "[W]e have to give birth to our thoughts out of our pain and, like mothers, endow them with all we have of blood, heart, fire, pleasure, passion, agony, conscience, fate, and catastrophe" (GS "Preface," 3. See also Z, "Prologue," 1). Nevertheless, Nietzsche's comparison of the poet-philosopher to the butterfly in third essay of *The Genealogy* highlights some attributes that are crucial to understanding the poet-philosopher and that would be obscured if Nietzsche used the metaphor of the fire-bird here.

One such attribute is the creature's name—"psyche"—which was given to it by Aristotle. In classical Greek, psyche means spirit or mind.[50] By comparing the evolution of the philosopher into the poet-philosopher to the metamorphosis of a caterpillar into a butterfly, therefore, Nietzsche draws attention to an augmentation to the philosopher's way of thinking and being in the world. The philosopher who is less evolved is, according to the metaphor, earth-bound. The activity that he is, including his thinking, crawls along the ground. It is as though, having learned something of the truth that the greatest thoughts are the greatest events in both the inner and the outer realm, he nevertheless continues to move as a crawling thing in both these realms. Speaking less metaphorically, his thinking is labored and relatively limited in scope because he is oppressed by the moral-theological prejudice. In keeping with this oppression, the philosopher in all of his earlier, simpler shapes is characterized by seriousness, by which we do not here mean integrity, intensity of focus or intellectual conscience. We mean an excessive graveness or gravity. In his occasional light-hearted moments, the simpler philosopher may dance, but he dances in chains. However, within the chrysalis or the tomb-like disguise of the religious type, he slowly evolves into the winged creature, psyche airborne.

Once he has transfigured into the poet-philosopher, his thinking and being in the world is no longer characterized by graveness. Rather, his spirit moves with the agility, grace, quickness, and levity that characterize a flying creature. To say he moves in this manner is also to say his activity or his being in the world is joyful and free in a new way. This newborn freedom consists partly in his liberation from the oppressive weight of the moral-theological prejudice, but it is also a positive freedom: namely, the freedom to read and write from the spiritual height that this comportment affords—that is, with astounding style, poetically, beautifully, in a way that inspires the reader and, by so doing, aims to elevate life. Nietzsche speaks of the manner of motion that belongs to the airborne spirit in "On Reading and Writing," the section from which the quotation prefixed to the third essay of *The Genealogy of Morals* is excerpted:

> I have learned to walk: ever since, I let myself run. I have learned to fly: ever since, I do not want to be pushed before moving along.
>
> Now I am light, now I fly, now I see myself beneath myself, now a god dances through me. (Z, "On Reading and Writing")

In *Thus Spoke Zarathustra*, the book from which this quotation is appropriated, the titular character elaborates on this mode of being. He does so in the context of sharing his wish for the grave warrior-philosopher, his immediate predecessor and one whom he likens to a lion (See Z, "On The Three Metamorphoses"). He hopes this warrior will learn to move with a lightness of being and joy, akin to a child at play. He knows such lightness in the context of philosophic thinking astounds the one who is grave (See Z, "On The Three Metamorphoses"). Like all who cannot fly, these grave ones falsely believe profundity must be accompanied by gravity and ponderousness. The beautiful prose Nietzsche attributes to Zarathustra as he expresses his wish testifies to the contrary. It is an excellent illustration of the poet-philosopher's mode of being, thinking, and communicating. It is so beautiful and its effects on the reader are so moving that we offer whole of it. One must experience it to understand it:

> Still is the bottom of my sea: who would guess that it harbors sportive monsters? Imperturbable is my depth, but it sparkles with swimming riddles and laughters.
>
> One who was sublime I saw today, one who was solemn, an ascetic of the spirit; oh, how my soul laughed at his ugliness! With a swelled chest and like one who holds in his breath, he stood there, the sublime one, silent, decked out with ugly truths, the spoil of his hunting, and rich in torn garments; many thorns too adorned him—yet I saw no rose.
>
> As yet he has not learned laughter or beauty. Gloomy this hunter returned from the woods of knowledge. He came home from a fight with savage beasts; but out of his seriousness there also peers a savage beast— one not overcome. He still stands there like a tiger who wants to leap; but I do not like these tense souls, and my taste does not favor all these who withdraw.

And you tell me, friends, that there is no disputing of taste and tasting? But all of life is a dispute over taste and tasting. Taste—that is at the same time weight and scales and weigher; and woe unto all the living that would live without disputes over weight and scales and weighers!

If he grew tired of his sublimity, this sublime one, only then would his beauty commence; and only then will I taste him and find him tasteful. And only when he turns away from himself, will he jump over his shadow—and verily, into his sun. All-too-long has he been sitting in the shadow, and the cheeks of this ascetic of the spirit have grown pale; he almost starved to death on his expectations. Contempt is still in his eyes, and nausea hides around his mouth. Though he is resting now, his rest has not yet lain in the sun. He should act like a bull, and his happiness should smell of the earth, and not of contempt for the earth. I would like to see him as a white bull, walking before the plowshare, snorting and bellowing; and his bellowing should be in praise of everything earthly.

His face is still dark; the shadow of the hand plays upon him. His sense of sight is still in shadows. His deed itself still lies on him as a shadow: the hand still darkens the doer. As yet he has not overcome his deed.

Though I love the bull's neck on him, I also want to see the eyes of the angel. He must still discard his heroic will; he shall be elevated, not merely sublime: the ether itself should elevate him, the will-less one.

He subdued monsters, he solved riddles: but he must still redeem his own monsters and riddles, changing them into heavenly children. As yet his knowledge has not learned to smile and to be without jealousy; as yet his torrential passion has not become still in beauty.

Verily, it is not in satiety that his desire shall grow silent and be submerged, but in beauty. Gracefulness is part of the graciousness of the great-souled.

His arm placed over his head: thus should the hero rest; thus should he overcome even his rest. But just for the hero the beautiful is the most difficult thing. No violent will can attain the beautiful by exertion. A little more, a little less: precisely this counts for much here, this matters most here.

To stand with relaxed muscles and unharnessed will: that is most difficult for all of you who are sublime.

When power becomes gracious and descends into the visible—such descent I call beauty.

And there is nobody from whom I want beauty as much as from you who are powerful: let your kindness be your final self-conquest.

Of all evil I deem you capable: therefore I want the good from you.

Verily, I have often laughed at the weaklings who thought themselves good because they had no claws.

You shall strive after the virtue of the column: it grows more and more beautiful and gentle, but internally harder and more enduring, as it ascends.

Indeed, you that are sublime shall yet become beautiful one day and hold up a mirror to your own beauty. Then your soul will shudder with godlike desires, and there will be adoration even in your vanity.

For this is the soul's secret: only when the hero has abandoned her, she is approached in a dream by the overhero.

Thus spoke Zarathustra. (Z, "On Those Who Are Sublime." See also Z, "On the Higher Man," 20; Z, "The Seven Seals," 6; Z, "On Old and New Tablets," 2; BGE 226)

The poet-philosopher's lightness of being, together with the perspective it affords him, are due to physio-psychological comprehensiveness, combined with super-abundant vitality. We highlighted in particular his incorporation of attributes and drives of both the artist and the philosopher, but he incorporates drives from a variety of other human types as well. Although such comprehensiveness is not necessarily or even typically accompanied by super-abundant vitality, in the poet-philosopher these various drives act with respect to each other in a manner that is super-abundantly vital and life-promoting for the community of drives as whole.

The incorporation of these drives into a new community or complex monad of drives transforms each of them, if not always directly, then by their interactions. Thus, they are no longer exactly what they were when they were part of a different community of drives. It is especially noteworthy that their incorporation into the poet-philosopher's comprehensive physio-psychology means the weaknesses or short-comings that characterized the human type from which these drives were appropriated are either substantially altered or they are countered by the life-promoting drives that characterize another human type that the poet-philosopher has also incorporated. The vitally potent combination of this variety of drives is represented in the butterfly metaphor by the creature's multi-colored wings. The kaleidoscopic colors indicate that the poet-philosopher's capacity to think as he does is due to this multiplicity of his perspectives, beautifully integrated into a complex whole, like the various colors on a butterfly's wings.

Nietzsche addresses this vitally potent comprehensiveness in several works, notably *The Gay Science, Thus Spoke Zarathustra,* and *On the Genealogy of Morals.* The latter book is our main focus here. We look to it to determine what drives come together to create the poet-philosopher. In the third essay of this book, the types the airborne psyche incorporates are the very ones Nietzsche identifies and analyzes as necessary to

understanding the value for life of the ascetic ideal. Work through them
to see the poet-philosopher's attributes in more detail and to understand
more fully why he alone so far has the will to oppose the ascetic ideal and
thus to accomplish the mission.

Begin with woman. As we noted previously, woman is scarcely mentioned in the third essay. Despite the fact that woman is not addressed
at length explicitly, Nietzsche's work—the thinking of a poet-philosopher—is profoundly an expression and celebration of woman's fundamental character as the human shape of maximum generation or becoming and as the seducer who can initiate generation. In this, the poet-philosopher contravenes the philosophic tradition, which over-estimates
the value of absolute being and thereby denigrates becoming. Nietzsche
knows philosophy is not the contemplation of this ascetic concept of
being but is instead equivalent to both genealogy and psychology; that is,
it seeks to understand the fluidity of being and to promote the growth of
the human being. By elucidating and celebrating generation, Nietzsche
aims to return the feminine principle of becoming to its rightful role in
a fecund, agonistic relationship with the masculine principle of being.
Although he is relatively silent about the woman, therefore, the feminine
principle permeates his philosophy because he incorporates the feminine. It is the very air that elevates the airborne psyche and in which this
spirit articulates its movements. If we draw upon Wagner's personified
interpretation of music and drama prior to his leap into his opposite,
we may say the poet-philosopher is the musical-lyrical-philosopher or
the feminine-masculine philosopher, where these terms signify affinities
with the principles of becoming and being respectively. These are all true
descriptors, and we invoke them all in speaking of the poet-philosopher.

When we discussed Nietzsche's analysis of the artist in the third
essay, we noted he is a human type to whom no ideals stick. He has a
kind of Teflon physio-psychology for ideals (GM 3.1; GM 3.5). In this,
the artist is akin to woman. The poet-philosopher shares this physio-psychological immunity insofar as he does not believe in any ideals
that have fixed content. His ideal embraces and promotes the motion of
ascending life.

In addition, recall that, in the context of discussing the scientist as the
embodiment of the ascetic ideal and thus as both unwilling and unable
to oppose it, Nietzsche briefly makes a very significant observation about

art and the artist. He tells us art is "much more fundamentally opposed to the ascetic ideal than is science" (GM 3.25). This fundamental opposition is rooted once again in the artist's physio-psychology, which enables him to lie with a good conscience. In his work, the artist sanctifies the lie. The poet-philosopher comprehends this capacity. Like the artist, he too can and will employ lies with a good conscience. His work also sanctifies the "lie" or the so-called lie, according to the ascetic ideal.

From Schopenhauer, the paradigm of the warrior-philosopher, the poet-philosopher incorporates the courage to face terrible truths and life-threatening opponents, including the most dangerous opponent, the ascetic ideal, as a "knight of a steely eye," without "first waiting for heralds and signs from above" (GM 3.5). The poet-philosopher, like the warrior-philosopher, stands alone, without even God. He has the courage and steadfastness necessary for spiritual solitude, for independent thought.

Although gifted in so many ways, Schopenhauer was unable to rise above the moral-theological prejudice and thereby oppose it effectively. His lack of success on this point is traceable to the fact that, while his warrior characteristics enabled him to face even the most terrible questions, his encounters with these questions were excessively grave. His gravity prevented him from acquiring the spiritual height necessary to review the ascetic ideal within the larger context of the genealogy of the human being. Without this overview, he could not see his way to life-promoting resolutions to ascetic questions. Instead, he fought his way to the question of the meaning of life, the penultimate question in the lifespan of the ascetic ideal. In keeping with his courageous, warrior nature, when Schopenhauer faced this question, he demanded an honest answer to it, regardless of how life-threatening it might be. Because he could not consider the question from an elevated perspective, however, he was left to answer it from within the confines of the moral-theological prejudice itself. He was forced to answer the question only on its own terms. To win on this ground is impossible! He was doomed to fail, and fail he did. Thus, he drew the hard and terrible conclusion that life is meaningless. He then did what his intellectual conscience demanded: he destroyed himself, for he was strong enough to take hold of the knowledge that a life without meaning is not worth living for a human being.

From the ascetic priest, the poet-philosopher comprehends that a reading or interpretation of human life, and of human suffering especially, is vastly more important than facts, including the unavoidable fact of suffering. He comprehends, in addition, that an interpretation that encompasses all significant aspects of human life and that directs the will by its narrative preserves the will. Finally, he extracts from the priest's raging antipodes—which in the priest seem to have the paradoxical configuration of life against life—the capacity and desire to see differently. These two things lay the necessary foundation for *real* objectivity. That is, a super-perspective, afforded by the incorporation of multiple perspectives, together with the will and desire to use each and all of them. We contrast what we here call a *super*-perspective with the sham, nonsensical notion of knowledge that transcends all perspectives. Moving forward, we shall call this impossible knowledge *supra*-perspectival.

The laborers among scientists, whom Nietzsche treats next, are not inspiring. Nevertheless, the poet-philosopher has something of their capacity to do the necessary, dry groundwork of scholarship. He shares something of this "nook-searching," even if only as something he must pass through, and then over. In *Beyond Good and Evil* Nietzsche speaks at greater length of the relationship these scientific laborers have to the genuine philosopher, which we identify as the mature philosopher, the poet-philosopher:

> I insist that people should finally stop confounding philosophical laborers, and scientific men generally, with philosophers; precisely at this point we should be strict about giving "each his due," and not far too much to those and far too little to these.
>
> It may be necessary for the education of a genuine philosopher that he himself has also once stood on all these steps on which his servants, the scientific laborers of philosophy, remain standing—have to remain standing. Perhaps he himself must have been critic and skeptic and dogmatist and historian and also poet and collector and traveler and solver of riddles and moralist and seer and "free spirit" and almost everything in order to pass through the whole range of human values and value feelings and to be able to see with many different eyes and consciences, from a height and into every distance, from the depths into every height, from a nook into every expanse. But all these are merely preconditions of his task: this task itself demands something different—it demands that he create values.
>
> Those philosophical laborers after the noble model of Kant and Hegel have to determine and press into formulas, whether in the realm of logic or political (moral) thought or art, some great data of valuations—that is,

former positings of values, creations of value which have become dominant and are for a time called "truths." It is for these investigators to make everything that has happened and been esteemed so far easy to look over, easy to think over, intelligible and manageable, to abbreviate everything long, even "time," and to overcome the entire past—an enormous and wonderful task in whose service every subtle pride, every tough will can certainly find satisfaction. Genuine philosophers, however, are commanders and legislators: they say, "thus it shall be!" They first determine the Whither and For What of the human being, and in so doing have at their disposal the preliminary labor of all philosophical laborers, all who have overcome the past. With a creative hand they reach for the future, and all that is and has been becomes a means for them, an instrument, a hammer. Their "knowing" is creating, their creating is a legislation, their will to truth is—will to power. (BGE 211)

Nietzsche treats the next group, "last idealists left among philosophers and scholars," relatively extensively. He may do so partly because they are promising in many ways. Indeed, the warrior-philosopher seems to belong to this group. Yet, as we know, despite their promise, they ultimately prove to be the very embodiment of the moral-theological prejudice today. Perhaps Nietzsche wishes, like Zarathustra, that his work will elevate at least some of them, so that they, too, can metamorphose into poet-philosophers. Such hopes are bolstered by a very significant attribute that Nietzsche shares with them: namely intellectual conscience. Nietzsche observes that the intellectual conscience is still "incarnate" today solely because it runs in their blood.

The final human type that Nietzsche treats is the modern historiographer. Can we conclude at this point that the poet-philosopher's subject matter in opposing the ascetic ideal must be history? If so, then he shares this interest with the historiographer. On the other hand, the modern historiographer writes ascetic histories. If the poet-philosopher is to counter the ascetic ideal by way of a new reading and writing of history, his work will be neither ascetic nor religious.

The most contemptible of the human types in the third essay of *The Genealogy* is the sham "contemplative," who is a sub-category of the historiographer. Does the poet-philosopher share anything significant with him? Perhaps. Nietzsche notes that the so-called "contemplatives" are the only enemy capable of harming the ascetic ideal today. They do not serve in this role intentionally. Rather, their buffoonery regarding the Christian-moral ideal unintentionally raises distrust in it. If the poet-philosopher shares anything with them, it is his use of humor to fight asceticism.

Unlike them, he consciously and artfully employs a much higher form of humor. By elevating it and combining it with a heartfelt interest in enhancing human life, the poet-philosopher's humor opposes nihilism, whereas the sham contemplative's buffoonery advances it, wittingly or unwittingly, by undermining the value of all red-blooded passion.

Having re-viewed at least some of the salient attributes of the poet-philosopher, the question becomes how this creature executes the mission. We have enough information now to make an educated inference. However, the inference becomes more authoritative and convincing if we find our way to it, or confirm it, by tracking more of the riddles that lead to it and that flow from our guiding riddle, which we have not forgotten. It is also more invigorating and more of an education in reading and writing to proceed this way.

We therefore begin a second leg of our investigation with the general observation that Nietzsche often uses patterns and stylistic oddities to draw attention to the fact that he is communicating indirectly with his reader. Such a pattern exists in *The Genealogy*. Specifically, the exclamation—"Enough! Enough!"—occurs in each of the three essays. In the first essay, it occurs in the fourteenth section, wherein Nietzsche takes us, along with Mr. Rash and Curious, to the workshop of ideals. The student is the first to utter the outcry. Nietzsche follows suit shortly thereafter. He utters the exclamation again in the last section of the second essay, section twenty-five. The final exclamation is in the penultimate section of the third essay, which is numbered as its twenty-seventh section. Delve further into each of these sections and note their immediate context in the plot of each essay to see what further meaning we might glean about the meaning of this pattern.

In the section on the workshop of ideals, the student utters this exclamation immediately after hearing the slavish valuators concoct an interpretation of weakness and strength according to which the vitally impotent are not only morally superior to the vitally potent, but also are more fortunate: "Enough! Enough! I can't take any more. Bad air! Bad air! This workshop where ideals are manufactured—it seems to me it stinks of so many lies" (GM 1.14). Nietzsche commands the student to rule himself and to keep listening, for he has not yet heard the "masterpiece" of moral mendaciousness. This masterpiece consists in the claim that *ressentiment*, not super-abundant vitality and the pro-action that belongs only to it, expresses God's justice. Once the student has heard this masterpiece, Nietzsche concludes both the lesson and the section with this same exclamation: "Enough! Enough!" (GM 1.14).

We noted earlier that, in Nietzsche's mouth, this exclamation is primarily a battle cry, signaling the onset of his attack. We also observe now that Nietzsche announces the specific target of his attack immediately prior to this exclamation. In this case, therefore, his specific target is the slave type's claim to be more just and more fortunate than the noble type. The slave type fleshes out this masterpiece of mendaciousness with the claim that, as a result of God's justice, slavish human beings will gain an everlasting kingdom in Heaven, whereas worldly rulers, who at that time are almost exclusively super-abundantly vital human beings, will be punished forever in Hell for having held political power for an incomparably short time period. Nietzsche's attack on this specific target begins in the section immediately following his battle cry (GM 1.15). It consists of revealing the logical and passionate incoherence of the slave type's claim on the one hand that it will be rewarded in Heaven with the characteristics and trappings of the noble type and, on the other hand, slave morality's condemnation of these same characteristics and trappings as evil.

When the exclamation is repeated in the twenty-fifth section of the second essay, the same basic plot pattern recurs, with minor variations. Rather than ending a section, this time the repeated exclamation opens one: "But what am I saying? Enough! Enough! At this point it behooves me only to be silent" (GM 2.25). Since this self-interruption and self-silencing begins the section, we must look to the section immediately prior to it to determine what provokes this outcry. In this prior section, Nietzsche again identifies the specific target of his attack. Here, it is the ascetic interpretation of life, which has given us an "evil eye" for our "natural inclinations" (GM 2.24).

He then tells us how to vanquish this target. Rather than continuing to believe the interpretation that weds moral guilt to all manifestations of thriving life, thereby condemning them as evil, we should develop an interpretation according to which all inclinations and efforts to undermine thriving life, and thereby threaten the growth of the human being, are bad:

> We modern human beings are the heirs of the conscience-vivisection

and self-torture of millennia: this is what we have practiced longest, it is our distinctive art perhaps, and in any case our subtlety in which we have acquired a refined taste. The human being has too long had an "evil eye" for his natural inclinations, so that they have finally become inseparable from his "bad conscience." An attempt at the reverse would *in itself* be possible— but who is strong enough for it?—that is, to wed the bad conscience to all the unnatural inclinations, all those aspirations to the beyond, to that which runs counter to sense, instinct, nature, animal, in short all ideals hitherto, which are one and all hostile to life and ideals that slander the world. (GM 2.24)

In the plot surrounding Nietzsche's exclamation in the first essay, we see Nietzsche himself execute his battle plan. By contrast, after making this exclamation in the second essay, he sketches his battle plan and then disconcertingly asks who could possible carry it out: "To whom should one turn today with *such* hopes and demands?" He articulates something of the problem in finding this individual. Such a one "would have precisely the *good* human beings against ... [him]; and, of course, the comfortable, the reconciled, the vain, the sentimental, the weary" (GM 2.24). He would therefore need an almost monstrous strength to stand alone, against almost everyone and everything of his day. Moreover, he needs this astounding strength not only for standing alone, but also for standing *against* the world, for his independence will attract hostility. Nietzsche observes that *nothing* today is as offensive as the self-love required for genuine independence or solitude. We see this fact in its converse. Identifying himself as such a person, Nietzsche observes that, because self-respect or genuine self-love is the telltale characteristic of a super-abundantly vital human being, and because we live in a democratic age that inclines to demand sameness in all things, including the demands we make of ourselves, self-respect is envied and is actually subject to opprobrium. People want this human being in particular to show signs of easing up on the severity with which he holds himself to the standard of noble behavior. Thus, "we" acquire "friends" and social approval precisely when we "'let ourselves go' like all the world!" (GM 2.24). Nietzsche fleshes out the characteristics of the only kind of human beings who can withstand the solitude required to win the spiritual battle against the ascetic ideal today:

[They must be] spirits strengthened by war and victory, for whom conquest, adventure, danger, and even pain have become needs; ... [this reinterpretation] would require habituation to the keen air of the heights, to winter journeys, to ice and mountains in every sense; it would require even a kind of sublime wickedness, an ultimate, supremely self-confident mischievousness in knowledge that goes with great health; it would require, in brief and alas, precisely this *great health!* (GM 2.24. See also GS 382)

He continues by repeating his query as to whether anyone today has the great health necessary for such a mission. Apparently, he is not sure such a one exists today, but he insists that, if he be not now, he will be one day:

Is this even possible today?— But some day, in a stronger age than this decaying, self-doubting present, he must yet come to us, the redeeming human being of great love and contempt, the creative spirit whose compelling strength will not let him rest in any aloofness or any beyond, whose isolation is misunderstood by the people as if it were *flight* from reality— while it is only his absorption, his immersion, penetration *into* reality, so that, when he one day emerges again into the light, he may bring home the *redemption* of this reality: its redemption from the curse that hitherto reigning ideal has laid upon it. This human being of the future, who will redeem us not only from the hitherto reigning ideal but also from that which was bound to grow out of it, the great nausea, the will to nothingness, nihilism; this bell-stroke of noon and of the great decision that liberates the will again and restores its goal to the earth and his hope to the human being; this Antichrist and anti-nihilist; this victor over God and nothingness—*he must come one day.*— (GM 3.24. See also Z, "On The Gift-Giving Virtue," 2; Z, "On The Three Evils," 2; Z, "At Noon"; Z, "The Sign")

The section ends. Even after the repeated exclamation that opens the subsequent section, Nietzsche still does not seem to execute the attack he outlines in the prior section. Instead, the exclamation or battle cry is followed by Nietzsche's self-interruption. He claims he should neither speak further about who is suited to carry out the attack strategy, nor should he execute it. If he were to take up this task, he explains, he would "usurp" the right of another who is coming to "redeem" reality (GM 2.24). Note, he does not to say outright that he is *unable* to enact his plan. He says it "behooves" him not to speak further of it, at least at this point. He has told us one reason why silence is prudent: one who would take up this task of revaluation would have almost everyone against him.

After subtly suggesting he is capable of enacting the plan, but that prudence now demands his silence, he goes on to speak as though the as-yet-unnamed other whose right he would usurp if he were to proceed, is truly better suited to the mission. He thereby implicitly adopts a role akin to that of John the Baptist in relation to Jesus Christ. However, in Nietzsche's appropriation and reinterpretation of these characters, Jesus Christ is replaced by an "Anti-Christ" who will redeem human beings and the entire earth by reversing the moral interpretation of bad conscience so that it comes to have a meaning that harmonizes and thereby promotes generation. He identifies this Anti-Christ as Zarathustra:

> But what am I saying? Enough! Enough! At this point it behooves me only to be silent; or I shall usurp that to which only one younger, "heavier with future," and stronger than I has a right—that to which only *Zarathustra* has a right, *Zarathustra the godless.*— (GM 2.25. See also BT, "Attempt At A Self-Criticism," 5; BGE 295)

Nietzsche's suggestion that he is less well suited than Zarathustra to tackle the ascetic interpretation of bad conscience must be taken with a grain of salt. The last time Nietzsche suggested he might remain silent was after he was interrupted by the sham free spirit in the first essay (GM. 1.9. Also contrast Z, "On the Gift-Giving Virtue" with Z, "The Sign"). Far from remaining silent, he went on to outline and execute his battle plan on various fronts in the subsequent sections of the first essay. Since Nietzsche communicates partly with plot patterns, we suspect he intends with this second interruption to remind us of the previous case and of what follows it directly. The reminder may be a hint that the prior pattern recurs here, despite appearances to the contrary. Chase this possibility, drawing on the ideas Nietzsche communicates in this book to test whether it is plausible.

Nietzsche emphasizes the fact that Zarathustra is his creation by way of the prefixed quotation from his book, *Thus Spoke Zarathustra*. In other words, after presenting Zarathustra simply as his superior, he indicates he created Zarathustra and therefore has some kind of command of the character. Consider further the relationship between this creator and this creature.

According to Nietzsche's own characterization of it, *Thus Spoke Zarathustra* offers a new reading and writing of history (EH, "*Thus Spoke Zarathustra*: A Book for All and None," 8). Specifically, in this book, Zoroaster or Zarathustra returns to humankind to give us a life-promoting philosophy. Just as Nietzsche seems to think at the end of the second essay that someone mightier than himself will perform the mission he announces, Zarathustra is also initially unclear about the central role he must play in living and thereby demonstrating his teaching. He, too, initially believes he is merely the herald of one who is stronger. Before attaining clarity about himself and his task, Zarathustra must first undo his original error—the absolute separation of good and evil (EH, "Why I Am a Destiny," 3). This separation is the first expression of the moral-theological prejudice. If we may still speak of it in the context of Nietzsche's philosophy, by this error Zarathustra commits the original sin against truth, life, and wisdom. He must redeem himself by learning the truth about life and about how to promote his own growth before he can redeem the world with his enlivening teaching.

Against that introductory backdrop and overview, focus now on the full section from which the pre-fixed quotation is excerpted. In it, we hear Zarathustra proclaim: "Of all that is written, I love only what a human being has written with his blood. Write with blood, and you will experience that blood is spirit" (Z, "On Reading and Writing"). What Zarathustra says here seems intended in part to tell us that he is *of* Nietzsche and *is* him or is some significant part of him. Stated differently, blood is spirit; Nietzsche's blood creates Zarathustra; hence, Zarathustra is Nietzsche's blood. Just as Nietzsche cannot be separated from his blood, so too Zarathustra cannot be separated from Nietzsche.

Alert to indications from both Nietzsche and Zarathustra that they are in some way one, reflect upon Nietzsche's account of his character. He claims Zarathustra is originally a moralist, but that he later leaps into his opposite, into an immoralist. By Nietzsche's own words, this immoralist is Nietzsche himself (EH, "Why I Am A Destiny," 3. See also EH, "*Thus Spoke Zarathustra*," 1). Thus, when Zarathustra leaves his erroneous ways and leaps into his opposite, he becomes one with Nietzsche, his father-creator. Far from subordinating himself to Zarathustra, therefore, Nietzsche instead presents himself as the initially superior entity, for he is the entity into which Zarathustra evolves. This evolution comes to full fruition when Zarathustra confronts and overcomes the moral-theological prejudice that still burdens the warrior-philosopher:

> I have not been asked, as I should have been asked, what the name of Zarathustra means in my mouth, the mouth of the first immoralist: for what constitutes the tremendous historical uniqueness of that Persian is just the opposite of this. Zarathustra was the first to consider the fight of good and evil the very wheel in the machinery of things: the transposition

of morality into the metaphysical realm, as a force, a cause, and end in itself, as *his* work. But this question itself is at bottom its own answer.

Zarathustra created this most calamitous error, morality; consequently, he must also be the first to recognize it. Not only has he more experience in this matter, for a longer time, than any other thinker—after all, the whole of history is the refutation by experiment of the principle of the so-called "moral world order"—what is more important is that Zarathustra is more truthful than any other thinker. His doctrine, and his alone, posits truthfulness as the highest virtue; this means the opposite of the cowardice of the "idealist" who flees from reality; Zarathustra has more intestinal fortitude than all other thinkers taken together. To speak the truth and *to shoot well with arrows*, that is Persian virtue.—Am I understood?—the self-overcoming of morality, out of truthfulness; the self-overcoming of the moralist, into his opposite—into me—that is what the name of Zarathustra means in my mouth. (EH, "Why I Am a Destiny," 3; see also BGE, "Preface").

By linking Zarathustra so intimately with himself, Nietzsche indicates he is not the artist whom he rejects as a plausible opponent of the ascetic ideal. Nietzsche tells us the artist, or at least the simple artist, must not be confounded with his artifact. By contrast, the same blood courses through both Zarathustra and Nietzsche. This is to say there is not merely a reciprocal interaction between Zarathustra and Nietzsche. Rather, it also means this reciprocal relationship is *ongoing*; they move or live in terms of each other. This is possible because, although Zarathustra has attributes or positive content, Nietzsche depicts him growing. Moreover, the point of this depiction is not to illustrate a character moving to a static end point, but to show the self-overcoming process—the Overman—by which one grows. In other words, the story is of the process that is growth. As a process, growth has no content and can therefore be ongoing. In this, it is akin to the supreme good. This process of growth by self-overcoming occurs or recurs in every good reader of this book. Hence, both Zarathustra and Nietzsche live in this good reader, too. Insofar as Nietzsche's artifact *lives*, it is reminiscent of a Platonic dialogue, which is similarly vivified by the reader's engagement, as an interlocutor of sorts, with the interlocutors that populate the pages of Plato's works. Plato himself, via his Socrates, speaks of his works in this way—as artifacts whose form enables them to defend themselves in a way that long speeches or treatises, which obfuscate the reader's need to interpret them and thus to become them, cannot.[51]

Furthermore, if Nietzsche were *only* an artist, he would not have the independence required to oppose the ascetic ideal. Rather, in the way Wagner relies on Schopenhauer and Homer relies on the ancient Greek gods, Nietzsche, too, would need an authority for protection and as a prop. Instead, Nietzsche incorporates both the artist and the philosopher. He demonstrates the capacity for solitude and his freedom from idealism in his reading and writing of the very this-worldly theory of generation. As a poet-philosopher, Nietzsche's artistry does not merely make independence possible. Instead, *his* artistry demands he stand alone against nihilism.

The same substantiality that enables Nietzsche to be solitary empowers him to generate original content for his creations out of himself; he acts as a super-abundantly vital creator. Speaking of Nietzsche in his capacity as a noble artist, we are better able to see why he cannot be separated from his creations, including his Zarathustra. His artistically or poetically philosophic creations are to him as each of the content-rich meanings of the good are of the noble valuator who generates them. Nietzsche's creations, especially Zarathustra, are expressions of *his* concept of the good.

Given that Nietzsche and Zarathustra are a complex unit, we must reconsider Nietzsche's apparent deference to Zarathustra, as the one with the "right" to execute Nietzsche's plan of attack against the moralization of bad conscience. His deference cannot be a complete abdication, if it is an abdication at all. With this conclusion in mind, consider the fourth and final occurrence of the repeated exclamations. As with its prior occurrence, it comes at the beginning of the section, thereby directing us to the prior section to determine its provocation. The topic of this previous section is the modern historiographer. Thus, something peculiar to, or most characteristic of, the modern historiographer is Nietzsche's specific and final target. Nietzsche directs us clearly to the attribute that most characterizes this modern reader and writer of history. He tells us historiography's "noblest claim nowadays is that it is a mirror; it rejects all teleology; it no longer wishes to 'prove' anything; it disdains to play the judge and considers this a sign of good taste" (GM 3.26). The claim to a supra-perspectival viewpoint is not only ascetic, but also "to an even higher degree *nihilistic*" (GM 3.26). The modern historiographer's claim to supra-perspectival objectivity is Nietzsche's specific target now.

This final target is most fully embodied in the sham contemplatives

amongst modern historiographers. Somewhat like the poet-philosopher, the sham contemplatives at least seem to comprehend a variety
of different human types. They are "whited sepulchers who impersonate
life … agitators dressed up like heroes … ambitious artists who like to
pose as ascetics and priests but who are at bottom only tragic buffoons"
(GM 3.27). Unlike the poet-philosopher, however, to the extent the
sham contemplative actually has any of these various attributes rather
than merely feigning them, he does not embody them in conjunction
with super-abundant vitality. Thus, in his reading and writing, the sham
contemplative employs "the word 'artist' as a glove," so as *not* to "touch"
his subject—so as *not* to write in blood. Because he lacks the strength
to be honest with himself about what he is and does, he lies dishonestly.
He presumes he is "good" and "pure" in his narratives, and of course
he equates goodness and purity with supra-perspectival objectivity.
With these presumptions in hand, he proceeds to amend those aspects
of recorded history that seem to him to have been told without the
supra-perspectivity he claims for himself and that he insists is necessary
for seeing facts truly.

Nietzsche offers Ernst Renan as an example of the sham contemplative. He does not provide much information about Renan's work.
However, it is helpful for understanding Nietzsche's criticism of these
historiographers to note that Renan wrote a *Life of Jesus* in which he
argues Jesus is laudable for having cast aside his Jewish heritage. According to Renan, this heritage was inhibiting Jesus' maturation, as a human
being, into a full-fledged Aryan. In keeping with Nietzsche's criticism of
modern historians generally, Renan claims his supra-perspectival objectivity enables him to see that Jesus is not divine. Although the historiographer purportedly disdains to judge, Renan nevertheless asserts that
his account of Jesus as merely human grants Jesus more dignity than he
would have if he were a god. In keeping with this interpretation, Renan
also dismisses the accounts of miracles in the gospels since, according to
him, they also are not recounted from a supra-perspectival standpoint.[52]

Having already told us the sham contemplatives dress up as heroes
and pose as priests, Nietzsche contrasts the sham contemplative and his
work with the ascetic priest and the ascetic ideal, as it is articulated and
employed by the priest. More specifically, he associates the sham contemplative with the "latest speculators in idealism, the anti-Semites, who

today roll their eyes in a Christian-Aryan bourgeois manner and exhaust one's patience by trying to rouse up all the horned-beast elements in the people by a brazen abuse of the cheapest of all agitator's tricks, moral attitudinizing" (GM 3.26). These latest speculators use ideals as a way of inducing orgies of feeling in the populace. In so doing, they recall the ascetic priest's use of such orgies, not only as a harmful means to temporary pain-relief, but also a means of increasing his influence over the many.

Partly by way of this comparison, Nietzsche invites us to notice that we are seeing a version of the workshop of ideals that we observed in the fourteenth section of the first essay, the section in which the repeated exclamation first appeared. As in that earlier instance, we once again find ourselves amidst "forgery in ideals, the most potent brandy of the spirit; hence also the repulsive, ill-smelling, mendacious, pseudo-alcoholic air everywhere" (GM 3.27). Yet, despite these similarities, the artifacts the workshop of ideals now manufactures are much more repulsive than they were formerly. It is true that even the less modern forms of the ascetic ideal or the moral-theological prejudice are ultimately nihilistic. However, in these less modern forms, nihilism is shrouded in narratives that give human life meaning by folding it into a larger picture that makes sense of it. This meaning directs the will and, by so doing, preserves it as something recognizably human—that is, as something with a determined goal and thus as the expression of a more evolved and more alive shape of the will to power than the blow-outs or undetermined expressions of will to power that characterize its more primitive shapes.

Largely because of the moral-theological prejudice itself, which posits absolute being and hence an ascetic notion of truth as authoritative, ascetic truth-seekers—including and most importantly the philosophers whose shapes are simpler than that of the poet-philosopher—have over time pulled these narrative veils off of the ascetic ideal. They expose it regardless and ignorant of the effects of their activity on thriving life. The stripping away of these veils brings us eventually to the warrior-philosopher, who actively seeks to face down the most dangerous questions. Yet, while a warrior-philosopher such as Schopenhauer concludes life is meaningless and thereby removes one more veil over the nihilism that is the essence of the ascetic ideal, he nevertheless actually experiences meaning precisely in facing this dangerous question. In other words, his meaning consists of an immature philosophic version of the meaning the ascetic priest finds in the torturous delight of attacking his own human-ity: "Triumph in the ultimate agony!" (GM 3.11). Not so for the sham contemplative.

Subtract vital potency from the warrior-philosopher's advance into the realm of nihilism. Thus, one is left, not with the noble warrior, but with the vitally impotent sham contemplative. Wrapped in his dishonest lies about his supra-perspectivity, his readings and writings loudly and clearly proclaim as true the ugly, nihilistic core of the ascetic ideal. He dismisses the very notion of a genuine future or growth for the human being as a *mere* interpretation and hence as valueless— More! as *immoral*. This denial of the validity of all perspectives and hence all interpretations is necessarily a simultaneous denial of all meaning and hence all direc-tion for the will. In the absence of a meaningful direction, the highly evolved *human* will degenerates; its exercise becomes increasingly undif-ferentiated, increasingly *pre-* and finally *non-human*.

With the specific target of supra-perspectival objectivity in our sights, Nietzsche shares his plan for an attack against it. He tells us we need an artist with a very free hand to write an alternative history to that which is proffered in various forms, including modern science or phi-losophy, by the ascetic ideal. This history will not claim to be supra-per-spectival. It will be a poetic and life-promoting reading of history. In this regard, it will be akin to Homer's histories. It will tell honest "lies" with a good conscience; it will sanctify the lie. —It will be entitled, "On the History of European Nihilism;" and it will be contained in the book, *The Will to Power: An Attempt At A Revaluation of All Values* (GM 3.27). This work was not written. —Right?

Return to the remark Nietzsche drops in the third essay when he directs his attention to the meaning of the ascetic ideal in the case of the priest:

> "What is the meaning of all seriousness?"—this even more fundamental question may perhaps be trembling on our lips at this point: a question for physiologists, of course, but one we must still avoid for the moment. (GM 3.11)

When we first came across Nietzsche pointing to this "more funda-mental question," we noted that, although he suggests he will return to this question, he does not do so in what remains of the third essay. This is not to say he does not do so at all. Truly, he does address this question, not in the third, but in the second essay of *The Genealogy*. Thus, by flagging the question of seriousness as even more fundamental than the meaning of the ascetic ideal, he directs us back to the second essay. However, he does so in such a way that the full meaning of this direction is only apparent at the end of the third essay, when he announces his third specific target, battle-plan, and both the title and specific subject matter of the work in which this battle-plan will be executed. The chapter and book he announces here may of course take the form of another book, but its subject matter is nevertheless sufficiently complete in the second essay of *this* book. Our guiding riddle, which we have not forgotten, indicates not only that he knows this, but also that he wants us to know this. Hence, while the second essay is entitled "'Guilt,' 'Bad Conscience,' and the Like," Nietzsche's riddle—our guiding and now un-raveled riddle—tells to return to it after interpreting the third essay and to re-read it as a chapter entitled, "*On the History of European Nihilism*" in a book called, *The Will to Power: An Attempt At A Revaluation of All Values*.

Loop back to it, this time at a higher level of comprehension. Pay special attention this time around to the more fundamental question of the value for life of all seriousness.

Seriousness or gravity has so far been associated with bad conscience, as interpreted morally by the ascetic ideal. This interpretation claims the pain that can accrue from our inwardly oriented drives is proof of our inadequacy in the face of an authoritative realm that transcends our world and what we are, as mortal beings. Using more religious language, bad conscience and the graveness associated with it have been interpreted as evidence of our inherent sinfulness. As he reads or interprets history, Nietzsche sees that our graveness is not a sign of our inadequacy or our sinfulness. It is the unavoidable by-product of mnemotechnics, the creation of memory in the human being.

We are familiar with Nietzsche's hypothesis that memory was produced in the context of the debtor-creditor relationship. In order for that relationship to be extended beyond immediate transactions, the human being must be able to make a promise, the foundation of which is the capacity to remember it. Although memory is necessary, however, we did not always have a memory adequate to making a contract in the present to which we could hold ourselves in the future. Memory had to be forged or amplified. This forging could neither be accidental nor passive because too much in our physio-psychology opposes retaining past events to the degree required for a promise. This opposition is especially strong when remembering seems to us to oppose our immediate interests. Thus, the creation of memory in the human being had to be done pro-actively, by us.

At the time this work was carried out, it was known that terrible and sustained pain could transform a person. This was precisely the method employed by mnemotechnics: memory was burned into our physio-psychology. Over time, the prevalence of mnemotechnics and hence of the awful pain associated with it depressed the human being's physio-psychology. This deficiency in levity or the feeling of freedom constitutes our graveness or seriousness. To borrow Nietzsche's metaphor, mnemotechnics made us caterpillars or earth-crawlers. This graveness has remained part of our physio-psychology. Wherever "solemnity, seriousness, mystery, and gloomy coloring still distinguish the life of the human being and a people," he tells us, "something of the terror that formerly attended all promises, pledges, and vows on earth is still effective: the past, the longest, deepest and sternest past, breathes upon us and rises up in us whenever we become 'serious'" (GM 2.3). In gravity, we see something of the terrible heritage of mnemotechnics (GM 2.3). Nietzsche goes on to identify all religions and all asceticism as "systems of cruelties" employed for memory-making:

> The human being could never do without blood, torture, and sacrifices when he felt the need to create a memory for himself; the most dreadful sacrifices and pledges (sacrifices of the first-born among them), the most repulsive mutilations (castration, for example), the cruelest rites of all the religious cults (and all religions are at the deepest level systems of cruelties)—all this has its origin in the instinct that realized that pain is the most powerful aid to mnemonics.
>
> In a certain sense, the whole of asceticism belongs here: a few ideas are to be rendered inextinguishable, ever-present, unforgettable, "fixed," with the aim of hypnotizing the entire nervous and intellectual system with these "fixed ideas"—and ascetic procedures and modes of life are means of freeing these ideas from the competition of all other ideas, so as to make them "unforgettable. The worse the human being's memory has been, the more fearful has been the appearance of his customs. (GM 2.3)

The gravity produced by mnemotechnics paved the way for grave or depressed thinking, the most significant expression of which is the moral-theological prejudice or ascetic ideal. Thus, asceticism is both a cause and an effect of a deficiency in physio-psychological levity (see also BGE 62).

Although Nietzsche hypothesizes that the proximate goal of mnemotechnics was to bolster and advance the efficacy of the creditor-debtor relationship, he sees something much more meaningful in this effort to transfigure the human being. He realizes the capacity and hence the right to make promises is tantamount to the capacity and right to create oneself. That is, one cannot genuinely make a promise unless one has the reasonable expectation that one has and will continue to have command over one's future self. To command one's future self is to create oneself. Thus, by Nietzsche's super-perspectival reading and writing of our genealogy, mnemotechnics is indicative of an instinctual, inter-generational, and eons-long project to create the human being who consciously rules and creates himself.

Nietzsche's super-perspectivity straddles the eons between the origin of this project and its fruition in the human being whom Nietzsche names the sovereign individual. He gives us a prolonged view of this creature, one that encompasses almost an entire section of the essay. This long look is helpful because Nietzsche never again speaks of the sovereign individual by name. In his silence on this point, he plays with us. Having told us his essay is about the creation of the sovereign individual and that the creation of this creature depends upon the prior development of memory, he then requires us to remember both what kind of being the sovereign individual is and the fact that this essay is explicitly about the genealogy of the human being in terms of the sovereign individual. If we do not hold onto this fact, the essay seems rather incoherent.

This seeming incoherence is, in fact, artful. It demonstrates that there is no mind and hence no narrative or storyline in either nature or history. A narrative is brought to beings and events only by way of a highly evolved mind that consciously perceives and interprets entities in the world in terms of their interrelations. In the case of our hodge-podge evolution—which, even as an assembly of facts is already an interpretation—Nietzsche's spirit reads and writes our human history. In so doing, he artfully brings coherence or intelligibility to what is otherwise mindless. Let us meet the rare, elusive creature—the sovereign individual—who emerges through this genealogical account of the human being:

If we place ourselves at the end of this tremendous process, where the tree at last brings forth fruit, where society and the morality of custom at last reveal *what* they have simply been the means to: then we discover that the ripest fruit is the *sovereign individual*, like only to himself, liberated again from morality of custom, autonomous and supra-moral (for "autonomous" and "moral" are mutually exclusive), in short, the human being who has his own independent, protracted will and the *right to make promises*—and in him a proud consciousness, quivering in every muscle, of what has at length been achieved and become flesh in him, a consciousness of his own power and freedom, a sensation of humankind come to completion. This emancipated individual, with the actual *right* to make promises, this master of a *free* will, this sovereign human being—how should he not be aware of his superiority over all those who lack the right to make promises and stand as their own guarantors, of how much trust, how much fear, how much reverence he arouses—he *"deserves"* all three—and of how this mastery over himself also necessarily gives him mastery over circumstances, over nature, and over all more short-willed and unreliable creatures? The "free" human being, the possessor of a protracted and unbreakable will, also possesses his *measure of value*: looking out upon others from himself, he honors or he despises; and just as he is bound to honor his peers, the strong and reliable (those with the *right* to make promises)—that is, all those who promise like sovereigns, reluctantly, rarely, slowly, who are chary of trusting, whose "trust is a mark of *distinction*, who give their word as something that can be relied on because they know themselves strong enough to maintain it in the face of accidents, even "in the face of fate"—he is bound to reserve a kick for the feeble windbags who promise without the right to do so, and a rod for the liar who breaks his word even at the moment he utters it. The proud awareness of the extraordinary privilege of *responsibility*, the consciousness of this rare freedom, this power over oneself and over fate, has in his case penetrated to the profoundest depths and become instinct, the dominating instinct. What will he call this dominating instinct, supposing he feels the need to give it a name? The answer is beyond doubt: this sovereign human being calls it his *conscience*. (GM 2.2)

By remembering that the sovereign individual is central to understanding the whole of this essay, we can infer he is the being whom Nietzsche describes in the essay's penultimate section. He is the one who can oppose the ascetic ideal with an interpretation of the human being that links bad conscience, not to what is vitalizing in us, but to what enervates us. In the ultimate section, Nietzsche identifies the sovereign individual by name: he is Zarathustra. Zarathustra, the sovereign individual, is the one who is "'heavier with future'" and who therefore has the capacity and hence the "right" to vouch for our future. Just as the poet-philosopher's capacity for action from a height results from the vitally potent incorporation of various human types for whom the ascetic ideal has meaning, so too, by bringing our human history together into himself, Zarathustra embodies a comprehensive height. That is, he incorporates our human history in a vitally potent shape. By comprehending our past in this potent and pregnant form, he not only vouches for our future, but also redeems our past. Everything significant in our history is enhanced or elevated and made meaningful in him (GM 2.25).

Like the narrative spun by the ascetic ideal, Nietzsche's genealogy of the human being in terms of our self-overcoming or our self-directed growth toward the sovereign individual gives meaning to human life, including and especially the suffering that necessarily attends it. As with the ascetic ideal's historiography, Nietzsche's narrative does this by folding human life into a larger narrative that elevates and makes sense of it in terms of an end-goal or North Star. In the case of the ascetic narrative, the end-goal is philosophic transcendence or Heaven. In Nietzsche's narrative, the North Star is growth, as determined by the interplay of the historical and supreme goods. Both the ascetic narrative and the narrative of the poet-philosopher direct the will according to this goal, and, by so doing, preserve it as something recognizably human.

The narratives differ, however, on two crucial points. First, whereas the ascetic narrative is metaphysical and therefore fundamentally and ultimately nihilistic, the poet-philosopher's reading and writing of history is cosmic or this-worldly. *It does not depend in any way upon metaphysics.* Second, the poet-philosopher's reading and writing of history has a decidedly different tone from the narrative offered by the moral-theological prejudice. From the perspective of the modern historiographer, who is oppressed by the moral-theological prejudice, our genealogy looks at best like a tragedy and at worst like mindlessness and buffoonery. By contrast, the height or vantage point to which the poet-philosopher can rise allows him to comprehend how our past may actually conduce to tremendous growth for the human being. The whole history of the moral-theological prejudice thereby finds its place, not as mere misfortune, but as part of a process that leads to our capacity for conscious self-creation. Such seeing, reading, and writing makes our genealogy tragicomic or comic.

This comic vision reveals the particular, content-rich goal for our immediate future, as well as the general goal for human life, always. The content-rich goal, the historical good, is now to embody more fully the characteristics of the sovereign individual, Zarathustra, or the poet-philosopher. For this is now and likely for some time to come the maximum shape of super-abundant vitality. In keeping with the supreme good, if and when we achieve this goal, we must overcome this particular shape with a more enhanced form of the human being. In sum, to be human, we must continue to strive to overcome what we are. Only in this way do we become what we are.

The riddle is unraveled; the mission accomplished. To speak in Nietzsche's words: "[A] *counter-ideal* was lacking—*until Zarathustra*. I have been understood" (EH, "*On The Genealogy of Morals: A Polemic*"). We have understood adequately this comedy written in blood, infused with spirit. Grace in deed.

THE END

Endnotes

1 Friedrich Nietzsche, "On The Genealogy of Morals" in *On The Genealogy of Morals and Ecce Homo*, trans. Walter Kaufmann (New York: Vintage Books, 1989), 17. All subsequent references to this book will be included in the body of the text with the appropriate section number. I have altered the translation in some cases for greater clarity.

2 What is true of differences between species is true at the more precise level of the individual. We have many experiences that are similar enough to allow us to conclude we are closely related to other human beings, but no individual is physio-psychologically exactly the same as any other. We might try to enter more fully into the experience of another individual, but, unless our physiologies are identical, our experiences will not be the same. This line of reasoning can be extended to the individual. Experiences an individual has at one time can also never be repeated exactly, unless this individual's physiology is exactly the same at both times.

3 This is not to say that only things we can know or that are available to us can have consequences for us. It is to say we cannot know anything of such causes; hence, we cannot recognize their effects for what they are. Speaking in moral terms, this means there might be an unknowable being who punishes us for certain actions, but, since we have no access to such a being and cannot recognize the punishments for what they are, we cannot mindfully adjust our behavior so as to avoid punishment. At best, we could modify our behavior because we see patterns in our actions and their effects, but this adjustment would not be morally motivated. We would not change our behavior because we know it to be evil. Since we can know nothing of this kind of supra-human being or the possible ills it might impose on us, they fall outside the realm of things that should properly attract our attention and interest.

4 The overthrow of these theological and moral prejudices does not mean all concepts of either the divine or of morality are disproved. The overthrow is specific to the prejudices as we have defined them.

5 Nietzsche offers a succinct account of morality, as it pertains to all commanding. In this quotation, he speaks of the human being's morality; however, what he says here is equally applicable to the human being's commanding drive:

> That the case of self-observation is indeed as desperate ... is attested best of all by the manner in which almost everybody talks about the

essence of moral actions—this quick, eager, convinced, and garrulous manner with its expression, its smile, and its obliging ardor! One seems to have the wish to say to you: "But my dear friend, precisely this is my specialty. You have directed your question to the one person who is entitled to answer you. As it happens, there is nothing about which I am as wise as about this. ... To come to the point: when a human being judges *"this is right"* and then infers *"therefore it must be done,"* and then proceeds to *do* what he has thus recognized as right and designated as necessary—then the essence of his action is *moral."*

But my friend, you are speaking of three actions instead of one. When you judge "this is right," that is an action, too. Might it not be possible that one could judge in a moral and in an immoral manner? *Why* do you consider this, precisely this, right?

"Because this is what my conscience tells me; and the voice of conscience is never immoral, for it alone determines what is to be moral."

But why do you *listen* to the voice of your conscience? And what gives you the right to consider such a judgment true and infallible? For this *faith*—is there no conscience for that? A conscience behind your "conscience"? Your judgment "this is right" has a pre-history in your instincts, likes, dislikes, experiences, and lack of experiences. *"How* did it originate there?" you must ask, and then also: "What is it that impels me to listen to it?" You can listen to its commands like a good soldier who hears his officer's command. Or like a woman who loves the man who commands. Or like a flatterer and coward who is afraid of the commander. Or like a dunderhead who obeys because no objection occurs to him. In short, there are a hundred ways in which you can listen to your conscience. But that you take this or that judgment for the voice of conscience—in other words, that you feel something to be right!—may be due to the fact that you have never thought much about yourself and simply have accepted blindly that what you have been told ever since your childhood was right; or it may be due to the fact that what you have called your duty has up to this point brought you sustenance and honors—and you consider it "right" because it appears to you as your own "condition of existence" (and that you have a right to existence appears irrefutable to you).

For all that, the *firmness* of your moral judgment could be evidence of your personal abjectness, of impersonality; your "moral strength" might have its source in your stubbornness—or in your inability to envision new ideals. And, briefly, if you had thought more subtly, observed better, and learned more, you certainly would not go on calling this "duty" of yours and this "conscience" of yours duty and conscience. Your understanding *of the manner in which moral judgments have originated* would spoil these grand words for you, just as other grand words, like

"sin" and "salvation of the soul" and "redemption" have been spoiled for
you. —And now don't cite the categorical imperative, my friend! This
term tickles my ear and makes me laugh despite your serious presence.
It makes me think of the old Kant who had obtained the "thing in
itself" *by stealth*—another very ridiculous thing!—and was punished
for this when the "categorical imperative" crept stealthily into his heart
and led him astray—back to "God," "soul," "freedom," and "immortality," like a fox who loses his way and goes astray back into his cage. Yet
it had been *his* strength and cleverness that had *broken open* the cage!

What? You admire the categorical imperative within you? This "firmness" of your so-called moral judgment? This "unconditional" feeling
that "here everyone must judge as I do"? Rather admire your selfishness at this point. And the blindness, pettiness, and frugality of your
selfishness. For it is selfish to experience one's own judgment as a
universal law; and this selfishness is blind, petty, and frugal because
it betrays that you have not yet discovered yourself nor created for
yourself an ideal of your own, your very own—for that could never be
somebody else's mind and much less that of all, all!

Anyone who still judges "in this case everybody would have to act like
this" has not yet taken five steps toward self-knowledge. Otherwise
he would know that there neither are nor can be actions that are the
same; that every action that has ever been done was done in an altogether unique and irretrievable way, and that this will be equally true
of every future action; that all regulations about actions relate only to
their coarse exterior (even the most inward and subtle regulations of all
moralities so far); that these regulations may lead to some semblance
of sameness, *but really only to some semblance*, that as one contemplates
or looks back upon *any* action at all, it is and remains impenetrable;
that our opinions about "good" and "noble" and "great" can never be
proved true by our actions because every action is unknowable; that
our opinions, valuations, and tables of what is good certainly belong
among the most powerful levers in the involved mechanism of our
actions, but that in any particular case the law of their mechanism is
indemonstrable.

Let us therefore *limit* ourselves to the purification of our opinions and
valuations and to the *creation of our own new* tables of what is good,
and let us stop brooding about the "moral value of our actions"! …
Let us leave such chatter and such bad taste to those who have nothing else to do but drag the past a few steps further through time and
who never live in the present—which is to say the majority, the great
majority. We, however, *want to become those we are*—human beings
who are new, unique, incomparable, who give themselves laws, who
create themselves. To that end we must become the best learners and

discoverers of everything that is lawful and necessary in the world: we must become physicists in order to be able to be *creators* in this sense—while hitherto all valuations and ideals have been based on ignorance of physics or were constructed so as to *contradict* it. Therefore: long live physics! And even more so that which *compels* us to turn to physics—our honesty! (GS 335; see also GS 2)

6 Nietzsche makes an analogous observation when reflecting on the difference between his thinking and what he articulates in words. Thinking is fluid, but this fluidity necessarily ceases as soon as one tries to capture the thoughts in words. He maintains that his thinking is more beautiful, more enlivening, than his written words, and he laments this difference (e.g. see BGE 296).

7 Nietzsche's comparison between the philosopher's commanding question and the sun of a world is especially apt, for the philosopher's soul is more akin to a world than to a single plant. It is sufficiently varied to liken it to a landscape with various topography. It consists of multiple aspects or drives that act and develop with some independence from each other, like different beings in the world. It has weather in the form of moods. It has regions that are in decline and others that are flourishing. This variety of distinct aspects in the philosopher's psyche shows us it is manifold. Yet, it is also a kind of whole rather than a disparate assemblage of uncoordinated drives.

The wholeness of the philosopher's soul is secured in part by the lack of chance, accident, or free will that is involved in its growth. No philosopher arbitrarily chooses his question, nor is he free to choose it (BGE 21). Rather, it is always an expression of his individual essence, which is given to him. He recognizes it over time, with surprise and fascination; always with recurring fear (see BGE 292). He cultivates what he is without necessarily knowing he does so or knowing how his actions nurture and develop what he is.

8 Lise van Boxel, "Nietzsche in Eden" in *The Pious Sex*, ed. Andrea Radasanu (Maryland: Lexington Books, 2010), 225–280. See also EH, "Why I Write Such Great Books," 5; EH, "The Birth of Tragedy," 3.

9 Carl Friedrich Gauss, a mathematician, is reported to have said, in 1856, that mathematics is the queen of the sciences, and number theory is the queen of mathematics. In the High Middle Ages, theology was recognized as the queen of the sciences.

10 Nietzsche maintains Socrates himself eventually came to realize he, like the aristocrats whom he criticized, was instinct rather than reason. Thus, he also realized dialectics and logic, which depend on the faith in opposite values for their authority, are not truly the opposite of the passions or instincts. Rather, reasoning is employed by the instincts for their own purposes:

The ancient theological problem of "faith" and "knowledge"—or, more clearly, of instinct and reason—in other words, the question whether regarding the valuation of things instinct deserves more authority than rationality, which wants us to evaluate and act in accordance with reasons, with a "why?"—in other words, in accordance with expedience and utility—this is still the ancient moral problem that first emerged in the person of Socrates and divided thinking people long before Christianity. Socrates himself, to be sure, with the taste of his talent—that of a superior dialectician—had initially sided with reason; and in fact, what did he do his life long but laugh at the awkward incapacity of noble Athenians who, like all noble men, were men of instinct and never could give sufficient information about the reasons for their actions? In the end, however, privately and secretly, he laughed at himself, too: in himself he found, before his subtle conscience and self-examination, the same difficulty and incapacity. But is that any reason, he encouraged himself, for giving up the instincts? One has to see to it that they as well as reason receive their due—one must follow the instincts but persuade reason to assist them with good reasons. This was the real *falseness* of that great ironic, so rich in secrets; he got his conscience to be satisfied with a kind of self-trickery: at bottom, he had seen through the irrational element in moral judgments.

Plato, more innocent in such matters and lacking the craftiness of the plebeian, wanted to employ all his strength—the greatest strength any philosopher so far has had at his disposal—to prove to himself that reason and instinct of themselves tend toward one goal, the good, "God." And since Plato, all theologians and philosophers are on the same track—that is, in moral matters it has so far been instinct, or what the Christians call "faith," or "the herd," as I put it, that has triumphed. Perhaps Descartes should be excepted, as the father of rationalism (and hence the grandfather of the Revolution) who conceded authority to reason alone: but reason is merely an instrument, and Descartes was superficial. (BGE 191; see also BGE 3; BGE 187; GS 340)

11 See Leo Strauss, "Natural Right and the Historical Approach" and "The Origin of Natural Right" in *Natural Right and History* (Chicago: The University of Chicago Press, 1953), 9–35; 81 - 120. See also Leo Strauss, "What is Political Philosophy?" in *What is Political Philosophy?* (Chicago: The University of Chicago Press, 1959), 9–55.

12 Aristotle agrees with Plato's Socrates on these points and offers a more explicit treatment of them than does Plato's Socrates. See Aristotle, *Nicomachean Ethics* (1170a3–1170b10; 1174b13–25; 1176a3–25). See also G.W. Hegel, "Introduction," *The Philosophy of History* (1956, 11–16).

13 See Aristotle, *Ethics* 1103b 1-5.

14 In GS 357, Nietzsche attributes the discovery of the historical sense to Hegel, which is not to say that Nietzsche understands this sense simply as Hegel does.

15 See also BGE 188, where Nietzsche argues all languages are moral, by which he means they all aim implicitly to form the physio-psychologies of the people who speak them. They do this at least partly by "the metrical compulsion of rhyme and reason" (BGE 188).

16 Compare Plato, *Symposium* (206c–208b).

17 *„Das Umgekehrte ist bei der vornehmen Werthungsweise der Fall: sie agirt und wächst spontan, sie sucht ihren Gegensatz nur auf, um zu sich selber noch dankbarer, noch frohlockender Ja zu sagen"* (GM 1.10).

18 See GS 162 for Nietzsche's explanation of what egoism is.

19 Nietzsche says here that the Greek nobles often felt pity for those whom they deemed bad. Elsewhere, he maintains pity is not characteristic of original morality. The two apparently contradictory claims are reconciled by the fact that he identifies two different kinds of pity, only one of which he associates with original morality. This original form of pity, to which he refers in this quotation, does not undermine human life. The other form of pity, which Nietzsche associates with the slave revolt in morality, can enervate those who experience it. In particular, it enervates and can destroy vitally potent human beings. It can do this because it focuses only on what is unfortunate and sick about individuals and the human being per se. It thereby promotes a sense of hopelessness for a return to health and for greater health in the case of both individuals and the human species. See GM, "Preface," 6; BGE 225; BGE 293; GS 338; Z, "On the Preachers of Death".

20 The three meanings of the original concept of the good correspond to the first three of the four virtues Nietzsche identifies in *Beyond Good and Evil*: courage, insight, and sympathy (BGE 284). With each new meaning of the original good, a new virtue is incorporated into the noble type. The fourth and final virtue—solitude—corresponds to the new content Nietzsche adds to the original concept of the good.

21 Friedrich Nietzsche, "Genealogy of Morals: A Polemic," in *Ecce Homo* in *On the Genealogy of Morals and Ecce Homo*, Translated by Walter Kaufmann. (New York: Vintage Books, 1989), 312–313.

22 See Leo Strauss, "What is Political Philosophy?" in *What is Political Philosophy* (Chicago: The University of Chicago Press, 1959), 9–55.

23 This notion of commensurability and its complex role in justice is richly illustrated by Aeschylus' *Oresteia*, especially the final of the three plays, *The Eumendies*. See Aeschylus, *Oresteia: Agamemnon; The Libation Bearers; The Eumenides*. Translated by Richmond Lattimore. Chicago: The University of Chicago Press, 1953.

24 In his *Nicomachean Ethics*, Aristotle subtly argues against the common notion that acts that benefit others seem to be acts of love but are, in fact, economic: the benefactor expects something in return for his seeming gift. Aristotle

corrects the error, noting to begin that true benefactors are not engaged in economics. Rather, in their benefactions their awareness of their existence is augmented. Extrapolating from this account of what makes generosity desirable to the benefactor to love more generally, Aristotle's implicit account of love is that it is the experience of the activity that is the fully actualized human being. This activity describes the philosopher in the activity of philosophizing. Thus, philosophy *constitutes* true love and more specifically true self-love. It is this activity, this love, that makes philosophy the most excellent, lovable, and desirable activity. The mirroring of this activity in conversation with another fully actualized or excellent human being constitutes true friendship or love of another. Thus, Aristotle's account is very consistent with Nietzsche's on this point (see Aristotle, *Nicomachean Ethics* 1167b18–1169a7; 1169b30–1170a6; 1173b35–1175a23; 1176a30–1179a33).

25 HH 108:

> *The twofold struggle against an ill.* - When we are assailed by an ill we can dispose of it either by getting rid of its cause or by changing the effect it produces on our sensibilities: that it to say by reinterpreting the ill into a good whose good effects will perhaps be perceptible only later. Religion and art (and metaphysical philosophy too) endeavor to bring about a change of sensibility, partly through changing our judgment as to the nature of our experiences (for example with the aid of the proposition: 'whom God loveth he chastiseth'), partly through awakening the ability to take pleasure in pain, in emotion in general (from which the art of tragedy takes its starting-point). The more a man inclines towards reinterpretation, the less attention he will give to the cause of the ill and to doing away with it; the momentary amelioration and narcoticizing, such as is normally employed for example in the case of a toothache, suffices him in the case of more serious sufferings too. The more the domination of the religions and all the arts of narcosis declines, the stricter attention men pay to the actual abolition of the ill: which is, to be sure, a bad lookout for the writers of tragedies—for there is less and less material for tragedy, because the realm of inexorable, implacable destiny is growing narrower and narrower—but an even worse one for the priests: for these have hitherto lived on the narcoticizing of human ills.

26 Compare Plato, *The Republic* 583c–586a.

27 I have altered the Master's translation in this sentence, as it appears in this edition of this book, to represent the original French more accurately.

28 Jean-Jacques Rousseau, *The Social Contract*, "On Civil Religion." Translated by Judith R. Masters. Edited by Roger D. Masters (New York: St. Martin's Press, 1978), 125–126. See also GM 2.20.

29 (i) See Lise van Boxel, "Contest as Context" in *Prefaces to Unwritten Works*, Edited by Michael Grenke (Illinois: St. Augustine's Press, 2005) 70–80.

(ii) See Friedrich Nietzsche, "Homer's Contest" in *Prefaces to Unwritten Works*, Edited by Michael Grenke (Illinois: St. Augustine's Press, 2005) 81–92.

30 Nietzsche identifies the virtues one might attribute to Dionysus as courage, daring honesty, truthfulness, and love of wisdom (BGE 295). These virtues are notably not the same as those that characterize the noble human being—namely, courage, insight, sympathy, and solitude. After listing the god's virtues, Nietzsche adds that Dionysus and the kind of philosopher who is like this philosopher-god would reject Nietzsche's characterization of them as virtues. They would counter that they have no need to obscure what they are with this redundant flattery, "virtue." Unlike modern human beings, they would say they are not ashamed of their nakedness—of the fullness of both their savagery and humanity.

While Dionysus has no qualms about the possibility that the human being could be made more evil and more profound, Nietzsche indicates explicitly that he does harbor hesitation. He identifies this hesitancy as an expression of his humanity. Perhaps part of his reaction is due to the fact that Dionysus expresses no interest in enhancing the human being's humaneness alongside an increased capacity for evil. Perhaps this oversight is at least partly attributable to what Nietzsche identifies as the god's lack of shame. Dionysus is uninterested in whether or not the various expressions of his will to power are characterized as virtuous; hence, he does not care whether increased vitality is called cruel or humane. He scorns such characterizations. Yet, the manifestation of the god's shamelessness is not a full explanation of Nietzsche's response to the god's musings. Upon learning of the god's intentions, Nietzsche not only recalls to us his earlier observation that the god lacks shame, but also adds to this recollection the additional observation that the god "could learn from us humans" in "several respects" (BGE 295). That is, Nietzsche notes not only the god's lack of shame, but also his ignorance regarding some things humans know. Given that Nietzsche associates these two observations in the same sentence, it is likely the god's shamelessness is the result of his ignorance. What knowledge do we possess that is relevant to Dionysus' ignorance in this context? Nietzsche associates the god's shamelessness with his nakedness: the god makes no apologies for his nature. This reference to nakedness is an allusion to the Biblical story of Eden. Adam and Eve cover their genitals after they learn about their sexuality, their generative capacity. Neither Dionysus nor Nietzsche is ashamed of generation. Indeed, Nietzsche wishes to rid us of this shame. Hence, he cannot mean to imply the god needs to learn this shame. Rather, despite working to rid us of this shame, Nietzsche knows that the weakness or sickness that accompanies this shame is at least partly responsible for prompting us to learn things about which we might otherwise have remained ignorant. The epoch of weakness deepened us and, while making us weaker, it also gave us the potential for new forms of growth or vitality. This connection between weakness and the possibilities for new growth it can introduce seems to be the thing about which the god is ignorant and the human being, or at least Nietzsche, as the human representative, is knowledgeable. This interpretation explains why Dionysus thinks only of how to increase the human being's cruelty and not his humaneness. This god associates humaneness with softness or weakness, which he scorns. By contrast, Nietzsche realizes humaneness, which does indeed originate in weakness, is as necessary to the ongoing vitality of the human being as the savagery to which it is linked. In other words, Nietzsche regards Dionysus' ignorance regarding shame as an indication that the god has not acquired the attributes that we human beings incorporated as a result of the Christian era of our genealogy.

31 Robert Solomon concludes the choice of a French word is meaningless at best and pompous at worst. For this reason, he decides to "dispense with the knowing tone of the French in favor of the more familiar and more easily typeset English word - [resentment]." He justifies this decision on the grounds that "both the origin and the meaning of the word in French seems close enough to both the English and the German" (Schacht 1994, 103). Max Scheler notes: "We did not use the word '*ressentiment*' because of a special predilection for the French language, but because we did not succeed in translating it into German" (Scheler 1961, 39). In fact, the German language did not seem to have had a word for resentment when Nietzsche was writing. The German word, "*ressentiment,*" did not seem to have appeared in German prior to Nietzsche's popularization of it.

Even if the German language did have a word for resentment when Nietzsche was writing, there would still be reason to hesitate before concluding Nietzsche's use of the French word is arbitrary. A writer is at liberty to choose whatever words he thinks will best express what he means. Given this freedom, a skilled writer will not choose to use a word on a mere whim. Rather, there will be a reason for the choices he makes. If it were the case that Nietzsche chose to use the French word, *ressentiment,* despite the fact a German approximation of it existed, we would be obliged to consider why he preferred the foreign word. One reason a writer might do such a thing is because he wishes to confront his reader with a term that is not quite familiar. In this way, he could help to alleviate the reader's tendency to assume he knows precisely what the author means by the word. Rüdiger Bittner takes this position. He argues the meaning of the German word "*ressentiment*" is not equivalent to the French word from which it seems to have been derived:

> The words need to be distinguished because they differ in sense - if only because the German word has, and the French word lacks, the connotations of a word of foreign origin. Actually, however, it seems

that both "to resent" in English and "*ressentir*" in French suggest a more straightforward annoyance, less of a grudge than the German word does. (Schacht 1994, 128)

32 Aristotle expands on his account of envy as follows:

> [W]e shall feel ... [envy] if we have, or think we have, equals; and by 'equals' I mean equals in birth, relationship, age, disposition, distinction, or wealth. We feel envy also if we fall but a little short of having everything; which is why people in high place and prosperity feel it—they think everyone else is taking what belongs to themselves. Also if we are exceptionally distinguished for some particular thing, and especially if that thing is wisdom or good fortune. Ambitious men are more envious than those who are not. So also those who profess wisdom; they are ambitious to be thought wise. Indeed, generally, those who aim at a reputation for anything are envious on this particular point. And small-minded men are envious, for everything seems great to them. (Aristotle, *The Rhetoric* 1387b21–1388a5)

33 Nietzsche claims Socrates himself is envious of the noble Athenians whose grace and authority he constantly undermines with his unmatched rhetorical prowess (TI, "The Problem of Socrates"; see also BT 15; BGE 191).

34 Nietzsche explains what he means by the intellectual conscience in GS 2.

35 (i) See Lise van Boxel, "Dignity and Decay," in *Prefaces to Unwritten Works*, Edited by Michael Grenke (Indiana: St. Augustine's Press, 2005), 36–43.

(ii) See Friedrich Nietzsche, "The Greek State," in *Prefaces to Unwritten Works*, Edited by Michael Grenke (Indiana: St. Augustine's Press, 2005), 44–59.

36 See also: Lise van Boxel, "Contest as Context" in *Prefaces to Unwritten Works*, Ed. and Trans. Michael Grenke (Indiana: St. Augustine's Press, 2005), 70–81.

37 The Greek word, λογος, which Plato's Socrates employs in his dialectical art, helpfully makes no distinction between speaking with someone and reasoning with someone, including with oneself.

38 The image of ripe fruit recurs, notably in GS 23 and Z, "The Honey Sacrifice."

39 In *On the Soul*, Aristotle offers an illuminating discussion of thinking that is helpful for understanding and for reflecting on Nietzsche's work on the same subject. See in particular 427b 20–433b 30. (Aristotle, "On the Soul" in *The Complete Works of Aristotle, Volume One*. Edited by Jonathan Barnes. Translated by J.A. Smith (New Jersey: Princeton University Press, 1984), 641–692.

40 The culture of the troubadours was destroyed by the Albigensian or Cathar Crusade (1209–1229), but it was resurrected and arguably enhanced by poets in the 1300's. The Crusade was initiated by Pope Innocent III in an effort to wipe out Catharism in Southern France. The Cathar's theology, which was

partly derived from early Gnosticism, was essentially dualistic. It maintained that there were two equal transcendental principles. The Cathars identified one of these principles as the good God. They believed this God to be the God of the New Testament, whom they regarded as the creator of the spiritual realm. They believed the other god to be evil, and they identify this evil god with the god of the Old Testament. Many Cathars also associated this god with Satan, The Evil One. They believed this evil god to be the creator of the physical world.

41 This re-start means each section following the first may be considered in terms of two numbers. The first is the number that is printed above the section—the explicit number—and the second, which is given by the restart and is implicit, is one less than the explicit number. Since Nietzsche does play with numbers as a way of communicating meaning, a full treatment of the third essay would require an analysis of whether and how this double-numbering affects its meaning. Our analysis here does not extend this far.

42 See Lise van Boxel, "Nietzsche in Eden," in *The Pious Sex*, ed. Andrea Radasanu (New York: Roman and Littlefield, 2010), 225–280.

43 Speaking of his relationship to truth and wisdom, both of whom are women, Zarathustra explains, secretly:

> [T]hus matters stand among the three of us: Deeply I love only life— and verily, most of all when I hate life. But that I am well disposed toward wisdom, and often too well, that is because she reminds me so much of life. She has her eyes, her laugh, and even her little golden fishing rod: is it my fault that the two look so similar?
>
> And when life once asked me, "Who is this wisdom?" I answered fervently, "oh yes, wisdom! One thirsts after her and is never satisfied; one looks through veils, one grabs through nets. Is she beautiful? How should I know? But even the oldest carps are baited with her. She is changeable and stubborn; often I have seen her bite her lip and comb her hair against the grain. Perhaps she is evil and false and a female in every way; but just when she speaks ill of herself she is most seductive."
>
> When I said this to life she laughed ... [mischievously] and closed her eyes. "Of whom are you speaking? she asked; "no doubt of me. And even if you are right—should *that* be said to my face? But now speak of your wisdom, too."
>
> Ah, and then you opened your eyes again, O beloved life. And I again seemed to myself to be sinking into the unfathomable. (Z, "The Dancing Song"; see also Z, "The Other Dancing Song")

44 Homer, *Odyssey*, 8.469–549, trans. Richmond Lattimore (New York: Harper Collins, 1967), 133–135.

45 For a further discussion of the difference between the artist and the artifact, see: Friedrich Nietzsche, "Homer's Contest," in *Prefaces to Unwritten Works*, trans. Michael Grenke (Indiana: St. Augustine's Press, 2005), 81–92; Lise van Boxel, "Dignity and Decay," ibid., 70–80.

46 The artist's so-called "unreality" is akin to woman's mercurialness. This kinship makes the artist, like woman, an object of suspicion according to the moral-theological prejudice. However, woman and the artist differ in that woman's primary realm of action is, unlike the artist, in the external realm. In other words, woman's so-called "unreality" consists in what the moral-theological prejudice would characterize as her deceptive nature. The artist's "unreality" manifests as a kind of inattention and disinterest in the realm of external actions in comparison to the inner actions of the mind.

47 Is the human being who embodies the highest sensuality and spirituality not the very creature at which Wagner aimed, prior to leaping into his opposite? Since the artist never stands alone but is always the valet of an authority, and since Schopenhauer's *ascetic* philosophy could not have served as Wagner's prop during the life-promoting or *non*-ascetic epoch of the artist's career, we conclude that Wagner's pre-leap work must have been directed by Nietzsche, regardless of whether or not Wagner was conscious of this fact or would admit it, even if he were conscious of it.

48 Joseph Conrad, *Heart of Darkness* (New York: W.W. Norton & Company, 2006), 27.

49 Nietzsche's description of the scientist's work harkens back to the sham free-spirit who interrupted Nietzsche in the first essay. Recall, the sham free spirit says he loves the poison—the ascetic ideal—that now courses through modern human beings, but he disdains the church as a non-essential, vulgar bobble to this ideal, one that should now be discarded. The sham free spirit may be a scientist (GM 1.9).

50 Aristotle, *The History of Animals*, ed. Jonathan Barnes (Princeton: Princeton University Press, 1984), 551a 13 - 30.

51 Plato, *Phaedrus*, trans. James Nichols Jr. (Ithaca: Cornell University Press, 1998), 275d–276b1.

52 Ernst Renan, *The Life of Jesus* (Amherst, New York: Prometheus Books, 1991).